NEW STRATEGIES FOR WICKED PROBLEMS

New Strategies for Wicked Problems

SCIENCE AND SOLUTIONS
IN THE TWENTY-FIRST CENTURY

Edited by
Edward P. Weber
Denise Lach
Brent S. Steel

Oregon State University Press   Corvallis

Library of Congress Cataloging-in-Publication Data

Names: Weber, Edward P., editor. | Lach, D. (Denise), editor. | Steel, Brent,
    editor.
Title: New strategies for wicked problems : science and solutions in the 21st
    century / edited by Edward P. Weber, Denise Lach, and Brent S. Steel.
Description: Corvallis, OR : Oregon State University Press, 2017. | Includes
    bibliographical references and index.
Identifiers: LCCN 2017009912 | ISBN 9780870718939 (paperback)
Subjects: LCSH: Environmental policy—United States. | Natural resources—
    Government policy—United States. | BISAC: BUSINESS & ECONOMICS
    / Decision-Making & Problem Solving. | EDUCATION / Decision-Making
    & Problem Solving. | POLITICAL SCIENCE / Public Policy / General.
Classification: LCC GE180 .N48 2017 | DDC 333.70973—dc23
LC record available at https://lccn.loc.gov/2017009912

Oregon State University Press
121 The Valley Library
Corvallis OR 97331-4501
541-737-3166 • fax 541-737-3170
www.osupress.oregonstate.edu

Contents

PART TWO
RESPONDING TO THE CHALLENGES WITH
NEW PROBLEM-SOLVING METHODOLOGIES

The U. G. Dubach Chair in Political Science
at Oregon State University

This volume would not have been possible without the financial support provided by the U. G. Dubach Chair endowment at Oregon State University. We, the editors of this book, are grateful for the support and for the opportunity to extend Dubach's legacy. As part of this, we wish to take this opportunity to familiarize readers with U. G. Dubach, an OSU and Oregon State legend.

Ulysses Grant Dubach has been hailed as one of Oregon's greatest educators, having devoted thirty-three years to OSU as a professor and administrator. Although he died in 1972 at the age of ninety-one, his Oregon State legacy continues to grow. Gifts from his estate as well as from his widow, Ida, and her estate have endowed the U. G. Dubach Chair of Political Science.

A Kansas native, Dubach earned his doctorate from the University of Wisconsin, then moved west and started his Oregon State career as a political science professor in 1913. In 1924 he was named head of the department and also appointed OSU's first dean of men, positions he held until he turned sixty-five, the state-mandated age for retirement. Dubach moved to Portland and served as head of the political science department at Lewis & Clark College for thirteen years. He retired a second and final time in 1960.

Despite his move to Lewis & Clark, part of Dubach remained at OSU. "My heart is in Corvallis, Oregon State, . . . an institution without any question that hasn't a peer in its field," he wrote in 1948.

In 1951 the *Oregonian* honored Dubach as one of the hundred people who had made the greatest contributions to the state in its first one hundred years. In 1967 Dubach received OSU's Distinguished Service Award in recognition of his career and his impact on countless people both in and out of the classroom. An inspiring lecturer, Dubach spoke frequently to civic, church, and youth groups on active participation in civic affairs. He gave seventy-five off-campus speeches in one year alone. His obituary notes that "a generation of Oregon State students remember that his office door was always open for what he called 'a gentlemanly meeting of the minds.'"

Introduction

Science and Problem Solving for Wicked Problems: Challenges and Responses

EDWARD P. WEBER, DENISE LACH, AND BRENT S. STEEL

Hydraulic fracturing (or "fracking") was first introduced in the 1940s as a technique for tapping unconventional oil and natural gas reserves that are otherwise inaccessible. In the late 1990s and early 2000s, energy companies began combining horizontal (or directional) drilling with hydraulic fracturing to tap these reserves. The process involves drilling horizontally through a rock layer and injecting a pressurized mixture of water, sand, and other chemicals that fractures the rock and facilitates the flow of oil and gas. These combined methods have allowed for expanded development in shale and other formations in the United States, Europe, Asia, Australia, and elsewhere. The rapid expansion of fracking is projected to make the United States a net exporter of natural gas in the coming years and, potentially, the world's largest oil producer by 2019 (IEA 2012). Shale gas, which in year 2000 accounted for only 1 percent of the nation's natural gas production, accounted for 23 percent in 2016 and is projected to increase to 49 percent by 2035 (US EIA 2012).

Hydraulic fracturing is just one part of the *unconventional* oil/gas development process, which also includes clearing land for well pads; constructing access roads and associated infrastructure (e.g., pipelines, compressor stations); transporting and processing extracted fossil fuels; transporting millions of gallons of water and wastewater for treatment and disposal; and bringing large (often transient) populations to a community. Fracking is also occurring in urban and suburban areas, as well as at the interfaces between suburban and rural areas, or, in other words, places where people are already living and working, which increases the number of issues at play. In addition to the increased potential for earthquakes, groundwater and well water contamination, and general pollution from installing and operating the drilling rigs, there are property rights and zoning conflicts, environmental justice concerns, environmental waste cleanup and disposal risks, air pollution issues (e.g., methane leaks), and the aesthetic concerns of drilling rigs in more populated places not accustomed to their presence (Pierce, Weible, and Heikkila 2014).

Yet, there is no scientific consensus, much less general certainty, in the science on the relationship between fracking operations and groundwater pollution or earthquakes, although some recent research does claim a causal relationship between fracking activities and small earthquakes. Nor is there agreement on what a proper "setback" should be for a fracking drilling rig from someone's already established home. Should it be five hundred feet, or a thousand, or fifteen hundred, or more? Should a neighbor within the viewshed of a rig have the right to prevent its installation if they deem it unaesthetic or otherwise detrimental to what they perceive to be the "right" view? How much risk is there with possible fracking fluid spillage from one property to the next, or into streams and wetlands, and who or what should bear the risk? And which level of government should regulate and manage these decisions about fracking—federal, state, local? All three? Only federal, or only state? Or . . . ?

In short, the fracking conundrum is a wicked public problem. Wicked problems are defined by three primary characteristics: they are unstructured, crosscutting, and relentless (Rittel and Webber 1973; Weber and Khademian 2008). First, "unstructured" means that causes and effects are extremely difficult to identify and model, thus adding complexity and uncertainty and engendering a high degree of conflict because there is little consensus on the problem or the solution (Roberts 2002). Second, wicked problems are crosscutting in that the problem space comprises multiple, overlapping, interconnected subsets of problems that cut across multiple policy domains and levels of government. Wicked problems, in other words, cut across hierarchy and authority structures within and between organizations, and across policy domains, political and administrative jurisdictions, and political "group" interests. And third, wicked problems, such as the fracking issue, are relentless. The problem is not going to be solved once and for all despite all the best intentions and resources directed at the problem, and efforts to solve the wicked problem will have consequences for other policy arenas as well. Similar to a stone dropped in the water, the ripples spread rapidly to impact other issue areas, thus adding new complications to an already complex situation (Weber and Khademian 2008).

The uncertainty, contestedness, and overall complexity of such wicked problems means that multiple citizens and groups, or stakeholders, are necessarily involved. And each participant tends to bring a different perspective, a different way of knowing, to the fracking problem. How do government, citizens, companies, environmentalists, and other stakeholders work toward effective solutions? In the past, we have relied on science (and applied science or technology) to help us through such problems, but in the case of wicked problems we seem to have need for more open-ended decision processes that integrate not just technical and scientific information, but experiential and values-based information as well.

Or think about the difficulties associated with forestry policy and logging on federal public lands in the Pacific Northwest region in the aftermath of the 1988 *Northern Spotted Owl v. Hodel* Supreme Court ruling on endangered owls. There was significant support within forestry science at the time to support a deep reduction in logging by more than 80 percent from prior levels in order to protect owl habitat. But the policy solution has contributed to well-documented and significant declines in the social and economic well-being of many rural, timber-dependent communities in the region. In short, the science-driven solution mandated by the federal Endangered Species Act (ESA) struggled to accommodate the full range of problem complexities that existed in the social, economic, and political spheres. Interestingly, forestry science has evolved since 1994, and there is now growing scientific support for changes in forestry practices that may well do an improved job of supporting forest health, spotted owls, and expanded logging opportunities (Franklin and Johnson 2010).

Fracking and forestry management, of course, are not the only wicked problems of importance today, problems that often seek to place science front and center in attempts to cut the Gordian knot and resolve them. Such a list would necessarily include climate change, genetic modifications of food (what critics derisively call "Frankenfood"), fisheries management (e.g., salmon recovery), water resource management, and ecosystem/watershed management, among others. And in fact, many scientists, but also advocacy organizations and activists on opposite sides of policy debates, are especially prominent in their calls for science to be a determining factor in policy decisions (e.g., Ehrlich and Ehrlich 1996; Ray, Riggenbach, and Guzzo 1997).

The calls for science in these situations refer to the traditional or, as some have termed it, the "normal" approach to science in the policy process. In the

traditional approach, the authoritative power of science stems from its treatment as a truth-seeking enterprise in which neutrality or objectivity—the idea
that what is true is independent of what we believe—is central. As such, the
core of the traditional scientific method involves testable hypotheses; experimentation; empirical, or evidence-based, conclusions; and replicability. It
also means that the traditional, or normal, role of scientists in the policy process is distinct and separate from that of policy makers or politicians, because
scientists' primary role is limited to discovering, purveying, and interpreting
objective facts. From this perspective, scientists test propositions, conduct
research, produce scientifically informed results, and advise policy makers relative to the science, while policy makers ultimately take science into
account when making decisions, along with other political, social, cultural,
and economic considerations. In short, science is traditionally treated in such
situations as having the capacity to unravel, identify, and effectively prioritize
the relevant causes and effects associated with problems of all types.

As a descriptor of science in the policy process, we think such advocates of the normal approach to science are on stronger ground with respect
to *some* public policy issues, especially those involving low complexity and
uncertainty, general value agreement, and low decision stakes. Under these
conditions the probability *is* higher that science will play a dominant role
in the policy process and will likely impact policy in the way traditionalists
assume and prefer (Funtowicz and Ravetz 1993).

But what about the highly contested wicked-problem scenarios noted
above? In these cases, where "facts are uncertain, values in dispute, stakes
high, and decisions [often] urgent," it is not at all clear that the traditional
science approach as a problem-solving methodology will work *if the goal is
effective problem solving* (Funtowicz and Ravetz 1993, 739, 744).[1] Moreover,
as Neal Lane, former presidential science adviser and former director of the
National Science Foundation, notes, the decline of science's influence on
such problems stems from the growing realization that they emerge out of
"complex patterns of overlapping consequences," including those of social,
economic, and cultural import; thus, effective solutions "will require more
than technical solutions" (Lane 1999; Pielke 2007). Adding to the chorus,
Sarewitz (2000) argues that, in the face of scientific uncertainties, ecological
vulnerability, and irreversibility, the policy process has to be open, transparent, and self-reflective, with this new, more overtly political decision process acting as a substitute or stand-in for scientific certainty. In this view,

traditional science is still important for effective problem solving in highly contested wicked-problem scenarios, but while it is necessary, it is unlikely to be sufficient by itself.

This is because the uncertainty and complexity of wicked problems such as fracking, forestry management, or salmon recovery means that scientific knowledge about them tends to be provisional, uncertain, and/or incomplete. This contributes to a legitimacy crisis for science in the policy process, because traditional science is no longer adequate by itself and thus struggles to justify its privileged position vis-à-vis other knowledges, much less provide the necessary knowledge required to resolve or effectively manage such problems. This reality also opens the door to science wars, competing scientists, and science for hire, as different interests seeking advantage in the policy process try to exploit the complexity, using science more as a weapon than as an objective representation of relevant truths. This politicization of science has eroded the authority of science as legitimate and credible in certain domains and prompted calls for making science, and the public decision processes that rely on it, more accountable and democratic.

The discussions in this volume respond to the three challenges noted above—more effectiveness, more accountability, more democracy. Taken together, the challenges suggest the need for new problem-solving methodologies, processes, institutions, and decision tools that can integrate science and other knowledges and values possessed by the diverse stakeholding groups typically involved in wicked-problem settings. What might these new problem-solving methodologies, processes, and institutions look like? Funtowicz and Ravetz (1993) suggested a different approach to science in the policy process—the idea of post-normal science. Unlike the traditional, or normal, approach to science, the post-normal approach is a "model for scientific argument . . . not [as] a formalized deduction, but an interactive dialogue . . . involv[ing] broader societal and cultural institutions . . . [including users of science, or those] persons directly affected by a [policy] problem." Essential to the post-normal science approach is an extended peer community that purposely involves a broad array of stakeholders in order to (1) increase public understanding and/or literacy through participation; (2) represent different viewpoints in the decisions about how problems are defined, what counts as evidence, what it means, and, in some cases, the selection of programmatic (policy implementation) alternatives; and (3) democratize knowledge production and its application to wicked-problem decisions.

Yet, Funtowicz and Ravetz (1993) stop short of demonstrating the empirical validity of their assumptions about post-normal science in highly uncertain, contested wicked-problem settings, while also providing only limited conceptual guidance for what a proper "extended peer community" problem-solving strategy looks like. This volume seeks to fill these gaps with the empirical examination of a series of examples demonstrating how a number of different alternative problem-solving methodologies might manage the challenge of extended peer communities and deliver more effective, accountable, and democratic problem solving for wicked problems.

But before we address the gap on problem-solving methodologies, we set the stage by illustrating how the uncertainty and complexity of wicked problems translate into decision-making contexts and dynamics ill-suited to the traditional approach to science and therefore unable to provide the full range of knowledge required for effective and accountable decisions. Using contemporary real-world studies of hydraulic fracking, salmon recovery, forestry management, and public health and environmental policy more generally, we explore and describe the actual challenges to science in wicked-problem settings. We also examine advances in social science as applied to individual decision-making to further explore the validity of the challenges to traditional science posed by wicked problems.

The discussion below turns to a historical review of the traditional approach to science before outlining some contemporary challenges to traditional science that are weakening science's authority and influence in the policy process. The challenges, particularly the specific dilemmas posed for science in wicked-problem settings, are then examined through the lens of Funtowicz and Ravetz's (1993) theoretical argument, which seeks to "provide guidance for the choice of appropriate problem-solving strategies" in what they term "post-normal science" settings (740). A final section provides a brief introduction to the chapters in the second half of the book, each of which outlines possible problem-solving strategies for dealing with the challenge of wicked problems.

THE TRADITIONAL APPROACH TO SCIENCE

As previously noted, in the traditional, or normal, approach to science in the policy process, scientists do not interfere with the political process and politicians do not interfere in the science; science is viewed as a uniquely truth-determining type of knowledge deserving of a privileged, even dominant, place in the policy process. Proponents of the traditional view on science also tend to equate scientific progress with societal progress, leading to the use of science as a trump card over competing policy proposals that conflict with the conclusions of science (Bush 1945; Pielke 2007; Scott 1998).

While there are many advocates of using science to inform policy, the strongest supporters of the potential of science to accurately and objectively predict various phenomena are adherents to various versions of positivism. Finding its roots in the Enlightenment, during the sixteenth and seventeenth centuries, positivism came to be identified with the writings of the philosopher Auguste Comte and physicist Ernst Mach, among others. Typically, supporters of this approach believed that the "scientific method and practice distinguished the people of the West from civilizations that the West had conquered" and that science "was a matter of truth" (Pyeson and Sheets-Pyeson 1999, 5). The scientific method was considered objective and therefore would bring about a new age of prosperity through the use of quantitative methods for understanding both physical and social affairs.

Although in contemporary times there are many doubts about positivism, as well as theoretical diversity evident among positivists themselves, similarities are found in the shared belief that science is the best way to get at truth, to understand the world well enough that we might predict the future and then possibly control and manipulate physical and social phenomena in specific ways. The underlying assumption is that the world and the universe operate by laws of cause and effect, which can be discovered through the scientific method.

William Bechtel (1988) and others affirm that most contemporary philosophers reject positivism in its various, original formulations, and the idea of positivism has come under critical scrutiny over the past forty years. Few scientists today would completely accept Comte's view of a logically ordered, objective reality that we can understand once and for all, even with the powerful resources of contemporary scientific research. As Nobel Prize winner John C. Polanyi states, "Science is done by scientists, and since scientists are people, the progress of science depends more on scientific judgment than on scientific instruments" (1995, 7). Moreover, the rise in importance of the history and sociology of science as academic disciplines has led to a more complex characterization of and debate about the nature of science and its relationship to social, political, and personal factors (e.g., Jasanoff et al. 1995). At the same time, Bechtel (1988, 49) argues, "the Positivists' picture of science remains the most comprehensive we have," and, in practice, even the reports scholars provide in peer-reviewed publications are still framed within the positivistic model. Simplified forms of the traditional model of science have filtered down into both the "culture" of contemporary science and popular depictions of science and scientists. According to some, this has created a mythical view of the nature and power of science that has remained prevalent in some quarters (e.g., Kitcher 2003).

While many contemporary scientists would not agree with all tenets of positivism, they would most likely agree with Levien (1979) that science and scientists can and should play an important and useful role in the policy process, especially for complex public problems such as those found in the natural resource management and policy spheres. He argues that this can occur in three ways. First, science and scientists can provide a clear understanding of the basic dimensions of environmental problems, identifying both what is known and what is uncertain. Second, science and scientists can then describe and identify options for the appropriate solutions of those problems, some of which might not be considered by political decision-makers. Finally, science can contribute to the resolution of environmental problems by estimating the economic, social, environmental, and political consequences of proposed solutions through time and space and across population groups (Levien 1979).

Accordingly, "science and technology play an unusual role in environmental policy . . . . Environmental policy rests on a foundation of scientific research without which it would not even exist" (Von Moltke 1996, 193). Sarewitz and Pielke have described these expectations as "justified in large part by the belief that scientific predictions are a valuable tool for crafting environmental and related policies" (2000, 11). They further argue that scientific prediction is not the same as predicting the outcome of an environmental law or policy, which is necessarily more complicated because of the number of ecological, social, economic, and political variables involved (Funtowicz and Ravetz 1999). This leads Von Moltke to conclude, "This creates a unique and uneasy relationship between scientists and policymakers" (1996, 193). Scientists often engage in basic research, which, because of differing time frames, research expectations, and so on, makes information difficult to "transfer from one jurisdiction to another" for use by managers (Von Moltke 1996, 193). Therefore, even scientists optimistic about their role in informing the policy process tend to be cautious concerning their efforts to provide correct predictions (e.g., Allen et al. 2001). At the same time, these same scientists are strong advocates of science and the scientific method and believe that "science still deserves to be privileged, because it is still the best game in town" (Allen et al. 2001).

CONTEMPORARY CHALLENGES TO THE TRADITIONAL SCIENCE MODEL

Current perspectives on the proper role for scientists in the environmental policy process are potentially related to how science is defined and under-stood. As discussed above, the traditional or "normal" model of science and scientists is an outgrowth of positivism. The role of scientists in this model is to provide relevant expertise about scientific data, theories, and findings that others in the policy-making process can use to make decisions, but not to make the decisions themselves or to advocate for particular policy positions. Moreover, scientists are not to become biased by involvement in environ-mental policy or to become policy advocates. In this model, science is revered by resource managers and the public, and has a special authority in environ-mental management because of its independence and its power to objectively interpret the world.

The problem for "traditional" science and scientists is that in recent decades the traditional role of science in the policy process has encountered significant challenges. In case after case, whether it is climate change, GMO food, forestry management, or fisheries management, for example, science and the scientists responsible for conducting and communicating the appli-cable research to decision-makers encounter more frequent and direct chal-lenges than ever before (Jasanoff 2007; Sarewitz 2004). The challenges are of four main types. The first takes aim at the veracity of science and tends to no longer view science and scientists/experts as unquestioned authoritative sources of credible information in policy debates. This line of critique instead identifies different sources of potential bias affecting science and its practi-tioners. The second argues for more science in the policy process, but with a twist, calling for a different, more assertive role and greater involvement of scientists in all phases of policy decision-making. The third challenge focuses on the "incompleteness" or inadequacy of science for successfully treating and resolving public policy debates, particularly those involving highly com-plex public problems. Fourth, and finally, the challenges from changing socio-political demands on natural resources management, which are the central "policy" concern of this volume, add new layers of complexity to decision-making and problem solving.

QUESTIONING THE VERACITY OF SCIENCE

The first challenge to traditional science critiques the privileged position of science in the policy process and questions its veracity. In doing so, this criticism highlights the contested nature of contemporary perspectives on science and its proper role in the policy process, along with the fact that citizens in developed countries such as the United States are less trusting of science, scientific experts, and government than ever before (Steel et al. 2004). The sources of bias, perceived or real, are several.

Part of the growing challenge to science is grounded in politics and is fueled by competing factions in highly contested policy areas; interest groups looking for any kind of advantage have been central to the growth industry of adversarial science, or "scientists as gladiators" (Weber, Leschine, and Brock 2010). As part of this, the emergence of normative science—information developed, presented, or interpreted based on an assumed, usually unstated, preference for a particular policy or class of policies (Lackey 2007)—challenges the credibility of science by using its "objectivity" as an overt political weapon on behalf of particular political interests (Braithwaite 1998). Moreover, scientists' strength, or "appeal as objective, neutral participants" with "truths" bearing on policy decisions, does not fit comfortably with "the necessary currency of the policy process—i.e., advocacy and persuasion" (Keller 2009, 1; Pielke 2007).

Similarly, questions arise regarding the presumed objectiveness of specialized experts participating in the policy process. The concern is that experts' training, practical experiences, professional norms, or career considerations will affect their preferences for analytic methods and models, types of information, and decision protocols, thus directly shaping decision outcomes (Mosher 1982). The idea that expertise represents a mobilization of bias (Weible and Moore 2010) means that it matters whether economists, lawyers, ecologists, or engineers dominate, or otherwise control, bureaucratic problem-solving processes because outcomes will most likely vary depending on the professional group in charge (Khademian 1992; J. Q. Wilson 1980). As Sarewitz (2004) argues, competing disciplinary approaches often bring with them their own normative and political baggage, which creates a "lack of coherence among competing scientific understandings" and hence an accompanying increase in scientific uncertainty, albeit from "normative" as opposed to "scientific" causes (385).

In addition, the objectivity and truth claims of traditional science have come under attack by postmodern scholars and others who see modern science as simply another expression of power that favors elites, while also seeking to discredit and marginalize other truth claims (Foucault 1980; Dryzek 2002). Others in this vein classify science, and the practice of scientists, as but another social institution with its own particular social and cultural "processes" that are inevitably replete with politics and values (Levins and Lewontin 1985). One does not have to be a postmodernist, of course, to make the link between power and the development and use of science, whether in terms of a military-industrial complex or simply as an expression of current entrenched economic interests (Paarlberg 2004; Melman 1970; Press and Washburn 2000). Other studies of the scientific process have shown that science and research processes are often socially defined (Latour and Woolgar 1979), or that knowledge is socially constructed to reduce political uncertainty and risks (Schneider and Ingram 1997). Such concerns have led to calls for greater citizen involvement and democratization of policy decision-making as a social "check" for scientific recommendations (Beierle and Cayford 2002; Ingram and Smith 1993).

THE SCIENCE IMPACT CHALLENGE:
A NEW SOCIAL CONTRACT FOR SCIENTISTS

The emerging "positive" alternative model posited by, among others, Kay (1998) and Lubchenco (1998) challenges the traditional science model, not so much on the authority of scientific information and the acceptability of positivism, but on the exclusion of scientists from natural resource management and policy processes. It proposes that scientists should become more integrated into management and policy processes. Put differently, research scientists need to come out of their labs and in from their field studies to directly engage in public environmental decisions within natural resource agencies and such venues as courts and public hearings. This has led the former president of the American Association for the Advancement of Science, Jane Lubchenco, to argue for a "new social contract" for scientists with society:

The new and unmet needs of society include more comprehensive
information, understanding, and technologies for society to move
toward a more sustainable biosphere—one which is ecologically
sound, economically feasible, and socially just. New fundamental
research, faster and more effective transmission of new and
existing knowledge to policy- and decision-makers, and better
communication of this knowledge to the public will all be required to
meet this challenge. (1998, 491)

There is a need for more science in these processes and decisions, the model
argues, but this can only be brought about if research scientists themselves
become more actively involved. Moreover, this model suggests that scientists
should not hesitate to make judgments that favor certain management alternatives, if the preponderance of evidence and their own experience and judgment
leads them to such conclusions (Lubchenco 1998). They are, after all, in the
best position to interpret the scientific data and findings and thus are in a special
position to advocate for specific management policies and alternatives.

Lubchenco's new social contract has also been called "integrative" science and is related to Kai Lee's "civic" science (1993). All of these models call
for more personal involvement by individual research scientists in bureaucratic and public decision-making, providing expertise and sometimes even
promoting specific strategies that they believe are supported by the available
scientific knowledge (Ravetz 1987). Funtowicz and Ravetz have articulated
this model as follows:

There is a new role for natural science. The facts that are taught
from textbooks in institutions are still necessary, but are no longer
sufficient. For these relate to a standardized version of the natural
world, frequently to the artificially pure and stable conditions of a
laboratory experiment. The world as we interact with it in working for
sustainability is quite different. Those who have become accredited
experts through a course of academic study, have much valuable
knowledge in relation to these practical problems. But they may also
need to recover from the mindset they might absorb unconsciously
from their instruction. Contrary to the impression conveyed by
textbooks, most problems in practice have more than one plausible
answer; and many have no answer at all. (1999)

The risk of the new social contract, however, is that scientists can lose their credibility as scientists if they cross the line between science and policy, science and management (Alm 1997–1998; Lackey 2007). This leads to a "separatist" role for scientists; ideally they are removed from management and policy and serve as experts or consultants only, called upon as the need arises and as policy makers, managers, and the public require.

COMPLEX PROBLEMS AND THE INADEQUACY OF SCIENCE

Concern is growing over the limits of science when it comes to extremely complex—or, wicked—policy problems. Wicked problems are those for which causes and effects are difficult, if not impossible, to establish and model, given their unstructured character, high degree of uncertainty, inescapable and numerous connections to other policy problems, and their tendency to generate the kinds of value trade-offs that spark significant conflict. Their complexity is such that wicked problems are characterized by a relentlessness and fluidity in which they are never "solved" once and for all, because resolving one part of the puzzle generally creates new, unexpected issues (Roberts 2002; van Brueren, Klijn, and Koppenjan 2003; Weber and Khademian 2008). Rebuilding broken urban neighborhoods, combatting climate change, securing the homeland against terrorism, (re)creating and maintaining environmentally sustainable communities, addressing non-point source pollution (e.g., urban storm water runoff), and managing ecosystems and watersheds are examples of wicked problems that are difficult to define and that cut across a complex maze of vertical and horizontal policy jurisdictions. The problem for science is that the high levels of system uncertainties mean that

> the [science] problem is not concerned with the discovery of a
> particular fact, but with the comprehension or management of
> an inherently complex reality . . . [in which] data on their effects,
> and even data for baselines of "undisturbed" systems, are radically
> inadequate. The phenomena, being novel, complex and variable,
> are themselves not well understood. [In such cases,] science cannot
> always provide well founded theories based on experiments for
> explanation and prediction, but can frequently achieve at best
> only mathematical models and computer simulations, which
> are essentially untestable. On the basis of such uncertain inputs,

decisions must be made. . . . Therefore policy cannot proceed on the basis of factual predictions, but only on policy forecasts. (Funtowicz and Ravetz 1993, 742, 744)

In addition, wicked problems tend to respond poorly to synoptic, rational plans or management by specialized agencies and experts, but instead require "clumsy solutions" that constructively engage with and listen and respond to "plural voices" or perspectives in order to develop politically feasible policies (Verweij and Thompson 2006; Frame 2008; Rayner 2006). Yet the call for plural voices—characterized by others as multiple knowledges or different "ways of knowing"—as essential to policy problem solving poses new challenges (Fortmann 2008; Lejano and Ingram 2009; Goodman, DuPuis, and Goodman 2012). Greater public participation in the policy process "entangles expert knowledge in others' knowledge domains and experiences. If expert knowledge is presented as uniquely 'truth determining'—thereby negating these other knowledge domains—confrontation, mistrust, or disengagement [and problem-solving ineffectiveness] typically results" (Stayaert and Jiggins 2007, 576–577). Scott comes to a similar conclusion while focusing on the exclusionary nature of science-based knowledge. He finds that the fundamental problem with the traditional science "high-modernist framework" is that it often feeds into

an imperial or hegemonic planning mentality . . . [that] is necessarily schematic; it always ignores essential features of any real, functioning social order . . . [and] excludes the necessary role of local knowledge and know-how. [In addition to such] . . . practical knowledge, informal processes and improvisation in the face of unpredictability . . . [are] indispensable [to the policy process] given the resilience of both social and natural diversity and . . . the limits, in principle, of what we are likely to know about complex, functioning order. (1998, 6, 7)

THE CHANGING DEMANDS OF NATURAL RESOURCES MANAGEMENT

Adding to the complexity of the actual problem setting are the changing demands associated with management for many different kinds of public problems, but especially for natural resource and environmental problems. In recent decades, the practice of public natural resource management has shifted from the long-standing multiple-use, commodity production paradigm to a multiscale ecosystem management perspective that emphasizes the sustainable provision of a much wider assortment of ecosystem services embedded in complex sets of social-ecological interactions at multiple spatial scales (Williams et al., 2013). Accompanying this shift is the perceived need for strategic planning and management capable of adaptivity across scales and time. Taken together, broader management agendas and adaptive management only heighten the complexity and uncertainty of fact-finding, further amplify the competing values at stake, and engage a broader array of political, social, and economic interests and values in every decision (Weber 2003).

RETHINKING SCIENCE AND PROBLEM SOLVING: CASTING A WIDER NET

Given these challenges and ideas, what kinds of problem-solving methodologies, processes, institutions, and decision tools might be effective at integrating the required mix of science, different ways of knowing, and political and cultural values into public policy and implementation decisions? Answering this question addresses what Keller (2009) and Rayner (2006) call a critical challenge for scholars and policy makers alike: determining what kinds of institutions and practices are best suited to managing the difficult negotiations along the science and policy boundary. And despite clear intellectual progress in reconceptualizing the role of science in the policy process, there are still gaps in the literature.[2] As McNie correctly notes, "It is essential that we develop a more robust understanding of experience and practical experiments regarding how relationships [and institutions] are constructed and managed across the science-society boundary" (2007, 29).

Moreover, answering this question provides valuable information that can be applied to the larger empirical trend in the United States, Europe, New Zealand, Australia, and elsewhere, to employ new alternative governance institutions for managing complex problems in the twenty-first century, natural resources or otherwise (Ansell 2011; Dietz and Stern 2009; Kamarck 2007; Kettl 2002; Margerum 2011; Salmon 2007).

Funtowicz and Ravetz (1993, 1999) get the conversation started by delineating the relationship between science and different problem types. Policy problems involving low complexity and uncertainty, general value agreement, and low decision stakes are likely to be the most amenable to the traditional, or "normal," science. Under these conditions, the probability is higher that science will play a dominant role in the policy process and will likely influence policy in the way traditionalists assume and prefer. Yet, for wicked-problem scenarios, where "facts are uncertain, values in dispute, stakes high, and decisions [often] urgent," it is not at all clear that the traditional-science approach as a problem-solving methodology will work, if the goal is effective problem solving (Funtowicz and Ravetz 1993, 739, 744).

This is because the inherent system uncertainties and differences in values in such cases mean that scientific or policy consensus is unlikely not only for "value-based" or political reasons, but also for purely scientific reasons.[3] In such situations, according to Funtowicz and Ravetz, it is better to conceive of "the model for scientific argument . . . not [as] a formalized deduction, but an interactive dialogue . . . involv[ing] broader societal and cultural institutions . . . [including users of science, or those] persons directly affected by a [policy] problem" (1993, 739–740, 752). This suggests a problem-solving process that necessarily recognizes and incorporates different views and approaches, including those of nonexperts who can contribute to knowledge production and other "legitimate" tasks in a variety of ways, including problem co-framing, quality assessment, policy debate, and citizen science (752).

In short, Funtowicz and Ravetz argue that for the kinds of natural resource and environmental problems being examined in this volume, traditional science is useful and necessary but is not sufficient. Moreover, they provide an important and logical conceptual framework that not only recognizes the importance of problem type associated with the science decision dynamic in the policy process, but also "provide[s] guidance for the choice of appropriate problem-solving strategies" (1993, 740) and takes the first rudimentary steps toward conceptualizing the key components of their new "post-normal" science problem-solving methodology.

Unfortunately, Funtowicz and Ravetz provide only limited conceptual guidance for what a proper problem-solving strategy looks like. Others do take it a step further and employ the concept of "clumsy solutions," yet stop short of recommending anything other than conceptual support for the idea that new institutions are needed (Verweij and Thompson 2006), or general prescriptions for the level of governance, or that government should not go it alone (Rayner 2006). Frame (2008) and Frame and Brown (2008) get more specific, arguing for "futuring" frameworks grounded in a dialogue among all the significant constituencies, or stakeholders. Yet even this "clumsy solution" approach assumes that, once disparate interests find common ground in a "future vision," the framework alone will suffice to guide participants toward the desired future as long as all voices continue to maintain a constructive dialogue.[4]

This volume builds on, extends, and refines this line of research with the presentation (in part 2) of four potential "problem-solving" methodologies, or institutions, norms, and decision tools that respond to, and therefore hold the potential to address successfully, the demands of highly wicked problems, where uncertainty, disputed values, and high stakes are the rule.[5] The four problem-solving methodologies are Knowledge-to-Action Networks (KTAN), place-oriented inquiry and practice, best practices and expectations for science and scientists, and collaborative governance arrangements.

In "An Experiment in Post-Normal Science," Denise Lach explores the construction and operation of a Knowledge-to-Action Network (KTAN) that addresses future water scarcity issues in a western US river basin in Idaho. KTANs are designed to bring together an evolving group of participants, including scientists, government officials, and local stakeholders, to pose and answer questions collaboratively and iteratively, with the goal of creating usable information (or knowledge) for policy decisions. One of the exercises critical for KTAN success is a process for developing shared information and meaning. While participants come into the network with different knowledge, perspectives, and values, the KTAN creates a venue for participants to pose problems, develop a shared understanding of the issue and its uncertainties, collect relevant information, and agree on ways to interpret the data. The KTAN in this case is organized around the key stages of a research project— problem identification and research question development, data collection and analysis, and data interpretation. The chapter provides a review of the opportunities and challenges for using KTANs for watershed-based resource dilemmas.

In "The Role of Place-Based Social Learning," Daniel Williams describes a potential path toward effective problem solving for wicked problems. Place-oriented inquiry and practice emphasizes bottom-up strategies for the adaptive, sustainable governance of complex dynamic landscapes. Adopting a spatial or place-based perspective helps with recognition that most knowledge is, to a significant degree, local or context-dependent, as all knowledge-holders occupy—by virtue of their biography, training, and geographic experiences—some particular, delimited position from which to observe the world. Wicked-problem conditions, the argument goes, require the cultivation, transmission, and application of existing bottom-up knowledge held by embedded actors in the landscape. This *emplaced* form of social learning is illustrated in two contexts of adaptive landscape governance. One example shows how informal structures of landscape governance have emerged to foster social learning in response to the mountain pine beetle infestation in the central Rocky Mountains. A second example examines a scenario-based social learning process for climate change adaptation. Both cases illustrate how actors and their potential adaptation strategies are situated within interacting social, political, and economic forces operating at multiple scales. For wicked problems, a place-based approach suggests that the path toward more sustainable governance is less about the application of science to inform policy and practice, and more about an expanded model of practice that can confront knowledge complexity, uncertainty, and controversy when applied to specific places or landscapes.

"Changing Expectations for Science and Scientists in Marine and Terrestrial Management and Policy," by Brent S. Steel and Denise Lach, shows how the expectations (norms) for scientists in the policy process are changing for both terrestrial and marine policy. The authors find growing support for the idea that research scientists should become more integrated into communities and management and policy processes, and directly engage in public policy and management decisions with communities and citizens. The final part of the chapter uses data from NSF's Long Term Ecological Research (LTER) program to develop several cases of "best practice" in the area of "collaborative research," or "joint fact finding and collaborative discovery."

The final chapter on potential problem-solving methodologies, "Collaborative Governance, Science, and Policy Outcomes," by Edward P. Weber and Anna P. Stevenson, starts with a brief, general discussion of the improved "fit" between collaborative governance institutions and wicked problems. The argument then turns to some of the ways that collaborative governance approaches might produce better knowledge and facilitate agreed interpretations of science, risk, and uncertainty, while also increasing the influence of science in policy-making, especially in cases of wicked problems where uncertainty is the rule. More explicitly, Weber and Stevenson examine two possible paths for how collaborative governance can help address the challenges of science/knowledge production and problem solving in wicked-problem settings. One case explores the application of "civic science" to the production and use of science in watershed-based salmon recovery, while the other develops the importance of a collaborative capacity building (CCB) mind-set for leaders in overcoming the challenges of knowledge sharing and use among diverse participants in a wicked-problem setting.

Before developing these potential problem-solving methodologies, however, we address, in chapters 1 through 5, the empirical specifics of the science and policy-making dynamic in wicked problem settings. We do this because Funtowicz and Ravetz stopped short of demonstrating the empirical validity of their assumptions about science in highly uncertain, contested, and wicked-problem settings. What actually happens to science in wicked problems loaded with uncertainty, contested values, and high stakes? Does it get integrated into policies that are then effective in managing or resolving the complex problem at issue? Or does it get overwhelmed by the "hard" values of political, social, economic, and cultural considerations? To answer these questions, we employ empirical studies focused on a series of wicked problems—hydraulic fracking, salmon recovery, forest management, and environmental policy more generally. We also examine advances in social science as applied to individual decision-making in order to further explore the validity of the Funtowicz and Ravetz (1993) argument. And, in fact, these cases find considerable support for their thesis that traditional science struggles to be effective, or influential, in wicked-problem settings.

Notes

1   Keller (2009) and Pielke (2007) take similar approaches in seeking to understand what happens to science in the policy process, but use scientists' roles as their dependent variable. Keller (2009) finds that the policy context has a direct effect on scientists' roles, and that different settings—agenda setting, legislation, and implementation—lead to different norms, and hence different roles for scientists participating in the policy process. Pielke (2007) also examines the roles of scientists in the policy process and argues that context should be an important consideration if scientists wish to be effective in decision processes. Yet his heuristic for helping scientists (and policy makers) decide the appropriate role for scientists in the policy process warns against trying to use a stakeholder-based, "honest broker" approach for the kinds of high-conflict-type post-normal problems this research is focused on.

2   Although see Ozawa (1991) for three cases in which the potential for consensus-based decision-making to create space for constructive civic science is evident; Susskind et al. (1999) for a number of illustrative cases; and Scholtz and Stiftel (2005) for a case of water resources seeking to

integrate science into policy-making. The work of the SLIM (Social Learning for the Integrated Management and sustainable use of water) group in Europe also qualifies here, given their development of a "diagnostic framework (DF) . . . that aims to transform the[ir] findings into a tool that could bring stakeholders, in other contexts, to understand better their own roles in complex natural resource management situations[, thus facilitating SLIM's goal of] . . . the development and deployment of scientific knowledge and research methodologies that are useful for action, and for actions that transform at socially and ecologically meaningful scales" (Scholtz and Stiftel 2005, 575). As well, there are other simple applications (see Clark and Illman 2001), but they do not apply here.

3   The model of scientific practice that they describe has elements similar to Don K. Price's (1965) four "estates," where scientists trade autonomy for policy relevance as they move closer to arenas of political power. Funtowicz and Ravetz's (1993) focus on uncertainty also has something in common with Alvin Weinberg's (1972) concept of "trans-science," or policy questions that push scientific inquiry beyond its most reliable methodologies.

4   While the concept of honest brokering (Pielke 2007) is implied both by clumsy solutions and the idea of trying to strike a balance among science, different knowledges, and political/cultural values, we argue that "brokering" results from the combination of individual brokers' (not necessarily scientists) actions *and* the constraints and opportunities provided by existing institutional (decision-making) arrangements.

5   Other approaches that bring nonexperts into both the production and evaluation of knowledge include consensus conferences, which have been used to bring together competing perspectives and values around topics like bioremediation of hazardous wastes (Lach and Sanford 2010), and citizen juries, which have been organized to assess the quality of biomedical research (Menon and Stefanski 2008).

References

Allen, T. F. H., J. Tainter, J. C. Pires, T. Hoekstra. 2001. "Dragnet Ecology—Just the Facts, Ma'am: The Privilege of Science in a Postmodern World." *Bioscience* 51:475–483.

Alm, L. 1997–1998. "Lost Credibility? Scientists, Advocacy and Acid Rain." *Journal of Environmental Systems* 26:249–263.

Ansell, Christopher K. 2011. *Pragmatist Democracy: Evolutionary Learning as Public Philosophy.* Oxford: Oxford University Press.

Bechtel, William. 1988. *Philosophy of Science: An Overview for Cognitive Science.* Hillsdale, NJ: Lawrence Erlbaum.

Beierle, Bruce, and Jerry Cayford. 2002. *Democracy in Practice: Public Participation in Environmental Decisions.* Washington, DC: Resources for the Future Press.

Braithwaite, John. 1998. "Institutionalizing Distrust, Enculturating Trust." In *Trust and Governance*, edited by V. Braithwaite and M. Levi, 343–375. New York: Russell Sage.

Bush, Vannevar. 1945. *Science the Endless Frontier: A Report to the President.* July. www.nsf.gov/od/lpa/nsf50/vbush1945.htm.

Clark, Fiona, and Deborah H. Illman. 2001. "Dimensions of Civic Science: Introductory Essay." *Science Communication* 23 (1): 5–27.

Dietz, Thomas, and Paul Stern. 2009. *Public Participation in Environmental Assessment and Decision Making.* Washington, DC: National Academies Press.

Dryzek, John S. 2002. *Deliberative Democracy and Beyond.* Oxford: Oxford University Press.

Ehrlich, P., and A. Ehrlich. 1996. *Betrayal of Science and Reason: How Anti-environmental Rhetoric Threatens Our Future.* Washington, DC: Island Press.

Fortmann, Louise, ed. 2008. *Participatory Research in Conservation and Rural Livelihoods: Doing Science Together.* Oxford: Wiley-Blackwell.

Foucault, Michel. 1980. *Power/Knowledge.* New York: Pantheon.

Frame, Bob. 2008. "Wicked, Messy and Clumsy: Long-Term Frameworks for Sustainability." *Environment and Planning* C 26:1113–1128.

Frame, Bob, and Judy Brown. 2008. "Developing Post-Normal Technologies for Sustainability." *Ecological Economics* 65 (2) (April): 225–241.

Franklin, Jerry, and Norm Johnson. 2010. *Applying Restoration Principles on the BLM O&C Forests in Southwest Oregon.* www.blm.gov/or/resources/forests/files/Franklin_Johnson_restoration_overview_Nov_30%20final.pdf.

Funtowicz, S., and J. Ravetz. 1992. "Three Types of Risk Assessment and the Emergence of Post-Normal Science." In *Social Theories of Risk*, edited by S. Krimisky and D. Golding. Westport, CT: Praeger.

———. 1993. "Science for the Post-Normal Age." *Futures* (September): 739–755.

———. 1999. *Post-Normal Science: Environmental Policy under Conditions of Complexity.* www.jvds.nl/pns/pns.htm.

Goodman, David, E. Melanie DuPuis, and Michael K. Goodman. 2012. *Alternative Food Networks: Knowledge, Practice, and Politics.* New York: Routledge.

Ingram, Helen, and Steven R. Smith, eds. 1993. *Public Policy for Democracy.* Washington, DC: Brookings Institution.

International Energy Agency (IEA). 2012. *World Energy Outlook 2012.* Paris: International Energy Agency.

Jasanoff, Sheila. 2007. *Designs on Nature.* Princeton, NJ: Princeton University Press.

Jasanoff, S., G. Markle, J. Petersen, and T. Pinch, eds. 1995. *Handbook of Science and Technology Studies.* Thousand Oaks, CA: Sage Publications.

Kamarck, Elaine C. 2007. *The End of Government . . . As We Know It.* Boulder, CO: Lynne Rienner.

Kay, J. 1998. *Ecosystems, Science and Sustainability.* www.ecologistics.com/nesh/scisust.html.

Keller, Ann C. 2009. *Science in Environmental Policy: The Politics of Objective Advice.* Cambridge, MA: MIT Press.

Kettl, Donald F. 2002. *The Transformation of Governance: Public Administration for Twenty-First Century America.* Baltimore, MD: Johns Hopkins University Press.

Khademian, Anne M. 1992. *The SEC and Capital Market Regulation: The Politics of Expertise.* Pittsburgh, PA: University of Pittsburgh Press.

Kitcher, Philip. 2003. *Science, Truth, and Democracy.* Cambridge: Oxford University Press.

Lackey, Robert. 2007. "Science, Scientists, and Policy Advocacy." *Conservation Biology* 21:12–17.

Lane, Neal. 1999. "The Civic Scientist and Science Policy." In *AAAS Science and Technology Policy Yearbook.* http://www.aaas.org/spp/yearbook/chap22.htm.

Latour, B., and S. Woolgar. 1979. *Laboratory Life: The Construction of Scientific Facts.* Beverly Hills, CA: Sage Publications.

Lee, K. 1993. *Compass and Gyroscope.* Washington, DC: Island Press.

Lejano, R. P., and H. Ingram. 2009. "Collaborative Networks and New Ways of Knowing." *Environmental Science and Policy* 12 (6): 653–662.

Levien, R. 1979. "Global Problems: The Role of International Science and Technology Organizations." In *Science, Technology and Global Problems,* edited by J. Gvishiani, 45–50. Oxford: Pergamon Press.

Levins, Richard, and Richard Lewontin. 1985. *The Dialectical Biologist.* Cambridge, MA: Harvard University Press.

Lubchenco, J. 1998. "Entering the Century of the Environment: A New Social Contract for Science." *Science* 279:491–497.

Margerum, Richard. 2011. *Beyond Consensus: Improving Collaborative Planning and Management.* Cambridge, MA: MIT Press.

McNie, Elizabeth. 2007. "Reconciling the Supply of Scientific Information with User Demands: An Analysis of the Problem and Review of the Literature." *Environmental Science and Policy* 10:17–38.

Melman, Seymour, ed. 1970. *Pentagon Capitalism: The Political Economy of War.* New York: McGraw Hill.

Mosher, Frederick C. 1982. *Democracy and the Public Service.* Cambridge: Oxford University Press.

Ozawa, Connie P. 1991. *Recasting Science: Consensual Procedures in Public Policy Making.* Boulder, CO: Westview Press.

Paarlberg, Robert. 2004. "Knowledge as Power: Science, Military Dominance, and U.S. Security." *International Security* 29, no. 1 (Summer): 122–151.

Pielke, Roger A. 2007. *The Honest Broker: Making Sense of Science in Policy and Politics.* Cambridge: Cambridge University Press.

Pierce, Jonathan, Christopher Weible, and Tanya Heikkila. 2014. "Hydraulic Fracturing." In *Science and Politics: An A-to-Z Guide to Issues and Controversies*, edited by B. S. Steel, 294–299. Los Angeles: Sage Press.

Polanyi, J. C. 1995. "A Laboratory of One's Own." In *Science and Society*, edited by Martin Moskovits. Concord, Ontario: House of Anansi Press.

Press, E., and J. Washburn. 2000. "The Kept University." *Atlantic Monthly*, March, 39–54.

Price, Don K. 1965. *The Scientific Estate*. Cambridge, MA: Belknap.

Pyeson, L., and S. Sheets-Pyeson. 1999. *Servants of Nature: A History of Scientific Institutions, Enterprises, and Sensibilities*. New York: Norton.

Ravetz, J. 1987. "Uncertainty, Ignorance, and Policy." In *Science for Public Policy*, edited by H. Brooks and C. Cooper, 48–63. New York: Pergamon Press.

———. 1990. *The Merger of Knowledge with Power: Essays in Critical Science*. London: Mansell Publishing.

Ray, Dixy Lee, Jeff Riggenbach, and Lou Guzzo. 1997. *Trashing the Planet: How Science Can Help Us Deal with Acid Rain, Depletion of the Ozone, and Nuclear Waste*. Washington, DC: Regnery.

Rayner, Steve. 2006. "Wicked Problems: Clumsy Solutions—Diagnoses and Prescriptions for Environmental Ills." Jack Beale Memorial Lecture on the Global Environment, James Martin Institute for Science and Civilization. July. Sydney, Australia. http://eureka.bodleian.ox.ac.uk/93/1/Steve%20 Rayner%2C%20Jack%20Beale%20Lecture%20Wicked%20Problems.pdf.

Rittel, Horst W. J., and Melvin M. Webber. 1973. "Dilemmas in a General Theory of Planning." *Policy Science* 2 (4): 155–169.

Roberts, Nancy C. 2002. *The Transformative Power of Dialogue*. New York: JAI Press.

Salmon, Guy. 2007. "Collaborative Approaches to Sustainable Development— Lessons from the Nordic Countries." Address to the Ninth Southeast Asian Survey Congress on Developing Sustainable Societies, October 31.

Sarewitz, Daniel. 2000. "Human Well-Being and Federal Science: What's the Connection?" In *Science, Technology and Democracy*, edited by Daniel Kleinman. Albany: State University of New York Press.

———. 2004. "How Science Makes Environmental Controversies Worse." *Environmental Science and Policy* 7:385–403.

Sarewitz, D., and R. Pielke. 2000. "Prediction in Science and Policy." In *Prediction: Science, Decision Making and the Future of Nature*, edited by D. Sarewitz, R. Pielke, and R. Byerly. Washington, DC: Island Press.

Schneider, Anne, and Helen Ingram. 1997. *Policy Design for Democracy*. Lawrence: University Press of Kansas.

Scholz, John, and Bruce Stiftel, eds. 2005. *Adaptive Governance and Water Conflict*. Washington, DC: Resources for the Future.

Scott, James. 1998. *Seeing Like a State: How Certain Schemes to Improve the Human Condition Have Failed*. New Haven, CT: Yale University Press.

Stayaert, Patrick, and Janice Jiggins. 2007. "Governance of Complex Environmental Situations through Social Learning: A Synthesis of SLIM's Lessons for Research, Policy and Practice." *Environmental Science and Policy* 10 (6): 575–586.

Steel, B. S., P. List, D. Lach, and B. Shindler. 2004. "The Role of Scientists in the Environmental Policy Process: A Case Study from the American West." *Environmental Science and Policy* 7:1–13.

Susskind, Lawrence, Sarah McKearnan, and Jennifer Thomas-Larmer. 1999. *The Consensus Building Handbook*. Thousand Oaks, CA: Sage Publications.

US Energy Information Association (US EIA). 2012. *Annual Energy Outlook 2012*. Washington, DC: US Department of Energy. www.eia.gov.

van Brueren, Ellen M., Erik-Hans Klijn, Joop F. M. Koppenjan. 2003. "Dealing with Wicked Problems in Networks: Analyzing an Environmental Debate from a Network Perspective." *Journal of Public Administration Research and Theory* 13 (2): 193–203.

Verweij, Marco, and Michael Thompson, eds. 2006. *Clumsy Solutions for a Complex World: Governance, Politics and Plural Perceptions*. New York: Palgrave Macmillan.

Von Moltke, K. 1996. "Environmental Goals and Science Policy: A Review of Selected Countries." In *Linking Science and Technology to Environmental Goals*. Washington DC: National Research Council.

Weber, Edward P. 2003. *Bringing Society Back In: Grassroots Ecosystem Management, Accountability, and Sustainable Communities*. Cambridge, MA: MIT Press.

Weber, Edward P., and Anne M. Khademian. 2008. "Wicked Problems, Knowledge Challenges, and Collaborative Capacity Builders in Network Settings." *Public Administration Review* 68 (2): 334–349.

Weber, E. P., T. M. Leschine, and J. Brock. 2010. "Civic Science and Salmon Recovery Planning in Puget Sound." *Policy Studies Journal* 38, no. 2 (May): 235–256.

Weible, C. M., and R. H. Moore. 2010. "Analytics and Beliefs: Competing Explanations for Defining Problems and in Choosing Allies and Opponents in Collaborative Environmental Management." *Public Administration Review* 70 (5): 756–766.

Weinberg, Alvin. 1972. "Science and Trans-science." *Minerva* 10:209–222.

Williams, D. R., W. P. Stewart, and L. E. Kruger. 2013. "The Emergence of Place-Based Conservation." In *Place-Based Conservation: Perspectives from the Social Sciences*, edited by W. P. Stewart, D. R. Williams, and L. E. Kruger, 1–17. Dordrecht: Springer.

Wilson, James Q., ed. 1980. *The Politics of Regulation*. New York: Basic Books.

Part One

Wrestling with Wicked Problems:
The Dilemmas

Chapter 1

Ways of Knowing and Relational Knowledge

MARCELA BRUGNACH AND HELEN INGRAM

Over the past several decades, the suitability of scientific knowledge for addressing public policy problems has been both championed and, as detailed in the introduction to this volume, questioned. Critics have argued that the exclusive use of scientific information, under the claims of objectivity, universality, and "truth," is no longer always the appropriate way to approach the scientific endeavour, particularly for wicked problems, as many chapters in this book demonstrate. A key reason that science has lost its privileged place in many public policy debates, even those that are not complex or wicked in form, is explained by the burgeoning literature on social construction. This approach to public policy finds that such problems emerge from the intersection of history, society, and materiality (Schneider and Ingram 1997). Reducing their description to a neutral body of statements, as science suggests, forgets that these problems are interpreted and subject to multiple meanings and values, and that many conceptual, procedural, and structural aspects of knowledge matter when coping with complex issues (Brugnach et al. 2014).

How public policy problems are defined and addressed deeply influences the type of knowledge used, how and by whom this knowledge is created, and whose values this knowledge represents (Brugnach et al. 2014). Public policy problems neither happen nor are they discovered. Instead, they are constructed or designed by people working together. The practice of problem construction is a mediated cognitive and emotional process that takes place in one or more social settings. Consequently, neither problems nor knowledge to address them are "out there" to be discovered, but instead are the result of social and social-psychological interactions contextually determined by the procedures, structures, and organizational processes within which they take place.

Interpretations of problems arise from many different perspectives: understandings of what evidence is valid and relevant; worldviews that posit how things are related; perceptions about impacts; and experiences and values. Different kinds of knowledge are generated and mobilized in distinct contexts, often related to the kinds of expertise that have a particular fix on research questions related to an established policy space, such as fisheries biology in salmon recovery efforts. Fragmentation and segmentation—the division of labor in the world of science—is augmented by constituencies and clientele that mobilize behind their preferred facts and interpretations. The result can be dueling science that is used for advocacy of specific policy outcomes instead of enlightenment or consensus (Van Buuren 2009). Rather than settling differences as additional scientific studies are supposed to do, more science often confuses the issue by raising more questions than answers. While studies may increase in sophistication and provide additional control over error, anomalies and explanations also tend to increase.

Many are the ways of knowing about public policy problems, and many the networks of actors concerned with them. Here we make the case that a more comprehensive and democratic understanding of contemporary public policy problems requires the integration of different ways of knowing about policy issues *if the goal is effective problem-solving in a democracy*. Seen from this perspective, decision choices must be able to accommodate a diversity of perspectives, interests, and ways of knowing, including, but not limited to, science. In short, we propose to reconceptualize knowledge as relational. This suggests a reformulation of knowledge and the knowledge creation processes that generate it, as well as a different role for science and scientists in policy-making.

Toward this end, we start by fleshing out the "ways of knowing" concept for public policy problems, paying particular attention to how cognitive and emotional pathways and issues of power, scale, and ambiguity all influence what is known about a problem and how a problem is addressed. We then propose and develop a relational conceptualization of knowledge, as more apt to address public policy problems effectively, before closing with a discussion of the implications this relational view may have for science and for the role scientists have in policy-making processes.

WAYS OF KNOWING PUBLIC POLICY PROBLEMS

Ways of knowing (WoK) link the knowledge of "what, why and how" with reality judgements, value judgements, and action judgements (Van Buuren

2009). A WoK is how one identifies and interprets important policy elements and makes sense of the relationships among those elements (Schneider and Ingram 2005). It is a story that holds all the pieces together in a relatively coherent way. The elements can include people, objects, and ideas, as well as the relationships among them. A WoK does not consistently refer to one particular domain or discipline, but associates heterogeneous elements from different domains as they are perceived to be related in a particular policy issue or problem. For example, a WoK for water scarcity may revolve around issues of water consumption by agricultural and other activities and how the different uses are balanced. Such a WoK can include diverse elements such as water availability, weather forecasts, water allocation patterns, farmers and other consumers, crops, ecologies, technologies, and formal and informal regulations, among others.

While ways of knowing emerge from processes of interpretation and negotiation, they are not fixed in stone and are subject to ongoing evolution and change. A WoK includes an active dimension of knowing, concerned with the way a policy issue or problem becomes significant and acquires meaning and is acted on. In WoKs, meaning-making is always done in relation to other elements and other contexts, so the meaning of any element is always contextually determined vis-à-vis other elements. In short, for WoKs, meaning lies in relationships.

When these ideas are applied to social problems, like the ones concerning public policy, the system of differences is enmeshed in very complex relationships that can involve disparity of power and resources, changing identities, and conflicts over resources. What counts as significant (i.e., the problem or issue of concern) depends on how these differences are established and valued. So, from the perspectives of WoKs, meaning-making is a situated process, inseparable from the context, history, and underlying ideologies wherein it happens. And, what is defined as a problem goes beyond a rational conceptualization, to reflect the subjectivities and lived experiences of those that define it.

Cognitive processes and emotions in policy decision knowledge

People draw on a wide range of cognitive and emotional pathways in knowing anything, and different pathways may be relevant in different contexts and circumstances. Personal intuition, inspiration, spirituality, ethics, and empathy often serve as guides as much as or more than rationality and logical reasoning.

Direct experience, as it is interpreted through cognitive and emotional pathways, is also a powerful source of knowledge. Human beings develop knowledge through experience and practices, and this knowledge can far outweigh the contribution of scientific understandings when making decisions. For instance, water project operators speak about the importance of their "craft" knowledge about the systems they manage. Only on-the-job experience can educate them as to what reactions are likely to result from operational choices they make (Rayner et al. 2005).

Experiential understanding filtered through spirituality and ethics that is bound to community is at the root of the traditional knowledge so important to many indigenous peoples. The observations of past generations become embodied in myths, stories, and traditions that hold powerful sway over present peoples, as respect for the experience of elders is reinforced by spiritual beliefs that unify peoples and strengthen community resilience. The Hopi people, for example, have lived in the same area in Northern Arizona for as long as a thousand years, developing a variety of strategies for survival in this land of little rain. A complex calendar of ceremonies and dances combine with planting at different times and places to respond to patchy and intermittent rainfall in order to maximize opportunities for crop growth and harvest. Ethics play a role in Hopi traditional knowledge, as drought is often interpreted as a problem created by failing to follow long-established Hopi rules of behavior (Waters 1963).

Modern-day thought supposes that individuals are liberated from the restraint of traditions and typically calculate for and act on their self-interest. But a great deal of social science evidence suggests that emotions such as empathy and common regard for humanity can trump instrumental reason. Researchers have shown that the neural connections between cognitive and emotional centers of the brain exist and that, absent emotions, decision-making ability deteriorates (Damasio 1994). Anger, fear, disgust, pleasure, and a host of other emotions affect not only cognition but relationships, and the emotional connections an individual has to others reflect back on reason. Taking a psychodynamic perspective on behavior in organizations, Prins (2006) argues that most human beings are inclined to avoid anxiety, uncertainty, and threats. They gravitate toward decisions and actions that promise to enhance control, predictability, and improved self-esteem. Social dynamics, especially as they affect emotions, greatly affect how people reason and understand problems within organizations, communities, and other social settings.

Shortcuts and decision heuristics can also lead to automatic or semiautomatic reliance on embedded behavior. Tversky and Kahneman (1974) draw attention to the way heuristics affect perceptions of risk, such as the availability heuristic that leads people to overestimate the probability of something if it is more immediate, vivid, and dramatic. While much of the scholarly literature blames heuristics for the poor record many people have in accurately estimating the probability of risk, Thatcher (2009) interprets availability not as error, but as reflecting experience and empathetic understanding of others. For Thatcher, judgements of outcomes must include the subjective, emotional sense, and availability of a resource as well as a bias. The availability heuristic lends social sensibilities, concreteness, and emotion-laden imagery that are essential for intelligent sense-making and choice (Thatcher 2009). Scientific efforts to objectify knowledge and strip away the emotional and value-laden pathways and social context through which people reason can lead to misunderstanding of the ways that public problems are likely to be defined and scientific evidence about those problems interpreted.

Issues of power in policy decision knowledge

Knowledge, supposedly, is power, but the reverse can be equally true. Power can shape public problems and the knowledge needed to address them. Power comes in a variety of forms including formal authority, voting strength, propensity to organize, wealth, social status, and social connectedness, among many others. Further, as Schneider and Ingram (1997) have argued, social constructions of the worthiness and entitlement of populations can combine with power so that those who are both powerful and viewed positively are more likely to have significant influence over public affairs, including problem definition and knowledge creation. In contrast, those who lack power resources and are also seen in negative terms as unworthy or as deviants tend to have little influence over how problems affecting them are defined or what knowledge is brought to bear in formulating solutions (Schneider and Ingram 1993).

Power and social construction have had strong influence in the way water resources have been managed in the American West. While water can be variously defined as a cultural or natural element, it has usually been characterized as property or the product of engineering processes. Such a definition serves the interests of water rights holders and water development interests. The growing political power of environmentalists has made some headway in shifting attention to water as a natural element tied to habitat and place (Whiteley et al. 2008). However, the cultural and community aspects of water continue to be relatively slighted. Rural populations and Native Americans, for example, have tried to protect access to water in order to preserve culture or ways of life, with limited success (Brown and Ingram 1987; Rodriguez 2006). Although the Winters Doctrine espoused by the Supreme Court in 1908 was supposed to protect sufficient water on Native American reservations for Native peoples to practice "the arts of civilization," it has generally been interpreted to mean economically profitable activities.

Power is reflected in strategic access to arenas where problems are framed and relevant knowledge identified. For instance, the Bureau of Indian Affairs is a relatively weak agency within the Department of the Interior, where much natural resources policy is formulated and implemented by officials historically accountable to resource development interests (McCarthy 2005). This lack of strategic access can be contrasted with that of the science establishment, which, by law, reviews a wide variety of administrative decisions through the National Academies of Sciences, Engineering, and Medicine. The science establishment is far from monolithic, however, and some kinds of science have more influence than others. Most social scientists believe that their insights are given less weight in public affairs than that of physical scientists, at least in part because their findings more often prove inconvenient to powerful interests. Schneider and Ingram (1997) agree with Mukerji (1989) that scientists, in general, can be influential by helping agency personnel avoid grave technical errors and in identifying scientific opportunities, but will be ignored when their advice is politically risky. Influence also depends on whether the voice of science is unified and coherent, something that can be difficult to achieve with wicked problems that engage multiple ways of knowing.

Issues of scale in policy decision knowledge

Public policy problems and scale are inseparable. How a problem is defined is commensurate with the scale at which it is examined (Brugnach et al. 2014). Scale refers not only to the geographical space (i.e., spatial scale) or time frames (i.e., temporal scale) at which a problem is conceptualized (e.g., local or global; daily or annual), but also to governance scale—the level at which society is organized to address the problem (e.g., community, national, etc.) (Termeer and Dewulf 2014). A problem may expand along different spatial-temporal and governance scales and involve interactions across scales and levels.

The scale at which a problem is defined influences knowledge, including production, transfer, dissemination, and use. Cash et al. (2006a) point out that a mismatch in spatial, temporal, or governance scale may lead to the production of scientific and technical information that lacks salience, credibility, or legitimacy. As Carroll and Daniels indicate in chapter 4 on the US Northwest Forest Plan process, the selection of a specific scientist leader, the staffing of the forestry science team, and the truncated sixty- day "science discovery" time frame for developing the complete management plan for the Pacific Northwest region assured that a certain type of expert knowledge and knowledge production process would shape final decisions: standardized data, terminology, and standards across states and between agencies, and the reliance on expert opinion to fill in knowledge gaps.

Different aspects of a problem and issues enter into play at different scales. Characteristics that are relevant at one scale may be irrelevant at another. Something positive at one scale may have negative consequences at lower or higher scales. While fracking may yield positive effects at the level of national economy (e.g., cheap and accessible energy), for example, it may yield negative effects at the level of local communities (e.g., water contamination). It is along these lines that many argue that the long-term negative effects of fracking may not be compensated by the short-term benefits (see chapter 2 in this volume). In short, choosing to address a public policy problem at one scale or another is not without assumptions regarding the dynamics of the problem and the ways that problem is chosen to be known and solved.

Issues of ambiguity in policy decision knowledge

Ambiguity is often the result of unrecognized contextual, methodological, and substantive differences among ways of knowing (Brugnach and Ingram 2012). For example, the stakeholders involved in a participatory process may subscribe to different scientific disciplines (e.g., social or natural sciences), come from very different knowledge traditions (e.g., indigenous communities or expert advisers), have different stakes in the situation (e.g., farmers associations or governmental agencies), or have different types of expertise and experience regarding the problem (e.g., laypeople or scientists). For instance, in the Upper Guadiana River Basin in Spain—much like battles over water resources in places like the arid states of the US West and the Canterbury region of New Zealand—different groups see the problem of water deficit differently (Weber 2013; Brugnach et al. 2008). Environmentalists consider it a problem of overexploitation of groundwater resources, claiming that extraction of water by farmers is too high and does not leave enough water for the wetland ecosystems of the area. In contrast, farmers consider it a problem of water shortage, claiming that there is not enough water to support their agricultural activities. The water agency administrators focus on water rights, and they see the problem as one of overextraction by certain rights-holders. This group frames water as a public right, accepting that water is a common property to be distributed by the water authority.

The presence of ambiguity can have varying implications. On the one hand, a diversity of WoKs can offer opportunities for innovation and the development of creative solutions. From this point of view, a certain degree of ambiguity is desirable to foster collaborative work and find innovative solutions (Dewulf et al. 2005). The presence of ambiguity can also be a source of tension or conflict in a group, and it may hamper the solution of problems (Gray 2004). When this happens, ambiguity can result in a polarization of viewpoints and may impede a groups' creation of a shared basis of communication for finding a solution.

Commonly, approaches to cope with ambiguity assume these differences do not exist, or that differences can be arbitrated by adopting a technical or scientific frame. However, doing so may slight consideration of the multiplicity of WoKs that exist, and may render problem definitions and solutions incommensurate with relevant social goals and values. Issues of ambiguity are also confounded with power, implying differing strategic access to decision-making arenas.

Relational knowledge and relational knowing

Ways of knowing public policy problems are influenced by the ways we think, feel, and interact. Knowing is a social process, and behind knowledge are social relations of production. Structural models and processes—such as science, policy, or religion—support the identification of what is significant, what is valued, and what is exchanged among actors and under what conditions. Attempts to identify relevant knowledge for policy cannot escape the intricate relationships established among different knowledge holders. When the social dimension of knowledge is taken into account, knowledge becomes a property of how individuals relate through certain practices and activities (e.g., managing water), and how they make sense of a problematic situation and act in consequence. And, knowing becomes the social relational activity that is concerned with how these interactions are carried out.

If we consider knowing as a social activity, knowledge can be redefined to have both a substantive, or *content*, aspect and a *relational* aspect (Bouwen and Taillieu 2004). The *content* aspect refers to what is being understood. This includes formal and systematic knowledge, such as hard and quantifiable data (e.g., scientific knowledge), as well as informal and experiential knowledge. The *relational* aspect refers to who is being included or excluded in problem understanding and how those included relate to each other to define what the problem is, engaging all the cognitive and emotional pathways and decision heuristics through which people understand problems. So, relational knowledge is not only about substance, but also about how this substance originates as a result of relational processes that are shaped by procedural, emotional, structural, and context-dependent characteristics that allow certain interaction patterns and inhibit others.

Adopting a relational view of knowledge (substantive content plus relations) changes the assumptions about how we know the world and how we bring forth meaning. When adopting a relational view, what is known about a problem is defined by how we experience the world in connection to others. It is through relating with others that people exchange meanings and make sense of situations, creating new knowledge. Knowledge is embedded in a network of possible connections and relations among people. So, what comes to be known depends greatly on the social interactions that are forged and the type of knowledge exchange that is enabled, suppressed, or neglected by these interactions. A relational view scales up knowledge from the individual to the group level and directs attention toward how group relations affect the transformation of data into knowledge.

Relational knowledge is intersubjective knowledge. Whereas science has been mostly preoccupied with the discovery and creation of objective explanations about how the world functions, a relational view of knowledge considers knowledge as inseparable from the knowing subject and considers how this subject relates through bodies, language, and social interactions with the objects, events, and persons in the world. Scientific knowledge has traditionally been defined as a neutral body of statements, void of subjective perceptions, that objectively describes a reality. This rationale is supported by a view of the world as separated from us, the objects, relationships, and functioning of which can be objectively described. From this point of view, the world and the knowing subject are regarded as two independent entities. Even though advances in sciences, particularly in cognitive sciences and neurosciences, have proven objectivism unfeasible (Kahneman 2011), it is still a preferred way of addressing public policy concerns.

The idea of a world independent and extrinsic to us is no longer appropriate when we consider knowledge as relational. Without an objective observer, reality is understood from the perspectives of knowing subjects who are in relation with one another. This goes beyond individual subjectivism to include an intersubjective understanding of reality. Under a relational view, knowledge is the result of two or more communicating selves and is conditioned on mutually reinforcing interpretations, beliefs, values, and assumptions (Weick 1995). A relational view of knowledge considers that knowledge lies in the relationships among knowledge subjects (Bouwen 1998).

Knowledge quality and validity. From a relational perspective, the type and quality of relationships held among the different actors, and how these relationships are organized to coproduce the knowledge needed, are as important as the substantive attributes of the knowledge produced. In chapter 4, Carroll and Daniels clearly illustrate that the biophysical and social science knowledge included in the Forest Ecosystem Management Assessment Team (FEMAT) report was largely determined by an already preexisting political and social agenda imposed on the participants. While the politics surrounding knowledge use and development in this high-stakes case does not come as a surprise, acknowledging it serves to reveal the assumptions underlying the use and development of knowledge and remind us that what is known about a public policy problem is not independent from who knows it.

When the relational aspects of knowledge are taken into account, knowledge production becomes concerned with how individual actors, groups, or organizations collaborate and organized their actions to produce knowledge that is credible, salient, and legitimate (see also Cash et al. 2006b). The conservation paradigm proposed by Dr. Thomas in FEMAT was just one among several suitable approaches, but nevertheless became the preferred framework. This reserve/matrix approach reduced the problem to apparently neutral technical facts (e.g., number of reserves, size, and type of use), slighting considerations of the negative social and economic implications the proposed approach could have in some communities. In this way, all controversies and ambiguities regarding FEMAT were erased.

Adopting a relational view of knowledge has implications for how the quality of knowledge and its validity are assessed. In a relational context, the quality of knowledge is inseparable from the quality of relationships through which the knowledge is generated. Processes of validation are also intersubjective and are concerned not only with differences in theoretical and methodological approaches among different ways of knowing, but also with how actors interact in framing the problem and in identifying and producing knowledge that is relevant. For FEMAT, this would have meant engaging participants (scientists and nonscientists) in a more inclusive and reflective process, where they could question their roles and participation in the coproduction of relevant knowledge in relation to the problem.

Ambiguity, power, and scale in a relational context. A relational view on knowledge suggests resolving ambiguities through the creation of new shared knowledge forms. When the ideal conditions for dialogue are met (Argyris and Schön 1978), the new shared knowledge forms can be reached through processes of dialogue, learning, and negotiation. This implies working through differences among participants, in ways that explore, enlarge, and connect existing WoKs to reflect common collective goals and mutually acceptable solutions (Brugnach and Ingram 2012). However, issues of ambiguity may be difficult to resolve in contexts that include conflicting interests, incommensurability in knowledge forms, or an unequal access to resources. Ambiguity in this sense is not amenable to commonly used approaches, in which it is assumed that differences do not exist or, when acknowledged, are arbitrated by adopting a technical or scientific frame. In these cases, particular attention must be paid to power differentials and the exclusion of actors. Dominant actors may tend to impose their ideas to favor their particular interests (Huxham and Vangen 2005). In this situation, dialogical approaches can be complemented with efforts and mechanisms that restore power balance (e.g., legal support, access to information, capacity building) and strengthen the negotiation capacities of excluded actors.

MEANING FOR SCIENCE AND NEW ROLES FOR SCIENTISTS

Thinking about the role of science in decision-making has evolved substantially from the model where scientists simply put out their findings in academic and technical journals and leave it to others to make sense of them to resolve policy problems. Initially, the turn toward enhancing public applications of science was a one-way street in which scientists promoted understanding through popularization of their ideas in more accessible venues and language. As some public problems worsened despite huge investments in science that was supposed to resolve them, attention turned to information transfer. Scientists in some fields came to recognize that insights gained from new theories, technologies, and methodologies were not being used in the field. The use of climate forecasting in water resources management is a familiar case in point. Despite the obvious relevance of long-term forecasting of temperature and precipitation, water managers continued with the comfortable, tried-and-true methods traditionally used within their organizations for hedging against risk (Rayner et al. 2005). Integrating new knowledge into existing ways of knowing requires time, resources, and investments. Knowledge external to an operating organization may be distrusted because it lacks clarity, credibility, and legitimacy, or may contain implicit biases at odds with organizational and professional values and goals (US Climate Change Program 2008).

The role of scientists changes when we move from knowledge transfer to knowledge translation. A translation gap exists between knowledge gained through the scientific process and knowledge gained through experience in the field involving specific historical, social, and physical contexts (Orlikowski 2002; Weber 2003). Scientists working across this boundary must fill the roles of brokers, mediators, and adaptive leaders who engage in inclusive management practices (Weber and Khademian 2008a; Carlisle 2004; Uhl-Bien et al. 2007; Lejano and Ingram 2009). Various authors have suggested the use of particular kinds of tools and structures to facilitate translation. Translation can involve creating a lexicon of common definitions, developing shared methodologies, formulating cross-organizational teams, and exercising strategies such as co-locating offices to facilitate interaction (US Climate Science Program 2008). Star and Griesemer (1989) note that boundary objects, such as public presentations or information sheets on which scientists and users work collaboratively, can build common knowledge. Guston (2001) proposes that the introduction of new structures like committees and advisory boards that engage people from different ways of knowing can be helpful.

Working across the boundaries of multiple, different ways of knowing to produce knowledge related to ambiguous issue areas requires a further evolution in the role of science and scientists that we wish to emphasize here. Carlisle (2004) identifies situations of great uncertainty requiring a pragmatic approach in which the iterative interaction of actors improves sharing and assessing each other's knowledge and developing a common knowledge. However, we have argued here that ambiguity is more demanding than uncertainty, and it requires an expanded repertoire of knowledge brokering, mediation, and leadership supportive of integrated knowledge creation.

Far more inclusive knowledge creation processes may be able to take place with open and fluid boundaries, progressing through nonlinear, iterative revisiting of issues from different directions and perspectives. Rather than narrowing in on the questions, relevant science, and stakeholders in order to identify reasonable alternatives, participants (including scientists) must accept ambiguity, especially in the case of wicked problems. In such cases, the degree of effectiveness for participatory processes is likely to be enhanced by engaging the widest possible array of ways of knowing, including not just experiential and traditional knowledge, but also ways of knowing that historically have been treated as unrelated or only marginally relevant. For example, bringing medical perspectives into criminal law has revolutionized the ways that addicts are treated by the justice system. And modern medical science now embraces many practices first developed in alternative medicine, including acupuncture, massage therapy, hypnosis, and naturopathic medications, among others. In addition, successful alternative farming operations now apply ideas once thought the province of pseudoscience, including biodynamic and organic agriculture (Lejano et al. 2013), while successful collaborative water resource management agreements in New Zealand actively seek out and incorporate holistic, culturally grounded knowledge of the indigenous Maori people (Weber 2013).

More inclusive knowledge creation processes bridging different ways of knowing will necessarily mean brokering the frictions and tensions that arise. Turnhout et al. (2013) quote one of their informants as remarking, "If people from different scientific paradigms, with different epistemological commitments, start to communicate, usually it ends up with chaos" (360). As Weber and Stevenson describe in chapter 9 of this volume, it is an important part of the knowledge-broker role to envision such chaos as productive, part of the process of recognizing the ambiguity inherent in considering different ways of knowing. This is a role of "meanings" management that can lead to the coproduction of integrated knowledge.

The roles of knowledge broker and mediator involve accepting emotion as a normal part of relational knowledge-creation processes. For instance, economists and economics are important to the creation of knowledge; but some people, alienated by individualism and perceived arrogance, dislike the field and its practitioners. This emotion may undercut the possibility of blended knowledge unless it is carefully mediated rather than dismissed or ignored. Failure to consider emotions is like disregarding an elephant in the room. In short, effective knowledge brokers and mediators consider the appropriate physical, social, and political contexts in which knowledge creation takes place (Weber and Khademian 2008a, 2008b).

CONCLUSION

In this chapter we have reconceptualised policy-relevant knowledge as containing both substantive content and relational aspects. Substantive knowledge that is based on scientific authority has proven insufficient for addressing many policy problems, including, but not necessarily limited to, those characterized by high uncertainty and high-decision stakes. In a relational view of knowledge, how relations are organized in knowledge production and use is as relevant as the actual substantive content. When the relational component of knowledge production is taken into account, knowledge becomes a property of how individuals and groups relate in certain practices and activities (e.g., managing a natural resource) to make sense of a problematic situation and to take action. Knowledge is generated through the coordinated action of actors who collectively generate knowledge that is ready for action. This interactive process results in usable knowledge that reflects many different ways of knowing and relies on a wide variety of reasoning, including rational, scientific, emotional, intuitive, and spiritual. This is not a mere juxtaposition of different ways of knowing, but the expression of a set of relationships enacted by collaborators that renders knowledge legitimate, credible, and trustworthy by participants in the knowledge processes. The quality of the knowledge that emerges is a reflection of the quality of relationships.

Given this, studies in the role of knowledge in policy decisions should refocus attention away from the conventional concerns of how and whether science is afforded its rightful, privileged place in governance. Scientists are only one of many participants in knowledge creation and use, and what kinds of relationships they forge with other participants with different perspectives is critical to their influence, which is seldom likely to be solely determinative.

Moreover, the importance of knowledge relationships to successful democratic policy-making requires interactive processes that are attentive to and, in the best cases, nurture productive problem-solving relationships, thus requiring continuous engagement by the many relevant actors. And yet, precisely because the inclusion of so many actors with differing worldviews, policy preferences, and ways of knowing is required for success, friction and tension are unavoidable. The realities of building and maintaining such knowledge relationships leads us to conclude that successful problem solving for public policy problems will be enhanced to the degree that scientists take on new roles as knowledge brokers and meanings managers.

References

Argyris, C., and D. A. Schön. 1978. *Organizational Learning: A Theory of Action Perspective*. Reading, PA: Addison-Wesley.

Bouwen, R. 1998. "Relational Construction of Meaning in Emerging Organization Contexts." *European Journal of Work and Organizational Psychology* 7 (3): 299–319.

Bouwen, R., and T. Taillieu. 2004. "Multi-party Collaboration as Social Learning for Interdependence: Developing Relational Knowing for Sustainable Natural Resource Management." *Journal of Community and Applied Social Psychology* 14:137–153.

Brown, F. L., and H. Ingram. 1987. "The Community Value of Water: Implications for the Rural Poor in the Southwest." *Journal of the Southwest* 29 (2): 179–202.

Brugnach, M., and H. Ingram. 2012. "Ambiguity: The Challenge of Knowing and Deciding Together." *Environmental Science & Policy* 15 (1): 60–71. doi:10.1016/j.envsci.2011.10.005.

Brugnach, M., M. Craps, and A. Dewulf. 2014. "Including Indigenous Peoples in Climate Change Mitigation: Addressing Issues of Scale, Knowledge and Power." *Climatic Change*. doi:10.1007/s10584-014-1280-3.

Brugnach, M., A. Dewulf, C. Pahl-Wostl, and T. Taillieu. 2008. "Toward a Relational Concept of Uncertainty: About Knowing Too Little, Knowing Too Differently, and Accepting Not to Know." *Ecology and Society* 13 (2): 30.

Carlisle, P. R. 2004. "Transferring, Translating, and Transforming: An Integrative Framework for Managing Knowledge across Boundaries." *Organizational Science* 15 (5): 555–568.

Cash, D. W., W. N. Adger, F. Berkes, P. Garden, L. Lebel, and P. Olsson. 2006a. "Scale and Cross-Scale Dynamics: Governance and Information in a Multilevel World." *Ecology and Society* 11 (2): 115–127.

Cash, D., J. Borch, and A. Patt. 2006b. "Countering the Loading-Dock Approach to Linking Science and Decision Making." *Science, Technology and Human Values* 31 (3): 465–494.

Damasio, A. 1994. *Descartes' Error: Emotion, Reason, and the Human Brain*. New York: Penguin Books.

Dewulf, A., M. Craps, R. Bouwen, T. Taillieu, and C. Pahl-Wostl. 2005. "Integrated Management of Natural Resources: Dealing with Ambiguous Issues, Multiple Actors and Diverging Frames." *Water, Science and Technology* 52:115–124.

Gray, B. 2004. "Strong Opposition: Frame-Based Resistance to Collaboration." *Journal of Community Applied Social Psychology* 14:166–176.

Guston, D. H. 2001. "Boundary Organizations in Environmental Policy and Science." *Science, Technology and Human Values* 26 (4): 399–408.

Huxham, C., and S. Vangen. 2005. *Managing to Collaborate*. London: Routledge.

Kahneman, D. 2011. *Thinking Fast and Slow*. New York: Farrar, Straus, and Giroux.

Lejano, R., and H. Ingram. 2009. "Collaborative Networks and New Ways of Knowing." *Environmental Science and Policy* 12 (6): 653–662.

Lejano, R., M. Ingram, and H. Ingram. 2013. *The Power of Narratives in Environmental Networks*. Cambridge, MA: MIT Press.

McCarthy, Robert. 2005. "The Bureau of Indian Affairs and the Federal Trust Obligation to American Indians." *BYU Journal of Public Law* 19 (2).

Mukerji, C. 1989. *A Fragile Power: Scientists and the State*. Princeton, NJ: Princeton University Press.

Orlikowski, W. 2002. "Knowing in Practice: Enacting a Collective Capability in Distributed Organizing." *Organization Science* 13 (3): 249–273.

Prins, S. 2006. "*The Psychodynamic Perspective in Organisational Research: Making Sense of the Dynamics and Emotional Challenges of Collaborative Work.*" *Journal of Occupational and Organizational Psychology* 79 (3): 335–355.

Rayner, S., D. Lach, and H. Ingram. 2005. "Weather Forecasts Are for Wimps: Why Water Resource Managers Do Not Use Climate Forecasts." *Climatic Change* 69:197–227.

Rodríguez, S. 2006. *Acequia: Water Sharing, Sanctity and Place*. Santa Fe, NM: School for Advanced Research Press.

Rosenberg, A. A. 2013. "Policy Tips: Heed Risks of Uncertainty." *Nature* 504 (7480): 376–376.

Schneider, A., and H. Ingram. 1993. "The Social Construction of Target Populations: Implication for Politics and Policy." *American Political Science Review* 87 (2): 334–347.

———. 1997. *Policy Design for Democracy*. Lawrence: University of Kansas Press.

———. 2005. *Deserving and Entitled: Social Constructions and Public Policy*. Albany, NY: SUNY Press.

Star, S. L., and J. Griesemer. 1989. "Institutional Ecology, Translations and Boundary Objects: Amateurs and Professionals in Berkeley's Museum of Vertebrate Zoology." *Social Studies of Science* 19 (3): 387–420.

Termeer, C., and A. Dewulf. 2014. "Governance of Wicked Climate Adaptation Problems." In *Climate Change Governance*, edited by J. Knieling and W. Leal Filho. Berlin: Springer Berlin Heidelberg.

Thacher, D. 2009. "The Cognitive Foundations of Humanistic Governance." *International Public Management Journal* 12 (2): 261–286.

Turnhout, E., M. Stuiver, J. Klostermann, B. Harms, and C. Leeuwis. 2013. "New Roles of Science in Society: Different Repertoires of Knowledge Brokering." *Science and Public Policy* 40:354–365.

Tversky, A., and D. Kahneman. 1974. "Judgment under Uncertainty: Heuristics and Biases." *Science* 185:1124–1131.

Uhl-Bien, M., M. Russ, and B. McKelvey. 2007. "Complexity Leadership Theory: Shifting Leadership from the Industrial Age to the Knowledge Era." *Leadership Quarterly* 18:298–318.

US Climate Change Science Program. 2008. "Synthesis and Assessment Product 5.3 Decision Support Experiments and Evaluations Using Seasonal to Interannual Forecasts and Observational Data: A Focus on Water Resources." http://www/gerio.org/orders.

Van Buuren, M. W. 2009. "Knowledge for Governance, Governance of Knowledge: Inclusive Knowledge Management in Collaborative Governance Processes." *International Public Management Journal* 12 (2): 208–235.

Waters, Frank. 1963. *The Book of the Hopi.* New York: Penguin Books.

Weber, E. 2003. *Bringing Society Back In: Grassroots Ecosystem Management, Accountability, and Sustainable Communities.* Cambridge, MA: MIT Press.

———. 2013. *Building Capacity for Collaborative Water Governance in Auckland.* Prepared for the Water Management Strategy and Policy Team, Auckland Council, New Zealand Regional Government. June.

Weber E., and A. Khademian. 2008a. "Wicked Problems, Knowledge Challenges, and Collaborative Capacity Builders in Network Settings." *Public Administration Review* 68 (2): 350–365.

Weber, E., and A. Khademian. 2008b. "Managing Collaborative Processes: Common Practices, Uncommon Circumstances." *Administration and Society* 40 (5): 431–464.

Weick, K. 1995. *Sensemaking in Organizations.* Thousand Oaks, CA: Sage Publications.

Whiteley, J., H. Ingram, and R. Perry. 2008. *Water, Place, and Equity.* Cambridge, MA: MIT Press.

Chapter 2

Understanding Positions on Hydraulic Fracturing

The Entangled Mix of Expertise, Values, and Group Affiliation

CHRISTOPHER M. WEIBLE AND TANYA HEIKKILA

As the introductory chapter makes clear, hydraulic "fracking" is a scientific and technical process of pumping a mixture of water, sand or similar material, and chemical additives, under high pressure, into vertically or horizontally drilled wells. The rapid expansion of fracking across the United States in recent years has created intense scientific and technical debates concerning its overall risks and benefits, including questions about whether hydraulic fracturing is a threat to public health, a cause of earthquakes, a source of air pollution and groundwater contamination, or an unnecessary public nuisance (e.g., noise, traffic, aesthetics), especially for established residential neighborhoods (Entrekin et al. 2011; Jackson et al. 2011; Lustgarten 2009; Mooney 2011; Pierce et al. 2013).

Others point to the benefits from fracking, including the value of natural gas as a cleaner fuel alternative, use of natural gas as a bridge fuel, energy independence through increased supplies of oil and gas, the contribution of industry-related jobs to economic development and growth, and the increased government revenues from severance taxes on oil and gas production.

Central to many of these debates over the wicked problem of fracking is intense political conflict over whether or how hydraulic fracturing should be regulated and by whom. A number of states, including Colorado, Pennsylvania, Texas, Wyoming, Arkansas, Ohio, Oklahoma and Louisiana (Davis 2012; Rabe and Borick 2013; Warner and Shapiro 2013; Heikkila et al. 2013), have responded to these debates and have passed new protective regulations and legislation, such as rules requiring the disclosure of chemicals used in hydraulic fracturing fluids. Local governments across states that overlie shale formations have also passed ordinances, such as bans and moratoria (e.g., New York State), to limit oil and gas drilling near population centers.

In these ways, the issue of hydraulic fracturing joins a litany of scientifically or technically complex environmental and natural resource topics (e.g., endangered species, non-point-source pollution, and nuclear energy) that are associated with divisive and entrenched political interests and governance challenges (Mazur 1981; Sabatier 1988; Jenkins-Smith 1990). Within this literature is some implicit recognition that the expertise of individuals involved in these issues may shape their political positions, as well as policy outcomes. The public bureaucracy literature is more explicit and finds that particular groups of experts with bureaucratic authority, such as lawyers, economists, and engineers, can and do shape decision outcomes differently based on their specific professional training and "career" demands (Khademian 1992; J. Q. Wilson 1980). In both literatures, this is because expertise provides a lens or way of knowing about the world that allows individuals to deal with the complexity of issues and therefore home in on particular positions or perceptions of the issue (Barke and Jenkins-Smith 1993; Lejano and Ingram 2009). At the same time, however, the literature on technically complex environmental issues acknowledges that other factors, such as values or group affiliation, are similarly important in understanding political positions. Despite the recognition that expertise, values, group affiliation, and political positions are intertwined, few have attempted to characterize these relationships.

This chapter helps fill this gap in the literature by answering the following question: What is the relationship among expertise, values, group affiliation, and positions about hydraulic fracturing? In examining this question, we consider, first, how expertise, values, and group affiliation relate individually to political positions and, second, the extent to which more nuanced interrelationships exist among these variables. Our analyses are based on data from a survey conducted in 2013 of policy actors in Colorado who are directly and indirectly involved in the issue of hydraulic fracturing. These policy actors include officials from all levels of government, environmentalists, representatives from the oil and gas industry, and academics and consultants.

We focus on Colorado for our study because, since 2009, hydraulic fracturing has been used in 90 percent of the approximately thirteen thousand new and adjusted oil and gas wells in Colorado (COGCC 2012). Additionally, the political disputes in Colorado on this issue are representative of those across the United States, in that the policy actors involved have diverging political positions on the problems and policy solutions (Heikkila et al. 2013). This includes the presence of pro- and anti- coalitions of actors visible across diverse political venues and forums (e.g., protests, media campaigns); state-level policy activity on specific issues such as the disclosure of chemicals in hydraulic fracturing fluids, setback distances between wells and occupied buildings, and groundwater monitoring rules; and growing local-level debates and policy processes such as municipal bans and county-wide moratoria.

Our analyses confirm two key observations related to the role of expertise in policy processes. First, for the policy actors involved in Colorado hydraulic fracturing debates, expertise is not as consistently significant as values and group affiliations for explaining variation in positions on hydraulic fracturing. This finding supports past observations that in high-conflict situations, individual-level expertise is of secondary importance in explaining differences in perceptions of problems and solutions (Norton 2005; Weible and Moore 2010). Second, expertise is entangled with values and organizational affiliations and should not be interpreted as politically detached or negligible but as a political resource unevenly distributed among policy actors. This supports observations that expertise is one source of political inequality (Dahl, 2006) and that expertise often serves as a means to achieve political objectives (Mazur 1981; Sarewitz 2004; Weible 2008).

A THEORETICAL BACKSTORY: EXPERTISE, VALUES, AND GROUP AFFILIATIONS

Policy issues involving complexities of science and technology and conflicts of values have been a challenging area of study among scholars for decades, especially in the area of the environment and natural resources (Mazur 1981; Sabatier 1988; Lee 1993). Part of the challenge has been determining individual-level attributes of expertise and values, two of the most important ways of knowing and interpreting the world, given that humans are bounded in their cognitive abilities to select and filter stimuli from events and experiences (Simon 1996). Another part of the challenge is to understand how expertise and values of individuals affect how they mobilize and participate in groups that often compete to shape the course of politics and policy-making (Bentley 1908).

The intersection of expertise with values and group affiliation is, however, arguably unimportant in understanding policy processes without relating them to political positions. We use political positions as a term to encapsulate policy actors' understanding of problems, perceptions of benefits, and preferences for policy action or inaction in relation to a particular policy issue. Political positions have been argued theoretically and shown empirically to be significant in understanding and explaining political behavior, as well as in shaping policy decisions and long-term outcomes (Putnam 1976; Sabatier and Jenkins-Smith 1993). Practically, the degree of divergence of political positions among policy actors, as might be found in highly contested environmental issues like hydraulic fracturing, can be indicative of the likelihood of intransigent conflicts or opportunities for cooperation on the issue.

To clarify the expectations surrounding the variables of expertise, values, group affiliation, and political positions, we derive four general propositions from across literatures and theories. These propositions are used to help clarify for the reader both the theoretical argument and interpretation of the data. The first three propositions focus on individual relationships between the different variables: expertise and political positions, values and political positions, and group affiliation and political position. The fourth proposition emphasizes the interrelationships among the four variables.

As previously noted, the expertise of actors in the policy process (i.e., an individual's training, experience, and knowledge in a given topical domain) may play a key role in shaping political positions. Expertise involves an individual's skills and methods of analysis and, thus, relates to formal academic training or to local or informal knowledge derived from experience and trial-and-error learning. Hence, among policy actors, expertise lies not only with those individuals from academia, think tanks, and consulting firms, but also with individuals from government and nongovernment organizations. For example, bureaucracies with technical expertise were initially praised for their scientific and technical leadership and later condemned for threatening democracy with technocracy (Ellul 1964; Jenkins-Smith 1990). Within policy processes, actors from outside government are recognized as sources of expertise in particular issue areas because they can bring information about problems to the public attention in shaping agendas as well as help formulate and design laws and regulations (Baumgartner and Leech 1998; Kerwin 1999).

Each form of expertise includes assumptions, tendencies to focus on some causal relations over others, and emphasis on, and tolerance for, different levels of uncertainty. Hence, expertise represents a mobilization of bias in approaching the world from a particular perspective (Snow 1959; Barke and Jenkins-Smith 1993; Norton 2005; Cohen 2006; Weible and Moore 2010). As a result, scholars recognize that the course of policy processes can be shaped by the types of expertise policy actors hold. For instance, limiting policy processes to particular types of experts can privilege particular types of information and limit the range of political positions that enter into policy processes (Healy and Ascher 1995; Fischer 2000; Ascher et al. 2010). Thus, scholars have emphasized the need for diverse forms of expertise to be represented in the policy process to improve decision-making (NRC 1996; Fischer 2000; Weber 2003). Others recognize that when policy actors hold divergent types of expertise, they may need to develop shared language and common understanding (Lejano and Ingram 2009) or new policy instruments or forums (Guston 2001) to reach agreements. Although the policy literature highlights different theoretical emphases in the study of expertise, one common theme is that *expertise is a significant factor in explaining political positions*.

Expertise is not the only factor that shapes how individuals understand complex political issues. Another key factor is values, which represent the normative principles that people use to help situate themselves within the world. The cognitive mechanisms explaining how values orient people to the world derive partly from the social psychology literature, which has documented the role of values and beliefs in affecting how people select and assimilate stimuli (Festinger 1957; Lord et al. 1979; Munro and Ditto 1997; Munro et al. 2002). These findings from social psychology have influenced the incorporation of values in many theories of behavior and politics. For example, value-belief-norm theory argues that values are the fundamental driver of beliefs, norms, and, eventually, behavior (Stern et al. 1999). The theory of planned behavior includes values as normative beliefs in shaping the intention to act (Ajzen 1991). In cultural theory, different categories of values have been theoretically and empirically found to be important factors in understanding a range of behaviors and positions (Douglas 1966, 1970, 1990; Wildavsky 1987). The advocacy coalition framework (ACF) assumes values are a primary source that individuals use to form their policy-related positions and then to choose their coalition of allies (Sabatier 1988). Each of these theories incorporates values differently in sets of hypotheses and models to describe and explain various forms of outputs and outcomes. Despite the differences in emphasis, a common thread across these theories is that people are boundedly rational and that values provide a useful heuristic, means, and general compass to help formulate positions across a range of topics. The fundamental proposition from this literature is that *values are significant factors in explaining political positions.*

In addition to expertise and values, group affiliation has been widely recognized in the political science and public policy literature as an important factor associated with political positions. Bentley (1908) made the formative argument that to understand government processes one must first understand the groups involved. Such an argument represents a core assumption of research on pluralism that emphasizes group competition and issues of power and influence in government affairs (Dahl 1961; Lowi 1969; Baumgartner and Leech 1998; McFarland 2004). The motivations and role of groups in politics depends partly on the group type and how groups relate to the policy issue. For example, private groups might be motivated by material and economic interests, and nonprofit groups might be motivated by purposive rationales or beliefs (Jenkins-Smith et al. 1991). Lowi (1964) also argued that certain types of policy issues will affect how groups relate to the policy process. Although this particular study does not attempt to unravel the motivating factors of individuals within groups, it does argue that group affiliation will have an independent effect on political positions. Therefore, our third proposition is *group affiliation is a significant factor in explaining political positions.*

Although the previous three propositions explore the independent effects of values, expertise, and group affiliation on positions, other scholars suggest a more complicated relationship among them. For example, the study of the scientific process has shown that science and research processes are often socially defined (Latour and Woolgar 1979) or that knowledge is socially constructed to reduce political uncertainty and risks (Schneider and Ingram 1997). Montpetit (2011) shows how credibility and disagreement among scientists is shaped by the level of value-based conflicts. Weible et al. (2010) finds that scientists are often the allies or opponents of belief-based advocacy coalitions, especially in high-conflict situations. Weible (2008) also posits that disciplinary training provides analytical skills to reinforce value orientations. At the same time, positions on issues may drive one's choice of professional training or group affiliation, which could reinforce fundamental values. Although the precise theoretical relationship among expertise, values, group affiliation, and political positions remains unclear, a common finding across this literature is that these concepts are not independent but are entangled in complicated ways. Thus, the expectation from this literature is that *differing types of expertise, values, group affiliation, and political positions will show distinct and divergent patterns of interrelationships.*

RESEARCH DESIGN AND METHODS

Data for this study come from a survey conducted in 2013 of individuals involved in the politics or policy processes related to hydraulic fracturing in Colorado. To identify these actors, we conducted a modified snowball sample. First, we interviewed fourteen key experts knowledgeable about hydraulic fracturing in Colorado, including individuals from government, industry, nonprofits, media, and the scientific community, and asked who we should include in our survey. Second, the Colorado Oil and Gas Conservation Commission, the regulatory body overseeing hydraulic fracturing in Colorado, produces lists of individual stakeholders who attended meetings on rulemakings in 2011 and in 2012–13, as well as those who commented on proposed rules by the agency. In addition, we attended public discussions, rallies, local government hearings, industry association meetings, and other events where hydraulic fracturing was being debated in Colorado from June 2012 to January 2013 to identify actors. Finally, we conducted an Internet search for documents of organizations with websites that take a position on the issue in Colorado.

From these different sources we developed a list of 398 stakeholders representing over 130 individual organizations operating in Colorado. This list includes individuals representing the federal government, regional governments, state government, local governments, oil and gas service providers and operators, industry and professional associations, environmental and conservation organizations, real estate developers and homebuilders, agriculture organizations, organized citizen groups, academics and consultants, news media, and other organizations. After the sample of direct and indirect stakeholders was completed, we launched an online survey in April 2012 to all 398 individuals and received 142 responses, for a response rate of 35.68 percent.

Our survey provided the data source for the measures of each of our key variables of interest—expertise, values, group affiliation, and political positions.

Expertise. To measure expertise, we use three indicators from our survey: (1) expert knowledge, (2) formal education/degree, and (3) years of involvement in hydraulic fracturing. Expert knowledge indicators are drawn from a

scale on two main knowledge areas: (1) policy management and law expertise and (2) natural/physical science expertise. These scales are drawn from a
subset of survey questions in which we asked respondents about their level of
knowledge on a range of professional fields or domains (0 = no knowledge;
4 = expert knowledge). See appendix table 2 for the factor loadings on the
two scales and specific professional fields within each of the two categories of
expertise. Formal education/degree was measured as a scale from our survey
question that asked each respondent to report their level of education (1 = no
high school degree; 6 = PhD or medical degree). To measure a policy actor's
years of involvement with this issue, our survey asked respondents to identify
their years according to a four-point categorization (0–1 years; 2–4 years;
5–9 years; 10–20 years; 21 or more).

Values. This study measures values using two indicators: (1) egalitarian
values and (2) pro-government values. These two indicators were measured
from our survey question that asked respondents to report on a four-point
scale their level of agreement with a variety of statements drawn from cultural
theory about the role of government in society and questions about their
perceptions of inequalities in society (Douglas 1966, 1970, 1990; Wildavsky
1987). Appendix table 3 reports the factor loadings from the sub-questions
used to create these scales.

Group affiliation. Indicators for group affiliation include multiple dichotomous measures for different types of organizations. These measures were
drawn from our survey question that asked respondents to identify the type
of organization they are affiliated with. Affiliation options on the survey
included federal, state, and local government organizations, environmental
and conservation groups, organized citizen groups (joined into the "environmental group" category), oil and gas industry organizations, academics/
consultants, and others (e.g., media, agricultural organizations). The other
category (n = 2) was excluded from this analysis.

Political positions. The measurement of political positions of actors con-
sists of three indicators. For the first indicator, we use our survey question
that assessed an actor's level of preference for expanding hydraulic fracturing
(1 = stop; 5 = expand significantly). This question represents a policy actor's
core policy position on the issue. The other two indicators are scales that capture policy actors' perceptions of the severity of two categories of problems:
(1) problems related to direct impacts of hydraulic fracturing, and (2) problems related to public perceptions and politics. Each of these two indicators

was created from multiple sub-indicators of these concepts, measured in the survey. The factor loadings on the two scales are shown in appendix table 1 (following this chapter).

FINDINGS

To analyze our data, we first present descriptive statistics on the survey respondents' expertise, values, group affiliation, and political positions. To test the first three propositions, we then present results from three ordinary least square (OLS) regression models that regress each of the indicators of positions on the variables representing expertise, values, and group affiliation. We then assess the fourth proposition, which focuses on the patterns of interrelationships among the different types of expertise, values, group affiliation, and positions, through ANOVA tests and cluster analysis and multidimensional scaling.

Summary statistics

Table 2.1 provides an overview of the data by including the means and standard deviations of the respondents. On average, respondents lie in the middle of the scale for expanding hydraulic fracturing, meaning they support the status quo. They are also more likely to perceive problems related to public perceptions and politics (mean = 3) than problems related to direct impacts of hydraulic fracturing (mean = 2). Respondents also report higher levels of expertise in policy, management, and law than in natural and physical sciences. On average, respondents report earning a graduate-level degree. Respondents tend to have somewhere between five and nine years of experience involved with the issue of hydraulic fracturing, or a mean score of 3 on the survey item. With respect to values, respondents on average report being in the middle of the pro-egalitarian and pro-government scales, with a slighter higher average reporting on the pro-government scale. Finally, there is a balanced representation of group affiliations, with oil and gas industry and local governments capturing the highest percentage of respondents and state government capturing the lowest percentage of respondents.

Explaining positions on hydraulic fracturing

Table 2.2 presents the results of OLS regression models for the three position measures on hydraulic fracturing. Unstandardized coefficients are presented.[1] The results show adequate fit with F-statistics ($p < 0.000$) and R^2 between 0.47 and 0.70. For the three dichotomous variables (environmental

Table 2.1. Summary Statistics of Variables

	Mean	Std Dev
Positions		
Expand Hydraulic Fracturing Beliefs	3	1.1
(1 = Stop Hydraulic Fracturing to 5 = Expand Extensively)		
Problems Related to the Direct Impacts of Hydraulic Fracturing	1.9	1.00
Problems Related to Public Perceptions and Politics	2.8	0.93
(0 = Not a Problem to 4 = Severe Problem)		
Expertise		
Policy, Management and Law Expertise	2.4	0.71
Natural/Physical Science Expertise	1.9	1.00
(0 = No Knowledge to 4 = Expert Knowledge)		
Level of Formal Education	4.7	0.75
(1 = No High School Diploma to 6 = PhD or MD)		
Years of Experience with Hydraulic Fracturing	3.1	1.1
(1 = 0–1 Years, 5 = 21 or More Years)		
Values		
Pro-egalitarian Values	2.6	0.99
Pro-government Values	2.9	0.74
(1=Strongly Disagree to 5 = Strongly Agree)		
Group Affiliation (Percent of Sample)		
Federal Government	10%	
State Government	7%	
Local Government	27%	
Oil and Gas Industry	28%	
Environmental and Citizen Groups	20%	
Academic or Consultant	8%	

affiliation, oil and gas industry affiliation, and academics and consultants), the base for comparison is government affiliation. For the purposes of the regression analyses, the categories of federal, state, and local government affiliation were collapsed into a single variable.

The findings from the OLS models indicate that the most consistent factors in explaining the variance of hydraulic fracturing positions are (1) pro-egalitarian values, (2) environmental group affiliation, and (3) oil and gas industry affiliation. These findings indicate that the more people hold egalitarian values, the more likely they are to oppose the expansion of hydraulic fracturing and to identify problems associated with the direct impacts of hydraulic fracturing, and the less likely they are to identify

Table 2.2 Explaining Positions on Hydraulic Fracturing

	Dependent Variables: Positions		
	Expand Hydraulic Fracturing Beliefs	Problems Related to the Direct Impacts of Hydraulic Fracturing	Problems Related to Public Perceptions and Politics
Expertise			
Policy, Management, and Law Expertise	0.25**	-0.17**	0.07
Natural/Physical Science Expertise	-0.04	-0.06	0.07
Level of Formal Education	-0.05	0.14*	-0.11
Years Involved	0.10*	-0.02	0.02
Values			
Pro-egalitarian Values	-0.30**	0.27***	-0.21**
Pro-government Values	-0.13	0.22**	-0.17
Group Affiliation			
Environmental Affiliation	-0.91***	0.88***	-0.60**
Oil and Gas Industry Affiliation	0.57**	-0.45**	0.51**
Academics and Consultants	0.45	-0.15	0.50*
Constant	3.6***	0.49	3.9***
R^2	0.59	0.70	0.42
N=	103	107	109

Notes: Omitted category of group affiliation is "government". Unstandardized coefficients provided and calculated from ordinary least square regression. $p<0.001$***, $p<0.05$**, $p<0.10$*

problems related to public relations and politics. Pro-government values are also significant and positively related to positions on problems related to the direct impacts of hydraulic fracturing but not the other two position-dependent variables.

Among the expertise measures, we find mixed results in explaining political positions on hydraulic fracturing. Policy, management, and law expertise is significant and positively associated with positions that prefer the expansion of hydraulic fracturing and negatively associated with positions on problems associated with the direct impacts of hydraulic fracturing. The level of formal education is positively associated with perceptions of problems with the direct impacts of hydraulic fracturing.

For the group affiliation indicators, the variables for environmental affiliations and for oil and gas affiliations are significant across all three models
in logical directions, compared with the baseline category of government
officials. The signs indicate that actors with environmental affiliations are
more likely to be against the expansion and more likely to perceive problems
with the direct impacts of hydraulic fracturing, but less likely to see problems
regarding public perceptions and politics. The direction of the relationships
between the variable for oil and gas industry affiliations and positions on
hydraulic fracturing is the opposite of the relationships between environmental group affiliation and positions. The variable representing academic
and consultant affiliation is only significant in the third model—suggesting
that academics and consultants are more likely to identify problems related to
public perceptions and politics, relative to government officials.

Overall, the results lend more support for the importance of values and
group affiliations, as opposed to expertise, in shaping political positions about
hydraulic fracturing.

Exploring interrelationships among expertise, values, group affiliation, and political positions

To explore the interrelationships suggested in proposition four, the variables
were combined and related in a multidimensional scaling analysis and cluster analysis, as shown in figure 1 (Wasserman and Faust 1994; Hanneman
2001; Borgatti et al. 2002). To derive the results in figure 1, all respondents
with complete responses to the variable items (n = 112) and the nine variables (as found in table 2.1) were used to create a 112x9 matrix. The variables
constituting the variables in vertical columns were rescaled from 0 to 1. The
matrix was then transformed using Pearson's correlation coefficients between
columns between variables. In other words, pro-egalitarian values for the 112
respondents were correlated with pro-government values for the same 112
respondents. The result is a 9x9 matrix with Pearson's correlation coefficients
constituting the cells and the nine variables in this paper constituting the row
and column labels.

This matrix was then analyzed using multidimensional scaling, an
approach for simplifying matrices of multiple rows and columns into two or
three dimensions. When mapped, as done in figure 1, objects that are close to
each other share similar correlation values, and objects that are farther apart
are dissimilar in their correlation values. The measure of fit is a stress value in

Figure 1. The Fracking Puzzle: Political Positions and Expertise

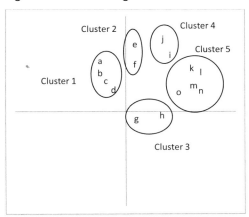

LEGEND

Cluster 1
a. Environmentalists
b. Problems Related to the Oil & Gas
    Industry
c. Pro-Egalitarian Values
d. Pro-Government Values

Cluster 2
e. Academics & Consultants
f. High Levels of Formal Education

Cluster 3
g. Local Government Officials
h. State Government Officials

Cluster 4
i. Natural/Physical Science Expertise
j. Federal Government Officials

Cluster 5
k. Many Years Involved
l. Industry Representatives
m. Problems Related to Public Relations
n. Pro Expand Hydraulic Fracturing Beliefs
o. Policy, Management & Law Expertise

Note: Letter placement was conducted by multi-dimensional scaling (Stress = 0.22). Clustering was conducted through Tabu Search Cluster Analysis (R2=0.62).

multidimensional scaling, with acceptable stress levels less than 0.20, though many conduct the technique for visualizing matrices with much higher stress levels (Knoke et al. 1996). The primary purposes of multidimensional scaling are to provide a visual layout of the different variables used in this analysis and to identify the major factors that relate them. Interpreting the dimensions in multidimensional scaling is an inductive exercise done by the researcher and reader. Based on the calculations in this paper, the placement of the variable represents high values for that variable. For example, the placement of pro-egalitarian values on one side of one dimension highlights its shared correlation with other objects on the same dimensional end; it also indicates negative association with objects on the other dimensional end.

The variables are then clustered using tabu search cluster analysis. Tabu search cluster analysis iteratively combines cells in a matrix to maximize within cluster correlations. One of the benefits of tabu search cluster analysis is the technique reports goodness of fit (R^2) that can be used to identify the optimal cluster number (Hanneman 2001; Borgatti et al. 2002).

The result from the multidimensional scaling and the tabu search cluster analysis is a two-dimensional depiction of the variables clustered into five groupings. The horizontal dimension divides the data set into variables for and against hydraulic fracturing. In cluster 1 on the left are environmentalists, problems related to the direct impacts of hydraulic fracturing, pro-egalitarian values, and pro-government values. On the other extreme, on the right of the horizontal dimension, is cluster 5, consisting of oil and gas industry representatives, many years of involvement, problems related to public perceptions and politics, and expertise in policy, management, and law.

The other three clusters spread along the vertical dimension represent government officials and academics and consultants. These group affiliations are isolated from the clusters 1 and 5 encircling the environmentalists and the oil and gas industry, respectively. Although the vertical dimension is open to interpretation, the most likely interpretation for the division is by expertise. Academics and consultants are isolated from the rest for their high levels of formal education and federal government officials are isolated for their expertise in natural and physical sciences.

Overall, figure 1 provides a visual depiction of the entanglement of expertise, values, group affiliations, and political positions, which cannot be captured in the OLS models. It also supports the findings from the regression models in table 2.2, where environmental and oil and gas affiliations were significantly different from each other and from those of government officials.

To help interpret and inform the cluster analysis, it is useful to consider the patterns of interrelationships among the variables as represented in table 2.3, which compares the mean scores of the variables representing expertise, values, and positions across different categories of group affiliations. Using ANOVA, significant differences in the mean values of each of these variables are found for at least one pairing among group affiliations.

The data in table 2.3 show distinct patterns among the group affiliations that support the findings in figure 1. For the oil and gas industry, they are more likely to expand hydraulic fracturing and perceive problems with public perceptions and politics, and are involved in the issue longer than other affiliations. For the environmental interests, they are the most against hydraulic fracturing and hold the strongest pro-egalitarian beliefs and beliefs in government. There tends to be uniformity across respondents for years of formal education with the exception of academics and consultants. Government officials from any level tend to hold more moderate political positions about hydraulic fracturing. Federal government officials also report higher levels of expertise in natural and physical science compared with other group affiliations. Comparing the horizontal dimension of figure 1 with the mean differences in table 2.3 supports the patterns found in the visual presentation of the multidimensional scaling and clusterings.

Table 2.3: Relating Group Affiliations to Positions, Values, and Expertise

	Measure	Group Affiliation					
		Oil and Gas	Acad /Con	Fed Gvt	State Gvt	Local Govt	Env
Positions							
Expand Hydraulic Fracturing Beliefs***	(1 = Stop Hydraulic Fracturing to 5 = Expand Extensively)	3.9	3.3	2.8	3.2	3.1	1.6
Problems Related to the Oil and Gas Industry***	(0 = Not a Problem to 4 = Severe Problem)	1.1	1.9	2.1	1.4	1.8	3.2
Problems Related to Public Relations with the Oil and Gas Industry***	(0 = Not a Problem to 4 = Severe Problem)	3.5	3.1	2.8	2.8	2.8	1.8
Expertise							
Policy, Management, Law Expertise**	(0 = No Knowledge to 4 = Expert Knowledge)	2.6	1.9	2.2	2.5	2.5	2.3
Natural/Physical Science Expertise**	(0 = No Knowledge to 4 = Expert Knowledge)	2.1	1.9	2.7	1.9	1.5	1.6
Level of Formal Education**	(0 = No Knowledge to 4 = Expert Knowledge)	4.6	5.6	4.5	4.7	4.5	4.7
Years Involved**	(1 = 0-1 Years, 5 = 21 or more Years)	3.7	2.5	3.5	2.9	2.9	2.6
Values							
Pro-egalitarian Values***	(1=Strongly Disagree to 5 = Strongly Agree)	2.0	2.8	2.8	2.6	2.4	3.5
Pro-government Values***	(1=Strongly Disagree to 5 = Strongly Agree)	2.4	3.0	2.8	3.0	2.9	3.4

Note: $*p<0.10$, $**p<0.05$, $***p<0.001$. Significant tests calculated by ANOVA models.

CONCLUSION

Hydraulic fracturing is one of the most contentious and complex environmental issues in recent US history. How do key actors in the policy process—defined as those individuals directly or indirectly involved in shaping policy, governance, and development of Colorado's hydraulic fracturing activities—come to their political positions? More specifically, what is the relationship among expertise, values, group affiliation, and political positions on fracking? The analysis first examined how expertise, values, and group affiliation *individually* relate to political positions, and then focused on the *interrelationships* among these variables. The findings for both research questions are integrated and summarized by the following points:

1. *Pro-egalitarian values and group affiliation explain political positions on hydraulic fracturing more consistently than expertise.* With regard to our first three propositions, we find support that values and group affiliations are important, but more mixed support for the proposition that expertise is important. Such a pattern supports the findings from other studies (Weible and Moore 2010) and adds refutation to arguments that disputes over environmental issues are motivated primarily by expertise. The finding suggests that values and group affiliations should be of primary consideration and expertise a secondary consideration in understanding policy-making processes.

2. *Expertise, values, group affiliation, and political positions entangle into patterned interrelationships.* In support of proposition four, we find evidence that expertise, values, group affiliations, and political positions show distinct patterns of interrelationships. Oil and gas industry affiliates are more likely to be involved for many years, have expertise in policy, management, and law, favor the expansion of hydraulic fracturing, and perceive problems with public perceptions and politics. Environmentalists are more likely to hold strong pro-egalitarian beliefs, strong beliefs in government, and perceive problems with the direct impacts of hydraulic fracturing. While the most polarized positions on hydraulic fracturing were taken by environmentalists and oil and gas industry affiliates, government officials and academics and consultants were more moderate in their beliefs. Unlike previous studies that found that government officials and academics were strongly aligned with one side of a political debate or another (e.g., Weible et al. 2010), this study finds that government officials and academics and consultants are more moderate in their beliefs and differ from those patterns of interrelationships associated with environmentalists and oil and gas industry affiliates. Academics and consultants and federal officials seem distinct from local and state officials in their level of expertise as well. The result supports observations that expertise is unevenly distributed among citizens (Dahl 2006). Further research is needed to understand the effects of expertise on policy processes over time.

This research also makes three additional contributions to the literature that explores the roles of expertise, values, and group affiliation in political debates. One contribution is the use of expanded measures of expertise. Rather than relying on categories of scientist, expert, or consultant only, this study includes measures of knowledge across a range of fields related to hydraulic fracturing. Additionally, expertise was measured by the number of years involved and, more traditionally, by level of formal education. Although these measures are self-reported and do not capture all the different components of expertise (Steel et al. 2004; Howlett 2009; Elgin and Weible 2013), the measures are more comprehensive collectively than alone. For example, this study finds that years involved and expertise in policy, management, and law is associated with pro-hydraulic fracturing positions and with the oil and gas industry.

A second contribution is in relation to the approach to data analysis. Rather than studying the independent effects of different variables, or even the interaction among two variables, on a dependent variable, this study uses multidimensional scaling and cluster analysis to uncover how the variables measured and used in this paper interrelate. The result is a more inclusive account of the entanglement of expertise, values, group affiliation, and positions.

Finally, a third contribution is substantive. This is one of the first quantitative studies of hydraulic fracturing—possibly the most contentious environmental issue that has emerged over a half century—and it provides insights using systematic procedures of data collection and analysis rarely seen (exceptions include Fisk 2013; Rabe and Borick 2013).

Drawing generalizable conclusions about this data set should be done with caution. The topic of hydraulic fracturing is arguably nascent, and policy actors may be continuing to formulate their positions. Hence, the data collected in Colorado in 2013 might very well differ from the data collected from the same population in the future. Similarly, the oil and gas industry operates with various levels of support and opposition across the United States. Obviously, the next step is to replicate the approach used in this paper cross-sectionally and longitudinally to better understand the stability of these relationships.

Appendix to Chapter 2

Appendix Table 1. Summary of Problem Perceptions

	Mean	Std Dev.	Factor Loading Two Scales	
Problems Caused Directly by Hydraulic Fracturing or Drilling				
1. Conflict between mineral rights and property rights owners	2.4	1.1	.67	.06
2. Inadequate or incomplete communication by the oil and gas industry about the risks, benefits and effects of hydraulic fracturing to the general public	2.4	1.17	.67	-.14
3. Nuisance to the general public caused by truck traffic, noise, and light from well site operations.	2.2	1.03	.77	.13
4. Competition for available water supplies from hydraulic fracturing.	2.1	1.3	.65	.48
5. Degradation of air quality from flares, diesel exhaust, and dust from well site operations.	2.1	1.3	.69	.55
6. Degradation of air quality from fugitive methane emissions	2.0	1.4	.69	.58
7. Ineffective monitoring by state regulatory agencies of hydraulic fracturing.	1.9	1.5	.66	.54
8. Influence of the oil and gas industry over state administrative and legislative branches	1.9	1.5	.67	.57
9. Boom-and-bust economic cycles from natural gas development	1.9	1.01	.71	.08
10. Destruction of public lands by well site operations, processing facilities, and pipelines	1.9	1.3	.72	.51
11. Surface degradation and erosion from access roads at well site operations.	1.8	1.2	.80	.36
12. Burdens on local government services from temporary employees for well site operations	1.8	1.0	.72	.04
13. Contamination of ground and surface water supplies from chemicals in hydraulic fracturing fluids (reversed)	1.7	1.4	.61	.61
14. Contamination of ground water from methane migration	1.6	1.3	.68	.55
15. Risks of induced seismic activity caused by hydraulic fracturing	1.1	1.2	.63	.46
Oil & Gas Industry Scale (Cronbach's alpha = 0.96)				
Problems Related to Public Perceptions and Politics				
16. Misinformation among the general public about the risks, benefits, and effects of hydraulic fracturing.	3.1	0.96	-.04	-.71
17. Public distrust of the oil and gas industry	2.8	0.99	.31	-.67
18. Distribution of biased information against hydraulic fracturing.	2.7	1.41	-.30	-.79
19. Scare tactics and demonizing of the oil and gas industry by opponents of hydraulic fracturing	2.6	1.33	-.22	-.82
Public Relations Scale (Cronbach's alpha = 0.79)				

Note: The question scale ranged from 0 = Not a problem to 4 = Severe problem. The factor loadings (with Varimax rotation) on the left provide the rationale for combining variables into the "Problems Caused Directly by Hydraulic Fracturing or Drilling" (factor ladings > 0.60) and on the right for combining variables into the "Problems Related to Public Perceptions and Politics (factor loadings > abs(0.70)).

Appendix Table 2. Summary of Expertise Scales

	Mean	Std. Dev.	Factor Loading on Two Scales	
Policy, Management & Law Expertise				
1. Law	2.4	1.1	0.15	0.67
2. Policy, Planning, and Management	2.9	0.9	-0.09	0.65
3. Public Relations	2.2	0.9	-0.07	0.72
4. Business Administration	1.9	1.1	0.12	0.61
Scale (Cronbach's alpha = 0.58)	2.4	0.7		
Natural & Physical Science Expertise				
5. Ecology or Biology	2.0	1.1	0.72	-0.08
6. Geology	2.0	1.2	0.86	-0.02
7. Chemistry	1.7	1.3	0.92	-0.12
8. Engineering	1.9	1.3	0.78	0.01
9. Mining	1.6	1.1	0.69	0.25
Scale (Cronbach's alpha = 0.85)	1.9	1.0		

Note: The question scale ranged from no knowledge = 0, little knowledge = 1, some knowledge = 2, moderate knowledge = 3, and expert knowledge = 4. The factor loadings (with Varimax rotation) on the right relate to "Policy, Management & Law Expertise" (factor loadings >0.60) and on the left relate to "Natural & Physical Science Expertise" (factor loadings >0.60).

Appendix Table 3: Summary of Egalitarian and Pro-Government Beliefs

	Mean	Std. Dev.	Factor Loading on Two Scales	
Pro-Government Values				
1. Government should put limits on the choices individuals can make so they do not get in the way of what is good for society.	2.1	0.95	0.74	0.17
2. The government should do more to advance society's goals, even if that means limiting the freedom and choices of individuals.	2.1	0.96	0.73	0.34
3. Sometimes government needs to make laws that keep people from hurting themselves.	2.7	0.91	0.74	0.14
4. It is not the government's business to try to protect people from themselves. (reversed)	3.5	0.95	0.73	0.15
5. The government should stop telling people how to live their lives. (reversed)	3.3	0.98	0.70	0.33
6. The government interferes far too much in our everyday lives. (reversed)	3.5	1.04	0.70	0.41
Scale (Cronbach's alpha = 0.85)	2.9	0.7		
Pro-Egalitarian Values				
7. We need to dramatically reduce inequalities between the rich and the poor, as well as between men and women.	2.7	1.0	0.25	0.90
8. Our society would be better off if the distribution of wealth was more equal.	2.5	1.0	0.25	0.92
Scale (Cronbach's alpha = 0.89)	2.6	1.0		

Note: The question scale range from 1=Strong Disagree to 5 = Strongly Agree. The factor loadings on the right relate to "Pro-Egalitarian Values" (factor loadings >0.90) and on the left relate to "Pro-Government Values" (factor loadings >0.60).

Notes

1 The results are robust for "expand hydraulic fracturing beliefs" when conducted with ordered logit models.

References

Ajzen, I. 1991. "The Theory of Planned Behavior." *Organizational Behavior and Human Decision Processes* 50 (2): 179–211.

Ascher, W., T. Steelman, and R. Healy. 2010. *Knowledge and Environmental Policy*. Cambridge, MA: MIT Press.

Barke, R. P., and H. C. Jenkins-Smith. 1993. "Politics and Scientific Expertise: Scientists, Risk, Perception, and Nuclear Waste Policy." *Risk Analysis* 13 (4): 425–439.

Baumgartner, F. R., and B. L. Leech. 1998. *Basic Interests: The Importance of Groups in Politics and in Political Science*. Princeton, NJ: Princeton University Press.

Bentley, A. F. 1908. *The Process of Government*. Cambridge, MA: Belknap Press of Harvard University Press.

Borgatti, S. P., M. G. Everett, and L. C. Freeman. 2002. *UCINET 6 for Windows*. Cambridge, MA: Analytic Technologies.

Cohen, S. 2006. *Understanding Environmental Policy*. New York: Columbia University Press.

Colorado Oil and Gas Conservation Commission (COGCC). 2012. Staff Testimony for Setback Rulemaking. December 11, 2012. http://cogcc.state.co.us/.

Dahl, R. A. 1961. *Who Governs?* New Haven, CT: Yale University Press.

———. 2006. *On Political Equality*. New Haven, CT: Yale University Press.

Davis, C. 2012. "The Politics of 'Fracking': Regulating Natural Gas Drilling Practices in Colorado and Texas." *Review of Policy Research* 29:177–191.

Douglas, M. 1966. *Purity and Danger: An Analysis of the Concepts of Pollution and Taboo*. New York: Routledge and Keegan Paul.

———. 1970. *Natural Symbols: Explorations in Cosmology*. London: Barrie & Rockliff.

———. 1990. *Risk and Blame: Essays in Cultural Theory*. New York: Routledge.

Elgin, D., and C. M. Weible. 2013. "Stakeholder Analysis of Colorado Climate and Energy Issues Using Policy Analytical Capacity and the Advocacy Coalition Framework." *Review of Policy Research* 30:116–134.

Ellul, Jacques. 1964. *The Technological Society*. New York: Vintage Books.

Entrekin, S., M. Evans-White, B. Johnson, and E. Hagenbuch. 2011. "Rapid Expansion of Natural Gas Development Poses a Threat to Surface Waters." *Frontiers in Ecology of the Environment* 9:503–505.

Festinger, L. 1957. *A Theory of Cognitive Dissonance.* Stanford, CA: Stanford University Press.

Fischer, F. 2000. *Citizens, Experts, and the Environment: The Politics of Local Knowledge.* Durham, NC: Duke University Press.

Fisk, J. M. 2013. "The Right to Know? State Politics of Fracking Disclosure." *Review of Policy Research* 30 (4): 345–365.

Guston, D. H. 2001. "Boundary Organizations in Environmental Policy and Science: An Introduction." *Science, Technology and Human Values* 26 (4): 399–408.

Hanneman, R. 2001. *Introduction to Social Network Methods.* http://faculty.ucr.edu/~hanneman/Soc157/TEXT/TextIndex.html.

Healy, R. G., and W. Ascher. 1995. "Knowledge in the Policy Process: Incorporating New Environmental Information in Natural Resources Policy Making." *Policy Sciences* 28 (1): 1–19.

Heikkila, T., and A. K. Gerlak. 2013. "Building a Conceptual Approach to Collective Learning: Lessons for Public Policy Scholars." *Policy Studies Journal* 41 (3): 484–512.

Heikkila, T., J. Pierce, S. Gallaher, J. Kagan, D. Crow, and C. M. Weible. 2013. "Understanding a Period of Policy Change: The Case of Hydraulic Fracturing Disclosure in Colorado." *Review of Policy Research* 31(2): 65–87.

Howlett, M. 2009. "Policy Analytical Capacity and Evidence-Based Policy-Making: Lessons from Canada." *Canadian Public Administration* 52 (2): 153–175.

Jackson, R. B., B. Rainey Pearson, S. G. Osborn, N. R. Warner, and A. Vengosh. 2011. *Research and Policy Recommendations for Hydraulic Fracturing and Shale-Gas Extraction.* Durham, NC: Center on Global Change, Duke University. http://www.nicholas.duke.edu.

Jenkins-Smith, H. C. 1990. *Democratic Politics and Policy Analysis.* Pacific Grove, CA: Brooks/Cole.

Jenkins-Smith, H. C., G. K. St. Clair, and B. Woods. 1991. "Explaining Change in Policy Subsystems: Analysis of Coalition Stability and Defection over Time." *American Journal of Political Science* 35 (4): 851–880.

Kerwin, C. M. 1999. *Rulemaking: How Government Agencies Write Law and Make Policy.* 2nd ed. Washington, DC: CQ Press.

Khademian, Anne M. 1992. *The SEC and Capital Market Regulation: The Politics of Expertise.* Pittsburgh, PA: University of Pittsburgh Press.

Knoke, D., F. U. Pappi, J. Broadbent, and Y. Tsujinaka. 1996. *Comparing Policy Networks: Labor Politics in the US, Germany, and Japan.* New York: Cambridge University Press.

Latour, B., and S. Woolgar. 1979. *Laboratory Life: The Construction of Scientific Facts.* Beverly Hills, CA: Sage.

Lee, K. N. 1993. *Compass and Gyroscope: Integrating Science and Politics for the Environment.* Washington, DC: Island Press.

Lejano, R. P., and H. Ingram. 2009. "Collaborative Networks and New Ways of Knowing." *Environmental Science and Policy* 12 (6): 653–662.

Lord, C. G., L. Ross, and M. R. Lepper. 1979. "Biased Assimilation and Attitude Polarization: The Effects of Prior Theories on Subsequently Considered Evidence." *Journal of Personality and Social Psychology* 37 (1): 2098–2109.

Lowi, T. 1964. "American Business, Public Policy, Case Studies, and Political Theory." *World Politics* 16:677–715.

———. 1969. *The End of Liberalism*. New York: W.W. Norton.

Lustgarten, A. 2009. "Natural Gas Drilling Produces Radioactive Wastewater." *Scientific American*, November 9. http://www.scientificamerican.com.

Mazur, A. 1981. *The Dynamic of Technical Controversy*. Washington, DC: Communications Press.

McFarland, A. S. 2004. *Neopluralism: The Evolution of Political Process Theory*. Lawrence: University Press of Kansas.

Montpetit, E. 2011. "Scientific Credibility, Disagreement, and Error Costs in 17 Biotechnology Policy Subsystems." *Policy Studies Journal* 39 (3): 513–534.

Mooney, C. 2011. "The Truth about Fracking." *Scientific American* 305 (5): 80–85. http://www.scientificamerican.com.

Munro, G. D., and P. H. Ditto. 1997. "Biased Assimilation, Attitude Polarization, and Affect in Reactions to Stereotype-Relevant Scientific Information." *Personality and Social Psychology Bulletin* 23 (6): 636–653.

Munro, G. D., P. H. Ditto, L. K. Lockhart, A. Fagerlin, M. Gready, and E. Peterson. 2002. "Biased Assimilation of Sociopolitical Arguments: Evaluating the 1996 U.S. Presidential Debate." *Basic and Applied Social Psychology* 24 (1):15–26.

National Research Council (NRC). 1996. *Understanding Risk: Informing Decisions in a Democratic Society*. Washington, DC: National Academy Press.

Norton, B. G. 2005. *Sustainability: A Philosophy of Adaptive Ecosystem Management*. Chicago: University of Chicago Press.

Pierce, Jonathan J., Jennifer Kagan, Tanya Heikkila, Christopher M. Weible, and Samuel Gallaher. 2013. "A Summary Report of Perceptions of the Politics and Regulation of Hydraulic Fracturing in Colorado." Denver: School of Public Affairs, University of Colorado.

Putnam, R. 1976. *The Comparative Study of Political Elite*. Englewood Cliffs, NJ: Prentice-Hall.

Rabe, B. G., and C. Borick. 2013. "Conventional Politics for Unconventional Drilling? Lessons from Pennsylvania's Early Move into Fracking Policy Development." *Review of Policy Research* 30 (3): 321–340.

Sabatier, P. A. 1988. "An Advocacy Coalition Framework of Policy Change and the Role of Policy-Oriented Learning Therein." *Policy Sciences* 21 (2-3): 129–168.

Sabatier, P. A., and H. C. Jenkins-Smith. 1993. "Policy Change and Learning: An Advocacy Coalition Approach." Boulder, CO: Westview Press.

Sarewitz, D. 2004. "How Science Makes Environmental Controversies Worse." *Environmental Science and Policy* 7:385–403.

Schneider, A. L., and H. Ingram. 1997. *Policy Design for Democracy*. Lawrence: University Press of Kansas.

Simon, H. A. 1996. *The Sciences of the Artificial*. Cambridge, MA: MIT press.

Snow, Charles P. 1959. *The Two Cultures*. Cambridge: Cambridge University Press.

Steel, B., P. List, D. Lach, and B. Shindler. 2004. "The Role of Scientists in Environmental Policy Process: A Case Study from the American West." *Environmental Science and Policy* 7:1–13.

Stern, P. C., T. Dietz, T. Abel, G. A. Guagnano, and L. Kalof. 1999. "A Value-Belief-Norm Theory of Support for Social Movements: The Case of Environmentalism." *Human Ecology Review* 6 (2): 81–98.

Warner, B., and J. Shapiro. 2013. "Fractured, Fragmented Federalism: A Study in Fracking Regulatory Policy." *Publius: The Journal of Federalism* 43 (3): 474–496.

Wasserman, S., and K. Faust. 1994. *Social Network Analysis: Methods and Applications*. Cambridge: Cambridge University Press.

Weber, E. P. 2003. *Bringing Society Back In*. Cambridge, MA: MIT Press.

Weible, C. M. 2008. "Expert-Based Information and Policy Subsystems: A Review and Synthesis." *Policy Studies Journal* 36 (4): 615–635.

Weible, C. M., and R. H. Moore. 2010. "Analytics and Beliefs: Competing Explanations for Defining Problems and in Choosing Allies and Opponents in Collaborative Environmental Management." *Public Administration Review* 70 (5): 756–766.

Weible, C. M., P. A. Sabatier, and A. Pattison. 2010. "Harnessing Expert-Based Information for Learning and the Sustainable Management of Complex Socio-Ecological Systems." *Environmental Science and Policy* 13 (6): 522–534.

Wildavsky, A. 1987. "Choosing Preferences by Constructing Institutions: A Cultural Theory of Preference Formation." *American Political Science Review* 81 (1): 3–21.

Wilson, James Q., ed. 1980. *The Politics of Regulation*. New York: Basic Books.

Chapter 3
Science and Salmon Recovery

ROBERT T. LACKEY

Efforts to restore declining wild salmon runs in California, Oregon, Washington, and Idaho have evolved into a "salmon recovery industry" with multiple local, state, and federal government bureaucracies and the associated contractors. Overall, the recovery industry employs thousands of scientists and other technical experts. Over many years and after hundreds of millions of dollars spent for scientific research, US Pacific Coast salmon are arguably the most studied group of fishes in the world. The vast bureaucracy and massive quantity of science have, however, failed to reverse the long-term decline of wild salmon.

The wickedness of the salmon recovery problem is easy to see along the West Coast of the United States. The scale of the problem is massive, involving hundreds of tributaries and watersheds in the Columbia River Basin of the Pacific and Inland Northwest (259,000 square miles; the size of France), more than thirty coastal rivers and watersheds, and ocean habitat that, given the migratory patterns of Pacific salmon, often extend hundreds of miles farther from the mouths of their home rivers. The scale means that complexity is endemic; the problem of salmon recovery cuts across international, national (e.g., Canada, tribal governments), state, and local boundaries, and involves values of great importance to the economy, Native American culture, recreational interests, food systems, and environmental protection. The nature, and tremendous size, of human settlements across this territory—millions of people, sizable industrial plants and processes, hydroelectric dams, and the general demands placed by human consumption and waste on waterways critical to fish survival—means that significant efforts to save salmon are likely to have profound effects on the region's established social, political, and economic patterns of living and working. Added up, these characteristics remind us that successful wild salmon recovery is not something that can be solved once and for all; instead, it has been, and will continue to be, relentless in character.

In fact, successful wild salmon recovery, if it ever occurs, rests squarely in the realm of the political process. Despite well over a century of failure to recover wild salmon, however, many in the salmon recovery industry insist that science continue to play a privileged, even dominant, role in helping decipher and decide key elements of this highly contested, wicked policy problem. The preference for science appears to be supported by both traditionally Democratic and traditionally Republican constituencies; in short, policy advocates from all parts of the political spectrum usually champion science as a critical or determining factor in policy decisions. But as this chapter makes clear, science is but one player in the larger, extremely complex drama of recovery, and to date it has not provided much in the way of successful sustained fish recovery across the region.

This chapter starts with a discussion of the policy context for salmon recovery, the paradox of apparent abundance existing simultaneously with salmon population declines, and the complexity added by the Endangered Species Act to an already wicked problem. A brief review of the difficulties associated with salmon recovery goals and objectives follows, before the analysis turns to a set of six lessons learned that illustrate how the wicked salmon recovery problem is most likely to stay wicked at the macro scale in the years to come. The conclusion brings us full circle by reminding us that it is not technical inadequacies that preclude successful recovery strategies from being implemented; rather, it is the unpleasant social and economic costs and consequences arising from implementation that feed into a politics in which the deck is stacked against the adoption of such strategies.

POLICY CONTEXT

The striking decline of salmon runs in California, Oregon, Washington, and Idaho has been typical of those that have occurred elsewhere. In other regions of the world where salmon were once plentiful, increasing human numbers, their activities, and consequent alteration of the landscape have coincided with decreasing salmon abundance. Thus, what *has* happened—and *is* happening—to wild salmon in California, Oregon, Washington, and Idaho is the latest example of a pattern that has played out numerous times in other regions of the world for salmon (Lackey et al. 2006a) and other fish species (Limburg and Waldman 2009; Limburg et al. 2011).

Prior to the 1800s, large spawning migrations (runs) of Atlantic salmon were found in many coastal rivers of western Europe and eastern North America (Montgomery 2003; National Research Council 2004). By the middle to late 1800s, many of those runs were drastically reduced, concurrent with human population increase and economic development (Limburg and Waldman 2009). Overall, salmon runs continue to be much reduced on both sides of the Atlantic Ocean. The largest remaining Atlantic salmon runs, although diminished by historical standards, occur in eastern Canada, Iceland, Ireland, Scotland, and the northern rivers of Norway, Finland, and Russia, locations with relatively few people and limited human impact on the aquatic environment. Nevertheless, Atlantic salmon are readily available in the retail market because commercial aquaculture provides an ample and consistent supply.

As with Atlantic salmon, Pacific salmon (Chinook, coho, sockeye, chum, pink, and steelhead) were historically abundant across a large region (Augerot 2005). Nevertheless, Pacific salmon, found on both sides of the North Pacific, have also declined substantially from historical levels, especially in the southern portion of their distribution, although not as dramatically as Atlantic salmon (Nehlsen 1997). Hatchery production has been used to maintain most runs in southern portions of the range (e.g., Japan, Korea, California, Oregon, and Washington). Today, in California, Oregon, Washington, and Idaho, runs that are sufficiently large to support commercial, recreational, and tribal fishing almost always comprise mainly hatchery-produced salmon. Runs of wild salmon in the northern portions of the range (e.g., Russian Far East, Alaska, Yukon, and northern British Columbia) are in better condition, though large hatchery programs exist in these regions as well (Nehlsen 1997). There are indications that salmon numbers are increasing in Arctic habitats, presumably caused by an overall warming trend (Nielsen et al. 2013).

The discoveries of gold in California (1848) and elsewhere later resulted in substantial adverse effects on many salmon runs (Lackey et al. 2006c). Efforts to protect and restore salmon populations in California, Oregon, Washington, and Idaho began in the early 1850s, and such efforts have been technically challenging, socially contentious, and politically painful (National Research Council 2012). Overall, past recovery efforts for wild salmon (in contrast to salmon bred and raised in hatcheries) have been largely unsuccessful (National Research Council 1996, 2012). Over many decades, thousands of scientists have been involved with salmon recovery efforts, but prospects for recovery of wild salmon remain elusive (Scarce 2000; National Research Council 2012). Of the nearly 1,400 distinct Pacific salmon populations that occurred prior to 1848 in California, Oregon, Washington, and Idaho, an estimated 29 percent have been extirpated (Gustafson et al. 2007). The remaining populations of wild salmon are greatly reduced, with almost all at less than 5 percent of their historical levels (Schoonmaker et al. 2003). Twenty-eight evolutionarily significant units (i.e., a group of salmon populations considered to be a "species" for purposes of regulatory protection) are formally listed as either threatened or endangered as defined by the Endangered Species Act (ESA).

Salmon recovery efforts are costly, though deciding which specific expenses should be deemed recovery costs is complicated and the subject of debate. Just within the Columbia River Basin, for example, salmon recovery costs have totaled approximately $10 billion since 1978 (Northwest Power and Conservation Council 2013), though part of this estimate reflects lost electricity sales (i.e., "forgone revenue") when the hydropower system curbed generation to meet constraints imposed by salmon recovery requirements (e.g., passing water downstream, but bypassing turbines that harm salmon).

As a public policy case study, wild salmon recovery in California, Oregon, Washington, and Idaho is characterized by many apparent conundrums:

- For well over a century, both scientists and the public have recognized the dramatic decline of wild salmon runs, but consensus remains elusive on a regional recovery policy that would actually work.
- At least several billion dollars has been spent to restore wild salmon, but their overall, long-term downward trajectory continues.
- Many populations of wild salmon are listed as "threatened" or "endangered," yet wild salmon are available seasonally in grocery stores— and farm-raised fresh salmon are sold year around.
- The various species of salmon are among the most thoroughly studied fishes in the world, but the failure of recovery efforts is often attributed to a lack of scientific information (Naiman et al. 2012).
- Thousands of scientists and other technological experts are employed to facilitate the recovery of wild salmon, but, over the long term, salmon populations have rarely responded positively to these recovery efforts (Lackey et al. 2006c).

- The Endangered Species Act, arguably the most powerful US environmental law, has been extensively used by some policy advocates to impose federal authority by listing various salmon species as either threatened or endangered; however, this approach has been insufficient to achieve salmon recovery (Lackey 2001b).
- The overarching goal of the ESA is to protect at-risk species and the habitat on which they depend, but this law, counterintuitively, may impede recovery of wild salmon in watersheds where the chances of recovery are greatest (Lach et al. 2006).
- To offset the effects on salmon runs of certain dams constructed for hydropower, irrigation, and other purposes, federal, state, and tribal governments are required to operate salmon hatchery programs to supplement runs to sustain fishing, but these programs may actually *weaken* wild salmon runs (Lichatowich 1999).
- Federal and state agencies are mandated with protecting and restoring wild salmon runs, but they are also tasked with promoting harvest (i.e., fishing), which can work, by definition, against recovery.

In sum, the salmon recovery issue is a classic example of the difficulties of effectively addressing wicked problems. Scientists engaged in salmon recovery issues tend to depict the policy debate as a scientific or ecological challenge, and the "solutions" they offer are usually focused on aspects of salmon ecology (Naiman et al. 2012). Even though there is an extensive scientific literature about salmon (Quinn 2005; Lackey et al. 2006a), experience thus far suggests that the future of wild salmon will largely be determined almost entirely by factors outside the scope of science (Williams et al. 1999; Montgomery 2003; Lackey et al. 2006b). More specifically, to effect a long-term reversal of the downward trajectory of wild salmon, a broad, interdependent, and complex suite of important public policy questions must be considered and effectively dealt with to successfully recover wild salmon to significant, sustainable levels:

- *Hydroelectric energy.* How costly and reliable does society want energy to be, given that wild salmon ultimately are affected by providing the relatively cheap, carbon-free, and reliable energy produced by hydropower?

- *Land use.* Where will people be able to live, how much living space will they be permitted, what activities will they be able to do on their own land, and what personal choices will they have in deciding how land is used?
- *Property rights.* Will the acceptable use of private land be altered, and who or what institutions will decide what constitutes acceptable use?
- *Food cost and choice.* Will food continue to be subsidized by taxpayers (e.g., publicly funded irrigation, crop subsidies), or will the price of food be determined solely by a free market?
- *Economic opportunities.* How will high-paying jobs be created and sustained for present and subsequent generations?
- *Individual freedoms.* Which, if any, personal rights or behavioral choices will be compromised or sacrificed if society is genuinely committed to restoring wild salmon?
- *Evolving priorities.* Is society willing to continue substituting hatchery-produced salmon for wild salmon, and, if so, will the ESA permit this?
- *Political realities.* Will society support modifying the ESA such that salmon recovery expenditures can be shifted to those watersheds offering the best chance of success?
- *Cultural legacies.* Which individuals and groups, if any, will be granted the right to fish, and who or what institutions will decide?
- *Indian treaties.* Will treaties between the United States and various tribes—guaranteeing Native American fishing rights and comanagement (with US states) of salmon stocks, and negotiated more than 150 years ago—be modified to reflect today's dramatically different biological, economic, and demographic realities?
- *Population policy.* —What, if anything, will society do to influence or control the level of the human population in California, Oregon, Washington, and Idaho, or indeed the United States as a whole?
- *Ecological realties.* Given likely future conditions (i.e., an apparently warming climate), what wild salmon recovery goals are biologically realistic?
- *Budgetary realities.* Will the fact that the annual cost of sustaining hatchery and wild salmon runs in California, Oregon, Washington, and Idaho exceeds the overall commercial market value of the harvest eventually mean that such a level of budgetary expenditure will become less politically viable?

These are all key policy questions germane to the public debate over wild salmon recovery policy, and they highlight how scientific information, while at some level relevant and necessary, is clearly not at the crux of the policy debate. In short, scientists can provide useful technical insight and ecological reality checks to help the public and decision-makers answer these policy questions, but science is only one input among many (Policansky 1998; Scarce 2000; National Research Council 2012).

THE PARADOX OF ABUNDANCE AND DECLINE

The question of whether wild salmon will continue to exist in the western United States is not new (Lichatowich 1999; Montgomery 2003). In California, Oregon, Washington, and Idaho, the decline started in earnest with the California gold rush. By the 1850s, excessive harvest and the impacts of mining activities on spawning and rearing habitat were decimating salmon in streams surrounding California's Central Valley. In response, by the 1870s, the federal government had begun what would eventually become a massive hatchery program in an unsuccessful attempt to reverse the decline (Taylor 1999). A similar salmon scenario followed gold discoveries in other locations. By the late 1800s, supplemental salmon stocking from hatcheries was widespread from California to Washington.

Even the massive Columbia River salmon runs had been greatly reduced by the end of the nineteenth century, largely because of minimally regulated fishing and loss of habitat caused by nominally regulated land practices such as mining, farming, ranching, and logging (National Research Council 1996; Lackey et al. 2006c). In 1894, the head of the agency that preceded NOAA Fisheries proclaimed to Congress that the Columbia's runs were in very poor condition and declining. Prior to 1933, the year the first main-stem dam on the Columbia was completed, the total Columbia salmon run had been reduced to one-fifth or less of the pre-1850 level. One can argue that the most severe Columbia River salmon decline took place in the nineteenth century—not the twentieth or twenty-first centuries—though that is not to suggest that the latter two centuries have been favorable ones for salmon.

In California, Oregon, Washington, and Idaho, supplemental stocking of juvenile salmon spawned and raised in hatcheries has long been used to sustain salmon runs at levels sufficient to support fishing (Taylor 1999). The majority of salmon runs in these states that currently support fishing are now of hatchery origin (Schoonmaker et al. 2003). Advocates for restoring wild salmon runs often assert that salmon originating from hatcheries are an imperfect substitute for naturally produced (wild) salmon (Williams et al. 1999). Further, many analysts have concluded that large-scale hatchery programs have actually hindered the recovery of wild salmon, because the relatively large numbers of hatchery-produced fish enable policy makers to allow salmon fishing to continue (Lichatowich 2013). Whether it is done in the open ocean, coastal waters, or river environments, fishing for salmon when a run is dominated by hatchery-origin fish will inevitably lead to the capture and death of some wild fish, even though fishing regulations may require the release of captured wild salmon. Other opponents of hatcheries argue that the straying or intentional dispersal of hatchery fish to different streams over many decades has resulted in a massive mixing (and weakening) of the native gene pool (Taylor 1999). Hatchery-origin salmon do interact ecologically with wild salmon and, depending on the desired management goal, the effect can be viewed as either positive or negative (Pearsons 2008). Given the current relatively low abundance of wild salmon, the absence of supplemental stocking from hatcheries would mean that salmon fishing would not currently be viable in California, Oregon, Washington, and Idaho, at least for the next few decades.

As indicated earlier, the salmon issue is full of paradoxes. For example, no biological species of Pacific salmon (Chinook, coho, sockeye, chum, pink, or steelhead) is currently in danger of extinction, but many distinct, locally adapted populations (also called runs or stocks) have been extirpated, and hundreds more are at risk (Gustafson et al. 2007). North American stocks that spawn in the "north" (northern British Columbia, Yukon, and Alaska) are generally doing well (with exceptions), but most wild stocks that spawn in the "south" (California, Oregon, Washington, and Idaho) are not (Augerot 2005).

The decline in wild salmon runs was caused by a well-known but poorly quantified combination of factors, including unsustainable harvests from earlier commercial, recreational, and subsistence fishing; blockage of upriver habitat by dams built for electricity generation, flood control, and irrigation, as well as for many other purposes; loss of spawning and rearing habitat from various mining, farming, ranching, and forestry practices; unfavorable ocean or other climatic conditions; reduced stream flow caused by diversions of water for agricultural, municipal, or commercial needs; hatchery production to supplement diminished salmon runs or to produce salmon for the retail market; predation by marine mammals, birds, and other fish species;

competition, especially with exotic fish species; diseases and parasites; and many others (Knudsen et al. 2000; National Research Council 1996, 2004, 2012).

Salmon experts continue to study and debate what proportion of the decline in wild salmon is attributable to which factor (Quinn 2005; Naiman et al. 2012). Having participated in many multi-organizational salmon science and policy meetings over the past several decades, I have observed that many affected organizations have developed, or funded the development of, sophisticated assessments of salmon populations that usually end up—probably not surprisingly—supporting their organization's favored policy preference. All the major organizations that participate in the salmon policy recovery disputes employ, or at least have access to, scientists. No one, not even the most astute salmon scientist, knows for sure the relative importance of the various factors that caused the decline of wild salmon, and therefore scientific debate is to be expected. Debate over scientific issues, however, often reflects clashing ethical attitudes, personal beliefs, and policy preferences (Policansky 1998; Scarce 2000).

There is also the incongruity of *apparent* high salmon abundance with simultaneous concern about extinction. Try explaining to the average shopper that salmon are at risk of extinction when fresh salmon are available year-round at the local grocery store. Most wild salmon sold in California, Oregon, Washington, and Idaho now come from Alaska and northern British Columbia. Salmon are still relatively abundant in these northern locations because of comparatively unaltered spawning and rearing habitat, reasonably restrictive regulations to control harvest, and favorable ocean conditions (Lackey et al. 2006c). Also, large quantities of "farm-raised" salmon are available year-round from many sources (e.g., British Columbia, Norway, Scotland, Chile, and New Zealand).

Yet, while the various Pacific salmon species are impressively resilient, the few recovery successes for *wild* salmon have been in locations where salmon spawning and rearing habitat was in comparatively good condition, migratory blockages from dams or other obstructions were not present or were minimal, and harvest occurred at levels that assured that sufficient numbers of adults reached the spawning grounds. The sockeye salmon runs of the Fraser River, British Columbia, are the best documented long-term example of at least partial recovery after decimation. In this case, the cause was the substantial 1914 Hell's Gate rockslide that hindered salmon migration (Roos 1991). Sockeye salmon runs recovered appreciably after fish passage was improved, stringent harvest controls were implemented, and other vigorous management actions were taken.

The resilience of salmon was also illustrated when a landslide (about five hundred years ago) blocked the Columbia River just east of Portland, and salmon were thus prevented from reaching upriver streams to spawn (O'Connor 2004). After the slide was breached naturally, salmon eventually reestablished themselves in streams above the blockage. Such blockages of the Columbia River and its tributaries almost certainly occurred at various other times over the past several thousand years.

In both the Fraser River and Columbia River blockages, freshwater salmon habitat was in excellent condition above the obstruction. Presently, however, there are few locations in California, Oregon, Washington, or Idaho where high-quality spawning and rearing habitats are intact (pre-1850 condition) and accessible to salmon. Today, river and stream blockages in California, Oregon, Washington, and Idaho have left 44 percent of this original spawning and rearing habitat inaccessible to returning salmon (McClure et al. 2008).

THE ENDANGERED SPECIES ACT:
ADDING COMPLEXITY TO AN ALREADY WICKED PROBLEM

For many reasons and for more than a century, salmon recovery has been a wicked policy problem. And particularly since the early 1990s, the Endangered Species Act (ESA) has greatly added to the inherent complexity, because it has become the major policy driver (Lackey 2001b; Lichatowich 2013). ESA places science in the policy driver's seat and does not, in practice, allow equal consideration of competing policy priorities. Advocates of salmon recovery have used the ESA successfully to force many changes in salmon policy, but these successes have also resulted in a number of policy paradoxes. For example, threatened or endangered salmon are the only ESA-listed animals for which government routinely licenses large numbers of people (i.e., fishermen) to harvest them. Further, if society's paramount salmon concern was with the depleted condition of wild salmon runs in California, Oregon, Washington, and Idaho, government agencies could simply close salmon fishing, cease supplementing runs with hatchery releases, and wait to see if wild salmon runs rebounded. Recreational, commercial, and Native American fishermen would object for obvious reasons, but most people would not be affected by a ban on fishing or stocking hatchery-origin salmon. Furthermore, farm-raised salmon (from British Columbia, Chile, Scotland, and Norway) and wild salmon (harvested in British Columbia and Alaska) would remain abundant and could continue to supply the retail market—and taxpayers would save hundreds of millions of dollars by closing the hatchery system and eliminating the subsidies currently needed to maintain existing salmon runs.

In addition to the ESA goal of restoring wild salmon, there is the broadly supported goal of sustaining recreational, commercial, and Native American fishing using fish hatcheries. Other support for continued hatchery operations comes from governmental organizations. State and tribal fish and wildlife agencies usually operate salmon hatcheries with funds provided by the Bonneville Power Administration, US Bureau of Reclamation, US Army Corps of Engineers, an assortment of private and public power companies, and the sale of fishing licenses. The loss of these funds and jobs would be bureaucratically traumatic to the recipient state agencies.

Ultimately, listing wild salmon as endangered or threatened as defined by the ESA means that all stakeholders, not just fishermen, are affected. As mandated by court decisions, efforts to protect or restore wild salmon often conflict with a suite of other individual and societal priorities (Policansky 1998). For example, two of the most visible contemporary examples of such conflict are the ongoing debate over how to balance Columbia River electricity generation with salmon survival, and the contentious lawsuits over how to divide up scarce Klamath River Basin water (in southern Oregon and Northern California) among threatened salmon, endangered suckers, migratory waterfowl, treaty Native American tribes, farmers, and a host of other demands.

I have often heard colleagues involved in ESA salmon conflicts, usually in informal settings, characterize the ESA as a naïve piece of legislation in search of a credible public policy goal. The ESA's consultation requirements, aimed at avoiding actions that could jeopardize the continued existence of protected salmon runs, apply only to "federal actions," but arguably some of the most important actions affecting at-risk species occur in the private sector, and these are usually beyond the scope of the ESA.

Supporters of the act, on the other hand, maintain that the ESA is forcing society to make the necessary, though painful, sacrifices for the future well-being of society or, perhaps, even society's very survival. What would be the status of wild salmon in California, Oregon, Washington, and Idaho had the ESA not been invoked? They assert that while the ESA may not be perfect, it is needed more than ever, as declines in salmon populations clearly attest. Although there may be references to the economic value of salmon fishing, salmon for some segments of society is a cultural icon. To other policy advocates, salmon may be a surrogate for the overall "health" of the natural environment. To yet other advocates, the fundamental policy debate is whether humans have a moral duty to save wild salmon from extinction.

THE DIFFICULTIES ASSOCIATED WITH RECOVERY GOALS AND OBJECTIVES

Presupposing, abstractly at least, that society regards "saving" or "recovering" wild salmon populations as a worthwhile endeavor, substantial tension exists over what the *unambiguous* and *specific* recovery goal ought to be (Lackey 2003). For example, should the policy goal be simply to save from extinction a biological *species*, an evolutionarily significant unit, or an individual salmon run? Such a policy objective (e.g., saving a species, evolutionarily significant unit, or run) can be achieved by conserving relatively low numbers of wild salmon (i.e., museum or remnant runs), but such numbers would be insufficient to sustain fishing. Conversely, from a treaty rights perspective, advocates argue that the appropriate salmon recovery goal must be at a population level sufficiently robust to permit sustainable tribal fishing. Or, from the perspective of recreational and commercial fishermen, maintaining salmon runs at the sufficiently high levels required to sustain their harvests should be the overarching goal, but achieving this goal requires heavy reliance on supplemental stocking from hatcheries. Perhaps even more contentious, who decides which goal is appropriate?

Beyond any ESA requirements, a much more challenging recovery objective is to increase runs of wild salmon to levels that would sustainably support fishing. Restoring wild salmon runs across their entire range to levels prior to 1850, or anything close to those levels, is not realistic. Almost certainly this objective is not achievable with wild salmon unless human impacts are reduced to pre-1850 levels. More fundamentally, will some advocacy groups continue to demand that salmon runs comprise entirely wild fish to achieve whatever level of recovery is demanded? If recovery success is constrained to wild fish, the project becomes much more challenging; it would be especially difficult to produce enough wild fish to support significant recreational, commercial, and tribal fishing. If hatchery fish are used to sustain large salmon runs and salmon fishing is permitted, there will continue to be adverse effects on the relatively small portion of that run that is wild-origin salmon, but what level of adverse effect on wild salmon is acceptable to society? Given the substantial societal and monetary costs to restore wild salmon, perhaps much of the public would continue to opt for using hatcheries to sustain salmon runs, in spite of the adverse effects on wild salmon. Thus, there is no inherently *best* approach to recovery, but rather a suite of alternatives, with "best" as largely a function of which vision of the recovery objective one accepts.

No one is bent on eradicating salmon. Further, scientists usually have a pretty solid assessment of the major causes of the long-term declines in salmon populations, even if the relative importance of the causes is open to debate (National Research Council 1996, 2012). Rather than acting on sinister motives or lack of knowledge, society makes choices by choosing between *desirable* but *conflicting* policy alternatives. For every recovery option, there are trade-offs: benefits come with costs. Thus, achieving the goal of restoring wild salmon engenders some of the features of a zero-sum game (Lackey 2006).

SALMON POLICY: LESSONS LEARNED

Given the complicated policy and ecological context of this natural resource case study, coupled with my personal observations while participating over many years in the bureaucratic process, what are the lessons learned? Whether these should be called lessons learned, frustrating truths, or candid realities, I propose that collectively they will circumscribe the future of wild salmon in California, Oregon, Washington, and Idaho. In different ways, each lesson highlights the inadequacies of using the traditional approach to science for resolving, or even coping with, the long-term decline of wild salmon populations. In every case, the policy dynamic suggests a need for innovative problem-solving methodologies that go beyond science and factor in social, institutional, economic, and political realities.

Lesson 1: Efforts to recover wild salmon will continue to struggle because of conflicting policy priorities and the constraints of the ESA's approach to species protection.

Beginning with the early listings of threatened or endangered populations of salmon two decades ago, the ESA has been a powerful tool in the hands of salmon recovery advocates. Lawsuits have forced the allocation of billions of dollars for salmon recovery, as well as untold additional billions in private costs (Williams et al. 1999; Lichatowich 2013). Some advocates press the claim that such expenditures are justified because the bureaucracy is responding to society's wishes. Conversely, others argue that such expenditures are largely a waste of money and, worse, society has never been asked to choose between wild salmon and other competing public policy priorities.

Once a species is deemed at risk of extinction, then the full force of ESA comes into play. In California, Oregon, Washington, and Idaho, many wild salmon runs are at risk because of varied and collective actions of the human population. Wild salmon runs in the worst condition are almost always in rivers and streams least likely to ever again support significant wild runs. There are, however, rivers and streams in relatively better condition (from a salmon perspective), but salmon runs in these environments are not at-risk and therefore receive little of the benefit of ESA-mandated expenditures. Some advocates argue that recovery resources ought to be spent on watersheds with the greatest chance of sustaining wild salmon, not in watersheds where success is very unlikely. Critics lambast this approach as a form of wild salmon triage. It is highly doubtful that ESA has the flexibility to permit writing off certain rivers and streams (for wild salmon) and moving the recovery dollars to places where achieving success would be much easier. For example, what if the billions of dollars spent on restoring wild salmon to the California Central Valley and the Columbia River had been spent on restoring salmon to the coastal watersheds of northern California, Oregon, and Washington?

After watching such recovery debates play out for decades, and in spite of the social turmoil caused by ESA, it looks to me like society has already made a choice relative to the future of "wild" salmon in California, Oregon, Washington, and Idaho. Salmon runs are now generally less than 5 percent of the 1850 levels, most of the current runs in these four states are of hatchery origin, and society is not willing to alter lifestyles to reverse the long-term decline. ESA will not greatly alter the long-term trajectory for wild salmon. To be fair, however, no one knows what would have happened to wild salmon had the money *not* been spent, although it is likely that they would be worse off and, very likely, in some cases, extirpated.

My interactions with senior government bureaucrats suggest they generally recognize most of the scientific and policy facts and realities surrounding wild salmon recovery. I have found that politicians also generally recognize the facts and realities, at least in private. Those in leadership roles with nongovernmental advocacy organizations recognize them. Most definitely, knowledgeable salmon technocrats (including scientists) recognize the facts and realities. In short, the overarching essential "facts of the case" are rarely in dispute, but the probability of success of a specific recovery effort often is in dispute.

As required by ESA and other laws and policies, hundreds of millions, if not billions, of dollars continue to be spent to recover wild salmon (Lichatowich 2013). Such funding distorts the behavior of individuals and organizations. Bureaucratic, professional, and personal conflicts of interest, both real and perceived, abound. Because agencies are obtaining large amounts of funding to try to reverse the decline, they are not likely to point out publicly the obvious inadequacies of current recovery plans. Because many scientists obtain significant research funding to work on interesting scientific questions, they are not likely to point out the obvious defects in recovery plans. Because advocates from nongovernmental organizations (and their lawyers) are well funded from membership fees and taxpayer-reimbursed costs for their lawsuits, they are not likely to point out the obvious. Because politicians use the argument that they are *already* allocating billions to recover salmon runs, additional unpopular decisions do not have to be made, so they too are not likely to point out the obvious flaws in salmon recovery strategies.

Lesson 2: Current institutional and political dynamics limit our ability to deal effectively with salmon recovery.

Over my career and involvement with salmon recovery, one fascinating and revealing aspect has been a recurring recommendation, even a plea, from some colleagues to "lighten up" and be more optimistic and positive in assessing the future of wild salmon (Lackey 2001a). Many scientists tend to urge their "realist" colleagues to abandon blunt assessments and forthright honesty in favor of offering a more encouraging tone of optimism for salmon recovery. For example, a common sentiment is illustrated by a reviewer's comment on a journal manuscript: "You have to give those of us trying to restore wild salmon some hope of success."

In contrast, some colleagues, especially veterans of the unending political conflict over salmon policy, have confessed their regret over the "optimistic" approach that they had taken during their careers in fisheries, and they now endorse the "tell it like it is" tactic. They feel that they had given false hope about the effectiveness of hatcheries and the ability of their agencies to manage mixed stock fishing. Many professional fisheries scientists acknowledge that they have been pressured by employers, funding organizations, and colleagues to "spin" fisheries science and policy realism to accentuate optimism. Sometimes the pressure on scientists to cheerlead is obvious; other times it is subtle. For example, consider the coercion of scientists by other scientists (often through nongovernmental professional societies) to avoid highlighting the importance of US population policy on sustaining natural resources (Hurlbert 2013).

These problems are compounded by other institutional and political dynamics. Many salmon scientists take professional refuge in the reality that senior managers or policy bureaucrats select and define the policy or science question to be addressed, thus constraining research. Consequently, the resulting scientific information and assessments are often scientifically rigorous, but so narrowly focused that the information is only marginally relevant to decision-makers. Rarely are fisheries scientists encouraged to provide "big picture" assessments of the future of salmon. Whether inadvertent or not, such constrained information often misleads the public into endorsing false expectations of the likelihood of the recovery of wild salmon (Lackey 2001a; Hurlbert 2011).

The problem with such optimism is that it does not convey what is happening with wild salmon, and it allows the public, elected officials, and fisheries managers to escape the torment of confronting species triage. No salmon expert ever seriously argues that you can have wild salmon everywhere they once were, but few are willing to be explicit about identifying those locations where the cost is high and chance of success is low (Lackey 2001a). The pressure to present an optimistic picture of the future also means that the public will be less likely to understand the difficult trade-offs required for effective salmon recovery. As well, the lack of accurate information about the long-term prospects of success increases the probability that public spending on ineffective recovery policies will continue rather than funding other, perhaps more important, policy priorities.

It is not only fisheries scientists, managers, and analysts who avoid explicitly conveying unpleasant facts or trade-offs to the public. Such an inclination exists on the part of elected and appointed officials. The 160-year track record of salmon policy makers in California, Oregon, Washington, and Idaho has demonstrated an unceasing propensity on the part of elected and appointed officials to slip into the behavior of "domesticating" the policy issue. By this, I mean the practice of taking difficult, divisive policy issues (i.e., salmon recovery) off the political table until a solution emerges or the problem disappears by solving itself (e.g., the species is extirpated or a political consensus emerges on a recovery strategy) (Lach et al. 2006). Relative to salmon recovery, the most common indicators of "domestication" are funding more research or scientific reviews, holding more workshops and venues to get stakeholders involved through collaboration, forming more planning teams to assess policy options, and tweaking current regulations or policies. Starting in the 1850s with the first efforts by politicians to reverse the decline of wild salmon in the California Central Valley, policy domestication through generous funding of such activities has provided the public with the illusion of progress in salmon recovery (Lichatowich 1999; Montgomery 2003).

And yet, for scientists at least, it has been easy to find comfort in debating the scientific nuances of hatchery genetics, evolutionarily significant units, dam breaching, fishing regulations, predatory bird and marine mammal control, habitat restoration, and atmospheric and oceanic climate trends. This focus on scientific details, often couched in optimistic rhetoric, can unintentionally mislead the public about the realities of the situation (Hurlbert 2011).

To appreciate the evolution of the current political circumstance, note that political actions to *domesticate* salmon recovery are easier than political actions that will *reverse* wild salmon decline. Thus, few elected or appointed officials explicitly propose ways to change political realities about recovery of wild salmon. Instead, they suggest permutations of existing policy options (e.g., revise the ESA, protect more or different salmon habitats, modify hatchery practices to reduce adverse effects on wild runs, change K–12 education to stress the importance of wild salmon, or somehow transform attitudes through public awareness).

Lesson 3: Market incentives and the rules of commerce tend to work against increasing wild salmon numbers.

The ongoing drive for competitive advantage and near-term, low-cost production in a globalized economy will continue to affect adversely wild salmon runs in California, Oregon, Washington, and Idaho (Lackey 2005; Lichatowich 2013). This is because noneconomic values, such as preserving at-risk wild salmon runs as required by ESA, tend not to get weighted very heavily in decision-making (Lichatowich 2013).

The tendency of market forces to put downward pressure on wild salmon runs is not inherently good or bad, but is a function of producers seeking the materials, labor, and location that give them a comparative cost advantage. For example, electronics are generally obtained from wherever they can be assembled at least cost. Automobile assembly plants typically end up wherever manufacturers can produce cars most inexpensively. Wheat is mostly produced where it can be grown most productively and consistently. Wood also tends to be produced where trees can be grown and harvested most efficiently and milled at the lowest price. Moreover, taxpayer subsidies and government regulations are often used to encourage certain behaviors and choices deemed socially important (e.g., renewable energy) or to discourage others (e.g., coal-fired power plants). And while there is considerable political rhetoric to modify the current rules of commercial (e.g., "fair") trade, it is not clear what such modifications would be, much less how they would affect salmon recovery (Lackey 2005).

The point here is that markets and costs matter greatly in developing an effective salmon recovery program. The requirements of large-scale salmon recovery (and the changes in economic practices that such a program would entail) will necessarily raise costs for individual consumers. How much more are people willing to pay for food, electricity, or transportation produced in ways that will not degrade salmon habitat? In short, as with all policy choices, there are winners and losers.

Lesson 4: Competition for critical natural resources, especially for water, will continue to increase and will work against recovering wild salmon.

Salmon need clean, cold water in abundant amounts to thrive and prosper, but this simple reality is often overlooked in policy analysis and forecasting. Many watersheds in California, Oregon, Washington, and Idaho suffer from human-induced water shortages, but unless the competition for scarce water explodes into open political conflict, most people are oblivious to the magnitude of the challenges. Even with media stories about impending water scarcity, most written in a doom-and-gloom style, our insatiable demand for fresh water shows little sign of easing. In such a setting, how will advocates for wild salmon fare relative to advocates for competing priorities such as water for domestic use, irrigation, manufacturing, generating electricity, and a host of other needs?

Without new problem-solving methodologies, the continuing water war in the Klamath Basin, along the California-Oregon border, gives us an indication of what many think is the probable future throughout California and the Pacific Northwest states. A decade ago, national newspapers described Klamath Basin farmers defying law enforcement agents and illegally opening locked valves and releasing water to irrigate their fields. Television news showed Klamath River choked with dying salmon caused by low water flows, poor water quality, and diseases.

Considering competition for water over a millennial time frame, it is likely that Earth's climate is returning to something closer to the Medieval Warm Period (years 900 to 1400). This was a period of mega-droughts that lasted for many decades, perhaps longer than a century (Ingram and Malamud-Roam 2013). Coupled with reduced snow and rain caused by a generally warmer climate, how will wild salmon recovery programs stack up against competing demands for scarce water?

Lesson 5: Dramatic increases in the human population of the Pacific Northwest will work against wild salmon recovery.

Assuming that there are not major changes in immigration/population policy in the United States, the most probable scenario for the human population trajectory through this century for places like California, Oregon, Washington, and Idaho is substantially upward (Lackey et al. 2006d). Any serious discussion about the future of wild salmon therefore must consider human population and the increasing demands placed on natural resources, as well as the impacts on land (National Research Council 1996; Hurlbert 2013).

The latest demographic forecasts show a slowing of the world population (currently 7.2 billion) growth rate through this century, with a leveling off toward 2100 (United Nations 2013). Yes, a leveling off is predicted, but at 10.9 billion people. But, especially for regions like the Pacific Northwest and the United States generally, there is a different story; it is largely one of past, current, and future immigration. Currently, Washington, Oregon, Idaho, and British Columbia are home to fifteen million humans. In the absence of policy changes, and assuming a range of likely human reproductive rates and migration to the Pacific Northwest from elsewhere in Canada and the United States, by 2100 this region's human population will not be its present fifteen million, but rather will be somewhere between fifty and one hundred million, a potential quadrupling, or more, of the region's population by the end of this century.

Consider those fifty to one hundred million people in the Pacific Northwest in 2100, and their demands for public and private infrastructure, whether for housing, schools, sewage treatment plants, industrial sites, roads, parking lots, airports, restaurants, stores, electricity, drinking water, pipelines, golf courses, and on and on. The consumer demand will be immense.

Visualize the western region of the state of Washington and southwestern corner of British Columbia in 2100, with its metropolis of Seattle-Vancouver, or "Seavan." Seavan is formed as smaller, discrete cities grow together and, by 2100, stretches from Olympia (Washington) in the south, along Puget Sound northward through the once stand-alone cities of Tacoma and Seattle, and on to Vancouver (British Columbia), east to Hope at the head of the Fraser Valley, and west to cover the southern half of Vancouver Island. Rather than the six million people of the early 2000s, Seavan in 2100 rivals present-day Mexico City or Tokyo, with thirty million inhabitants. Think of it as the New York City to Boston corridor, transplanted to the Pacific Northwest.

At the same time, it is not simply the number of people that causes problems for wild salmon, but it is also their individual and collective ecological footprint and the fact that humans and salmon tend to use the lower elevations of watersheds. Protected public lands (e.g., national parks, wilderness areas, and national forests) are often at higher elevation, and streams in these locations usually provide little habitat for wild salmon.

Lesson 6: Individual and collective lifestyle preferences are important, and substantial changes must take place in these preferences if long-term downward trends in wild salmon abundance are to be reversed.

For most fisheries scientists and others involved with salmon recovery, it is easy to assume that wild salmon are near the top of the public's concerns. It seems that everyone supports salmon, and especially wild salmon. But the fact is that salmon recovery is only one of many priorities that individuals, when not forced to make a choice, profess to rank highly. When forced to make a choice, salmon recovery drops substantially in importance compared with other priorities.

Consider the following brief history as an example of where wild salmon rank as a societal priority. In 1980, the Northwest Power and Conservation Act elevated the importance of salmon runs within the Columbia River Basin by acknowledging the important role dams played in the decline of salmon. This legislation forced dam operators to balance the public interest of reducing the impacts of hydropower on salmon against the public interest in sustaining affordable, reliable electricity supply. Further, in 1991, the first Columbia River salmon "evolutionarily significant unit" was listed under the terms of the ESA. Starting with this first 1991 ESA listing, followed by many others, it would appear that wild salmon had won out over electricity as a societal priority.

However, despite the new and formal Columbia River policies favoring salmon, crises serve as reminders of real-world priorities when the needs of salmon are pitted against other important societal wants. In 2001, two decades after passage of the Northwest Power and Conservation Act and only a decade after the first salmon listing, ongoing electrical blackouts and brownouts in California prompted the US Bonneville Power Administration to declare a power emergency, abandon previously agreed-upon interagency salmon recovery commitments, and generate electricity at maximum capacity using water reserved to help salmon migrate. In short, electricity for air conditioners and refrigerators won out over both wild and hatchery-bred salmon. Perhaps even more instructive, there was scant public opposition. There were minimal legal challenges. There were no elected officials publicly pleading to save the water to help salmon. Nor were any environmental groups blanketing the Internet with calls to mobilize in defense of salmon. Even among wild salmon advocates, the silence was nearly complete.

The lesson here is that many people will support "saving wild salmon" so long as *their* individual lifestyles are not greatly affected. For well over a century, there have been many of these societal trade-offs, and the choices made reflect the *relative* low priority of recovering wild salmon vis-à-vis other societal values and policy goals.

CONCLUSION

Based on my experiences with salmon recovery programs, among the scientific community there remains a common delusion that wild salmon in California, Oregon, Washington, and Idaho *could* be greatly increased concurrent with the present upward trajectory of the region's human population coupled with most individuals' apparent unwillingness to reduce substantially their consumption of resources and standard of living. Few salmon advocates argue publicly that society *must* make these substantial and contentious changes to recover wild salmon. Further, the implicit public optimism of salmon scientists and technocrats about restoring wild salmon tends to perpetuate this avoidance of reality.

Strategies exist that could successfully restore wild salmon to California, Oregon, Washington, and Idaho, but each requires major and politically divisive choices (Lackey et al. 2006). It is not technical inadequacies that preclude such recovery strategies from being implemented. Rather, it is the unpleasant resulting consequences arising from implementation. The economic and societal costs of implementing a wild salmon recovery strategy that has a good chance of restoring wild salmon runs to significant, sustainable levels in California, Oregon, Washington, and Idaho would be extremely high. Based on the experience of the past 160 years or more, it appears unlikely that society collectively is willing to bear such costs except in an ad hoc, case-by-case fashion that, when all is said and done, is unlikely to make a major difference in overall salmon recovery numbers in the Pacific Northwest. Examples here include the 1992 congressional approval for the removal of two dams on the pristine Elwha River on the Olympic Peninsula in Washington State, and the private, collaborative agreement to remove four dams on the Klamath River in southern Oregon and northern California in 2016.

What is not clear at this time is whether these two cases are harbingers of the future or exceptions to the general rule that politics and economics, and the other factors noted in this chapter, often stand in the way of substantial, effective, widespread salmon recovery. It is significant that these midsize dams have been, and are being, breached in order to restore historical, natural seasonal water flows of benefit to the fish. Combined with the explosion of small-scale, watershed-based collaborative management efforts (see chapter 9) across the US West designed to restore ecological functions, including conditions supportive of salmon, steelhead, and bull trout restoration, there is some hope, albeit one might argue that it is at the margins of the overall wicked problem. This less sanguine view finds at least some support in the fact that one of the Elwha River dams (Elwha Dam) was not removed until 2011, almost twenty years after congressional approval, that the second Elwha dam (Glines Canyon) was not removed until 2014, and that the Klamath River dam removal agreement came only after sixteen years of a highly contentious process and failure to gain congressional approval. Yet even at this glacial pace of change, an optimistic person might imagine a world a hundred years hence and find that such small, limited steps toward recovery have resulted in the removal of another fifty to a hundred small to medium dams, and perhaps even a few of the larger dams in the Columbia River system.

Nonetheless, to succeed over the larger region of the Pacific Northwest, a wild salmon recovery strategy must change the trajectory of the major policy drivers, or that strategy will fail even if dams are successfully removed from the system. If society continues to spend billions of dollars only in quick-fix efforts to restore wild salmon runs, then in most cases these efforts will be only marginally successful. The same holds true for the possible solutions presented in the second half of this volume. For while the application of one, or several, of these problem-solving changes might well address adequately salmon recovery in some watersheds in the Pacific Northwest region, such efforts are unlikely to improve the region-wide status of wild salmon except at the margins *unless they are tied strategically to a larger, basin-wide plan capable of making the difficult trade-offs described herein.*

In the opinion of this author, the billions spent on salmon recovery might be considered "guilt money"—modern-day indulgences—a tax society and individuals willingly bear to alleviate their collective and individual remorse. It is money spent on activities not likely to achieve recovery of wild salmon, but it helps people feel better as they continue the behaviors and choices that preclude the recovery of wild salmon. It also sustains a job program for scientists and other technocrats by funding the salmon recovery industry.

References

Augerot, Xanthippe. 2005. *Atlas of Pacific Salmon.* Berkeley: University of California Press.

Gustafson, Richard G., Robin S. Waples, James M. Myers, Laurie A. Weitkamp, Gregory J. Bryant, Orlay W. Johnson, and Jeffrey J. Hard. 2007. "Pacific Salmon Extinctions: Quantifying Lost and Remaining Diversity." *Conservation Biology* 21 (4): 1009–1020.

Hurlbert, Stuart H. 2011. "Pacific Salmon, Immigration, and Censors: Unreliability of the Cowed Technocrat." *Social Contract* 21 (3): 42–46.

———. 2013. "Critical Need for Modification of U.S. Population Policy." *Conservation Biology* 27 (4): 887–889.

Ingram, B. Lynn, and Frances Malamud-Roam. 2013. *The West without Water: What Past Floods, Droughts, and Other Climatic Clues Tell Us about Tomorrow.* Berkeley: University of California Press.

Knudsen, E. Eric, Cleveland R. Steward, Donald D. MacDonald, Jack E. Williams, and Dudley W. Reiser, eds. 2000. *Sustainable Fisheries Management: Pacific Salmon.* Boca Raton, FL: Lewis Publishers.

Lach, Denise H., Sally L. Duncan, and Robert T. Lackey. 2006. "Can We Get There from Here? Salmon in the 21st Century." In *Salmon 2100: The Future of Wild Pacific Salmon*, edited by Robert T. Lackey, Denise H. Lach, and Sally L. Duncan, 597–617. Bethesda, MD: American Fisheries Society.

Lackey, Robert T. 2001a. "Defending Reality." *Fisheries* 26 (6): 26–27.

———. 2001b. "Pacific Salmon and the Endangered Species Act: Troublesome Questions." *Renewable Resources Journal* 19 (2): 6–9.

———. 2003. "Setting Goals and Objectives in Managing for Healthy Ecosystems." In *Managing for Healthy Ecosystems,* edited by David J. Rapport, William L. Lasley, Dennis E. Rolston, N. Ole Nielsen, Calvin O. Qualset, and Ardeshir B. Damania, 165–166. Boca Raton, FL: Lewis Publishers.

———. 2005. "Economic Growth and Salmon Recovery: An Irreconcilable Conflict?" *Fisheries* 30 (3): 30–32.

———. 2006. "Axioms of Ecological Policy." *Fisheries* 31 (6): 286–290.

Lackey, Robert T., Denise H. Lach, and Sally L. Duncan, eds. 2006a. *Salmon 2100: The Future of Wild Pacific Salmon*. Bethesda, MD: American Fisheries Society.

———. 2006b. "The Challenge of Restoring Wild Salmon." In *Salmon 2100: The Future of Wild Pacific Salmon*, edited by Robert T. Lackey, Denise H. Lach, and Sally L. Duncan, 1–11. Bethesda, MD: American Fisheries Society.

———. 2006c. "Wild Salmon in Western North America: The Historical and Policy Context." In *Salmon 2100: The Future of Wild Pacific Salmon*, edited by Robert T. Lackey, Denise H. Lach, and Sally L. Duncan, 13–55. Bethesda, MD: American Fisheries Society.

———. 2006d. "Wild Salmon in Western North America: Forecasting the Most Likely Status in 2100." In *Salmon 2100: The Future of Wild Pacific Salmon,* edited by Robert T. Lackey, Denise H. Lach, and Sally L. Duncan, 57–70. Bethesda, MD: American Fisheries Society.

Lichatowich, James A. 1999. *Salmon without Rivers: A History of the Pacific Salmon Crisis*. Washington, DC: Island Press.

———. 2013. *Salmon, People, and Place: A Biologist's Search for Salmon Recovery*. Corvallis: Oregon State University Press.

Limburg, Karin E., and John R. Waldman. 2009. "Dramatic Declines in North Atlantic Diadromous Fishes." *BioScience* 59 (11): 955–965.

Limburg, Karin E., Robert M. Hughes, Donald C. Jackson, and Brian Czech. 2011. "Human Population Increase, Economic Growth, and Fish Conservation: Collision Course or Savvy Stewardship?" *Fisheries* 36 (1): 27–34.

McClure, Michelle M., Stephanie M. Carlson, Timothy J. Beechie, George R. Pess, Jeffrey C. Jorgensen, Susan M. Sogard, Sonia E. Sultan, et al. 2008. "Evolutionary Consequences of Habitat Loss for Pacific Anadromous Salmonids." *Evolutionary Applications* 1 (2): 300–318.

Montgomery, David R. 2003. *King of Fish: The Thousand-Year Run of Salmon.* Boulder, CO: Westview Press.

Naiman, Robert J., J. Richard Alldredge, David A. Beauchamp, Peter A. Bisson, James Congleton, Charles J. Henny, Nancy Huntly, et al. 2012. "Developing a Broader Scientific Foundation for River Restoration: Columbia River Food Webs." *Proceedings of the National Academy of Sciences* 109 (52): 21201–21207.

National Research Council. 1996. *Upstream: Salmon and Society in the Pacific Northwest.* Washington, DC: National Academies Press.

———. 2004. *Atlantic Salmon in Maine.* Washington, DC: National Academies Press.

———. 2012. *Sustainable Water and Environmental Management in the California Bay-Delta.* Washington, DC: National Academies Press.

Nehlsen, Willa. 1997. "Pacific Salmon Status and Trends—A Coastwide Perspective." In *Pacific Salmon and Their Ecosystems*, edited by Deanna J. Stouder, Peter A. Bisson, and Robert J. Naiman, 41–50. New York: Chapman and Hall.

Nielsen, Jennifer L., Gregory T. Ruggerone, and Christian E. Zimmerman. 2013. "Adaptive Strategies and Life Cycle Characteristics in a Warming Climate: Salmon in the Arctic?" *Environmental Biology of Fishes* 96 (10-11): 1187–1226.

Northwest Power and Conservation Council. 2013. *2012 Columbia River Basin Fish and Wildlife Program Costs Report.* Portland, OR: Northwest Power and Conservation Council, Document 2013-04.

O'Connor, Jim E. 2004. "The Evolving Landscape of the Columbia River Gorge: Lewis and Clark and Cataclysms of the Columbia." *Oregon Historical Quarterly* 105 (3): 390–421.

Pearsons, Todd N. 2008. "Misconception, Reality, and Uncertainty about Ecological Interactions and Risks between Hatchery and Wild Salmonids." *Fisheries* 33 (6): 278–290.

Policansky, David. 1998. "Science and Decision Making for Water Resources." *Ecological Applications* 8 (3): 610–618.

Quinn, Thomas P. 2005. *The Behavior and Ecology of Pacific Salmon and Trout.* Bethesda, MD: American Fisheries Society.

Roos, John F. 1991. *Restoring Fraser River Salmon: A History of the International Pacific Salmon Fisheries Commission, 1937–1985.* Vancouver: Pacific Salmon Commission.

Scarce, Rik. 2000. *Fishy Business: Salmon, Biology, and the Social Construction of Nature.* Philadelphia, PA: Temple University Press.

Schoonmaker, Peter K., Ted Gresh, Jim Lichatowich, and Hans D. Radtke. 2003. "Past and Present Pacific Salmon Abundance: Bioregional Estimates for Key Life History Stages." In *Nutrients in Salmonid Ecosystems: Sustaining*

Production and Biodiversity, edited by John G. Stockner, 33–40. Bethesda, MD: American Fisheries Society.

Taylor, Joseph E. 1999. *Making Salmon: An Environmental History of the Northwest Fisheries Crisis*. Seattle: University of Washington Press.

United Nations. 2013. *World Population Prospects: The 2012 Revision, Key Findings, and Advance Tables*. Department of Economic and Social Affairs, Population Division, Working Paper No. ESA/P/WP.227.

Williams, Richard N., Peter A. Bisson, Daniel L. Bottom, Lyle D. Calvin, Charles C. Coutant, Michael W. Erho Jr., Christopher A. Frissell, et al. 1999. "Scientific Issues in the Restoration of Salmonid Fishes in the Columbia River." *Fisheries* 24 (3): 10–19.

Chapter 4

The Science and Politics of Forest Management: President Clinton's Northwest Forest Plan

MATTHEW S. CARROLL AND STEVEN E. DANIELS

It has now been twenty-four years since the publication of the report of the Forest Ecosystem Management Assessment Team (FEMAT), *Forest Ecosystem Management: An Ecological, Economic, and Social Assessment*. The FEMAT report was the culmination of a process put in place by President Bill Clinton that attempted to resolve a bitter twenty-year political struggle over the management of federally owned forestlands in a region commonly known as the "spotted owl region" of western Washington, western Oregon, and northern California. The struggle pitted much of the forest products industry in the Pacific Northwest, along with many rural residents of "timber communities," against a coalition of largely urban-based environmental groups. At the center of the battle was the wicked problem of managing social-ecological systems across more than a dozen national forests and many more US Bureau of Land Management forests totaling millions of acres of public forestlands. Trying to come up with an integrated, effective forest plan, covering the entire region and capable of affording adequate protection for endangered and threatened species, was rife with high levels of uncertainty, contested values, and high stakes, especially given the economic prominence of the timber industry during the 1980s and early 1990s. In short, it was a classic battle framed in terms of industrial production and blue-collar jobs versus species and habitat protection.

The conflict was also broadly viewed as a rural versus urban struggle, particularly in rural areas of the Pacific Northwest. Each side brought forth spokespeople and symbols as various skirmishes were fought in administrative, legislative, and legal arenas. As the battle approached its denouement, media coverage increased. It reached a climax during a one-day, nationally televised stakeholder conference in Portland, Oregon, during April of 1993. The stakeholder conference was chaired by President Clinton, and attended by Vice President Gore, the region's governors, cabinet secretaries, prominent religious figures, leaders of the wood products industry, and others. The president dramatically announced, at the closing of the conference, that he was appointing a team of primarily government scientists to create a plan that would balance protection for old-growth-dependent species (of which the northern spotted owl was only one) with the economy and livelihoods of the spotted owl region. That team ultimately issued the FEMAT report in 1993, which has shaped federal forest management in the region ever since.

The FEMAT team was divided into six major working groups, organized along disciplinary lines: aquatic/watershed management, terrestrial ecology, resource analysis, economic assessment, social assessment, and spatial analysis. The authors of this chapter were university faculty members from land grant universities in the Pacific Northwest at the time of FEMAT and were invited to join the social assessment team to supplement the few government social scientists with expertise in assessing social impacts of public land management decisions on human communities.

This chapter explores the interplay of science and politics in the FEMAT process and asks what actually happens to science for a wicked problem characterized by uncertainty, contested values, and high stakes? Based largely on the recollections and reflections of the authors regarding the roles played by biophysical and social sciences in the FEMAT process, we use specific examples to discuss how the ideas and analyses of these disciplinary scientists were juxtaposed against other, primarily political, considerations that ended up being the main drivers of the decision process. The first vignette deals with the timing and details surrounding the creation of the FEMAT team; the selection of its leader, Jack Ward Thomas of the US Forest Service; and the highly publicized 1993 Timber Summit in Portland, Oregon. The second vignette revolves around a key aspect of the social assessment conducted by the social assessment team, and how the leadership of the FEMAT process responded to it. The third vignette offers one view of how the standards were set for the width of forested buffer zones along streams within the analysis area.

Our experiences, and the evidence presented here, suggest strongly that while the *external* view of the Clinton administration's Timber Summit and Northwest Forest Plan (NWFP) science-decision dynamics present a picture of an extended peer community per the post-normal science model, the reality was one of symbolic gestures in which the political dynamic was largely hidden from public view. This finding helps remind us of how difficult it often is to apply either the traditional model of science or the post-normal model to wicked problems at such a large scale.

We start by developing the three vignettes and then turn to a final discussion, wherein we reach some conclusions and draw lessons about the use of biophysical and social science in FEMAT that appear to be applicable to other issues.

THE BATTLE OVER SPOTTED OWLS IN TIMBER COUNTRY

Providing a brief description of the multi-decadal process that culminated in the policy gridlock over federal forest management in the early 1990s is daunting, given that others (e.g., Yaffee 1994) have devoted entire books to the story. At the risk of oversimplifying, the episode can be understood as a collision between an unstoppable change and an immovable status quo. The unstoppable change was the inevitable shift away from an old-growth-based timber economy to a small-log/second-growth timber economy in the Pacific Northwest. Ever since industrial timber harvesting began regionally in the late nineteenth century, the trees that were being harvested were extremely large, old trees that were native to the land—ones that Europeans "inherited" upon settling the area. Every museum in the region is replete with photos of massive trees of eight to fifteen feet in diameter at the base being harvested by stoic men with saws and axes. But these native forests needed to be understood as a nonrenewable resource, one that would eventually be completely exhausted if there were no efforts to preserve them. These native forests are home not only to massive trees, but also to a broad suite of species referred to as "old-growth obligates"—species that are found only in the rich, cool, shady temperate rain forests of the Pacific Northwest. The old-growth forests are a source of biological diversity and magnificent beauty that the much simpler second-growth forests that would replace them could not match.

The immovable status quo was the extensive timber industry that had grown up in the Pacific Northwest around harvest from federal public lands managed by the US Forest Service (USFS) and the US Bureau of Land Management (BLM). Sawmills used technology designed to transform these large logs into lumber for homes and other products; entire communities were located near USFS and BLM lands to support the timber industry; and people had their self-identities constructed around their traditions and skills as loggers and mill workers. In short, a huge economic and social investment was dependent on the large old-growth logs coming from the federal forests. As part of this, the federal land management agencies were under considerable congressional pressure and federal budget incentives to "get the cut out." This created and sustained a powerful national political coalition in support of continued harvesting of old-growth timber on federal lands.

Beginning about 1975, scientific research began to show that the northern spotted owl had a marked preference for old-growth forests. This was also the "golden era" for the passage of federal environmental legislation: the National Environmental Policy Act (NEPA) was enacted in 1970, the Endangered Species Act in 1973, and the National Forest Management Act in 1976, which contained a new requirement to maintain "species diversity" on federally managed lands. Between new science and new legislative mandates, by the early 1980s the decision environment for USFS and BLM forest managers was very different than it had been only a decade before. The first spotted owl–related administrative appeals were filed against the Forest Service and the BLM in early 1980. And even though they were unsuccessful, subsequent legal actions, NEPA documents, scientific panels, and public relations campaigns filled the region's newspapers for the rest of the decade. As harvesting on federal lands became increasingly gridlocked by litigation, Oregon's Senator Mark Hatfield introduced legislation in 1989 to implement a set of agreements arrived at during a "timber summit": it set the Forest Service harvest level, restricted administrative and legal review of timber sales, and also established the Interagency Scientific Committee on National Forests (ISC), which was chaired by a Forest Service researcher, Jack Ward Thomas. In large measure, the summit that US Senator Hatfield convened was the precursor to the one that President Clinton led some four years later, and many of the players and themes from the ISC report were reprised in the FEMAT report as well.

In short, the region's timber economy was going to make an inevitable transition from relying on old-growth trees to smaller, second-growth trees. The only question was how many old-growth acres and old-growth-obligate species were going to be left when that transition was over. Using the spotted owl as the photogenic archetype of the biodiversity at risk, the mounting evidence was that much of the region's remaining old growth, particularly the essentially contiguous blocks of significant size, needed to be preserved. (In the end that preservation also put off-limits to harvest significant amounts of second-growth forest as well.) President Clinton's challenge, if he was going to follow through on his campaign promise to resolve this contentious debate, was to craft a sufficiently legitimate plan that the various political constituencies in the region would accept. Surely the best science would provide a foundation for such a plan.

VIGNETTE 1: THE FOREST SUMMIT AS POLITICAL THEATER

The Northwest Forest Conference, commonly referred to as the "Timber Summit," was arguably the pivotal event in the long spotted owl/federal forests saga. As a presidential candidate, Bill Clinton pledged to convene a process to resolve the issue and followed through on this campaign promise on April 2, 1993. By making that promise, he was making a commitment to two traditional, powerful Democratic Party constituencies in the Pacific Northwest: organized labor and the members of environmental advocacy organizations. Clinton carried California, Oregon, and Washington in the election, although in the latter two states, he might not have won except for the effect that third-party candidate Ross Perot had in dividing the conservative/Republican vote.

Given that he had taken office only on January 21, 1993, this summit occurred quite early in his time in office, and indicates that it was a high priority in his administration. The Forest Summit was held in Portland, Oregon, chaired by the president himself, and attended by the vice president, four cabinet members, and a who's who of Pacific Northwest politicos, labor leaders, environmentalists, and scientists. The summit received national news coverage, and the local coverage was extensive, including gavel-to-gavel television broadcast. Hopes were incredibly high that the rancorous political logjam over federal forest practices could be busted loose once and for all.

The language used by the administration focused on strongly shared interests and the opportunity for mutual gains; it was very collaborative in tone. The president's opening statement concluded with the following call for creativity and unity:

A healthy economy and a healthy environment are not at odds with each other. . . . We all understand these things. Let's not be afraid to acknowledge them and to recognize the simple and powerful truth that we come here today less as adversaries than as neighbors and coworkers. Let's confront problems, not people.

Today I ask all of you to speak from your hearts, and I ask you to listen and strive to understand the stories of your neighbors. We're all here because we want to help the economic environment and a healthy natural environment, because we want to end the divisions here in the Northwest and the deadlock in Washington. If we commit today to move forward together we can arrive at a balanced solution and put the stalemate behind us. Together we can make a new start. (FEMAT 1993, 7–8)

The various panels of stakeholders echoed this collaborative, unified, problem-solving frame throughout the first day. One of the last panels of the day included scientists whose work had been central to the various challenges to the environmental adequacy of federal timber management, and upon whom the creation of a new paradigm of forest management would surely rely. One of these scientists, Jack Ward Thomas of the US Forest Service, had built his career studying elk biology and management in eastern Oregon. In his remarks, he told the president that there were perhaps only a few hundred scientists who understood how these forests work, and that the president should convene a team of scientists to develop a comprehensive management plan for the federal forests across the three states in the spotted owl region.

At the end of the summit, the president announced that he was indeed convening a working group of scientists just as Dr. Thomas had recommended. The timing of the formation of this team is the aspect of the spotted owl parable that is the focus of this vignette. The decision to form this working group did not emerge from dialogue at the Timber Summit, or from Dr. Thomas's pointed suggestion that such a group was needed. He had in fact already agreed to chair the new FEMAT team even before he publicly argued for its creation. In fact, space for the team had already been leased in a Portland office building, and other scientists had been contacted about their willingness to serve on the team. The day after the summit, Vice President Gore's press secretary confirmed this, when he stated that "teams have been working for weeks . . . to devise a new logging policy in the Pacific Northwest" (Sonner 1993). In short, the Clinton administration knew exactly what the outcome of the Timber Summit was going to be, even before the television lights were turned on. The various people who were admonished to "speak from their hearts" were merely unwitting players in a political drama that had already been carefully scripted. The openness and honesty the president sought was in fact not reflected in the underlying process itself.

For students of politics and political processes, and for those with experience in the world of policy-making, it is naïve to be shocked that the policy path after the Timber Summit was a fait accompli. In general, White House staffers or politicians who leave major policy outcomes to chance tend to have short careers. In this instance, it is clear that the White House was thinking several moves ahead on the chessboard. The more interesting question is, if the entire summit served to justify a predetermined conservation strategy, what confidence ought we have that the use of science in the subsequent planning and regulatory processes were no less scripted? If the political stakes were so high that the outcome could not be left to the unpredictable vagaries of authentic dialogue, might it not hold equally true that the FEMAT science informing the actual Northwest Forest Plan could itself not be left to unpredictable authentic scientific inquiry?

In the first case, choosing Jack Ward Thomas to chair FEMAT foreshadowed a critical element of the outcome: that the NWFP would utilize a species conservation paradigm known as the "reserve/matrix" approach. In this approach, reserves are areas where human activity is greatly constrained in order to protect the old-growth character of the reserve and matrices are the areas between the reserves. Dr. Thomas was well known for supporting that conservation paradigm, but other approaches had equally articulate proponents. However, scientists with alternative viewpoints were not appointed to the team, thus effectively ending debate over the science at that level. The only real questions were how many reserves there would be, how large they would be, where they would be located, and what types of uses would be permitted in the reserves and in the matrices.

A second case also signals that the Clinton administration did not want anything really new to emerge from the science teams. Scientists were given only sixty days to complete a region-wide forest management plan. That is breathtakingly quick, especially when it is considered that drafting the management plan for a single national forest often takes two to three years, and that the spotted owl region contains a dozen national forests and a comparable amount of public forestlands administered by the US Bureau of Land Management. The sixty-day structure for reviewing and integrating science into the NWFP ensured that virtually no new data would be generated.

Rather, the analysis would be required to rely mostly on existing knowledge and expert opinion to fill in gaps.

This quick deadline also precluded any meaningful public dialogue or feedback in formulating the plan. Furthermore, in order to work at the pace required by this deadline, the science teams disappeared into an office building and provided no meaningful information about their progress. In this sense, the FEMAT science efforts in Portland were a bit like the Vatican on "pope watch," when the media and interested parties maintain a constant vigil on the Vatican's secretive, cloistered process for selecting a new pope. The main differences being that it was occurring in Portland, not Rome, and it was (ostensibly) more about science than religion. In the end, many of the people whose hopes were so high in April in the wake of the "collaborative" summit felt disappointed by both the subsequent process and the outcome.

It may well be that, just as the participants in the Timber Summit were trapped in a larger national political drama, selecting Jack Ward Thomas as FEMAT's leader and deciding to constrain scientific inquiry (as well as the production of a complete NWFP) to an extremely short sixty-day schedule also owed more to the need for political symbolism than to a desire for unbiased, deliberate, thoroughly reviewed science as a critical foundation for federal forest management in the region. Given that, how could the scientists on the team understand their role? The scientists on the team had to choose one of several philosophical bases for their involvement: they could ignore that the summit was hollow political theatre (which would be doubly hard to do if they were invited to serve before the summit even occurred); they could admit that even though the summit participants were kept in the dark, scientists are surely too smart to be similarly fooled; they could believe that their science would be "right," and by its virtue carry the day; or they could recognize that their efforts were only going to be used if the result was politically expedient.

VIGNETTE 2: THE DISAPPEARING DOT MAPS

Among the FEMAT sub-teams was a group of social scientists charged with examining a broad suite of social impacts of the plan. Certainly the element of their efforts that received the most attention was their effort to estimate the potential impacts of various federal timber-harvest scenarios on those communities in the owl region most likely to be affected by such reductions. Among the challenges the social assessment team faced was the sheer magnitude of the task: how to assess potential impacts of multiple timber harvest reduction scenarios for some three hundred separate communities within a matter of weeks.

These estimation efforts began with a paper and pencil survey of state extension specialists familiar with particular communities in their respective states. This provided the starting point for two workshops consisting of "local experts" who were highly familiar with specific communities in the potentially affected areas. The local experts were public employees: often extension agents or people funded through public sources such as local government, school boards, and the like. Individuals were selected to achieve reasonable coverage of the geographic expanse of communities in the owl region within each of the three states. Each workshop consisted of approximately fifty individuals. Workshop participants were provided census and other available secondary data relating to individual or groups of communities. They were then asked to estimate the likely social consequences of each of three scenarios of possible timber harvest reductions for the communities they knew, based on their own firsthand knowledge of the particular characteristics of communities. They were asked to rate on a seven-point scale from highly negative to highly positive the likely consequences for individual communities. They were also asked to rate the *capacity* of such communities to deal with said consequences.

Finally, in an effort to depict geographic patterns of possible impacts, both workshop groups were presented (as a group) with large maps showing the locations of all three hundred–some communities, broken out by state. Each individual was provided with three colors of sticky dots of different sizes and asked to use the dots to rate the overall consequences of each of three harvest reduction scenarios on communities with which they were individually familiar. Communities estimated to suffer severe negative consequences were to be given a large red dot, minor negative consequences a small red dot, moderate consequences a yellow dot, and those with negligible (or even positive) consequences, green dots. Individuals were asked to rate only individual communities with which they were familiar. Some communities received ratings from several individuals, while others received fewer ratings. While this was hardly an exercise in fine precision, it was aimed to depict rough spatial patterns in probable community impacts from harvest reductions.

Of all the activities undertaken as part of the FEMAT social assessment, the "dot maps" depicted potential impacts in the most visually striking and readily interpretable manner. They showed areas within each state with clusters of red dots, clearly indicating that some areas within each state were likely to suffer more severe social consequences from harvest reductions than others. They also showed how the red color deepened and spread as harvest levels went down. These dot maps represented a powerful new integration of expert opinion from across the region, and made the community impacts undeniably stark.

So what role did these dot maps have in FEMAT? Did they influence the choice of the final option or inform the public debate? The originals of the maps were whisked off to Washington, DC, to be shown to higher-level decision-makers, who would presumably determine how best to use them. The assessment team was thrilled that their work was being taken so seriously. The decision soon relayed back to the team members was that the maps were not to be released or used for publication purposes. It became apparent that the dot maps were not going to be included in the final report. The final report did contain statistics on how many communities fell into which estimated impact levels across harvest scenarios, but the spatial depiction never saw the light of day. All extraneous copies of the dot maps held within the team were ordered in the end to be destroyed.

It is fair to say that team members were initially surprised at the reaction within the FEMAT hierarchy to the dot maps. What soon became apparent was that the administrators feared that the maps, if released, could be seized upon by the opponents of harvest reduction as a kind of "redlining" of communities and subregions—not unlike the practice of some mortgage lenders at the time, which had been receiving negative attention in the press and US Congress. In short, the dot maps, created as an analytical exercise by the team (and not unlike wildlife habitat maps created by other teams within FEMAT) were perhaps seen as having the potential to provide ammunition to the political opponents of federal timber harvest reduction in the region. In the end, the only discernible impact of the "dot maps" on the final report and management plan was the placement of "adaptive management areas" within the areas of federal forest affected by the plan. These (relatively small) areas were designed to allow for some additional management flexibility within what was an otherwise highly structured and restrictive set of forest management guidelines.

VIGNETTE 3: AQUATIC BUFFERS—HOW WIDE IS WIDE ENOUGH?

Even though the spotted owl was the focal point of controversy over federal forest management in the Pacific Northwest, protection of aquatic resources was quickly overtaking it as a regional concern. Although the level of legal challenge over aquatics had not yet risen to that of the spotted owl, the geographic extent of fish-bearing streams and the declines in anadromous fish populations meant that protection of riparian areas had the potential to dwarf the disruptions caused by protecting old-growth-dependent species such as the owl. Fisheries habitat management was therefore integrated into the FEMAT process, a fact that contributed to the increased protection of second-growth along with old-growth forests in the "owl region."

Although uplands management undeniably affects aquatic resources, management within the riparian zone itself is the more direct determinant of habitat quality. Intact (unmanaged or minimally managed) riparian areas are critical to maintaining aquatic resources. A number of key effects that riparian areas have on streams include shading, recruiting coarse woody debris, providing litter fall, mediating soil and air temperature, wind speed, relative humidity, turbidity, and so on. FEMAT figures show that most of these effects, with the exception of relative humidity, increase dramatically as the width of a buffer strip increases, but that the increase is achieved once the buffer width is roughly one tree height (FEMAT 1993, figures V-12 and V-13).

FEMAT established the following standard:

> *Fish bearing streams*—Riparian Reserves consist of the stream and the area on either side of the stream extending from the edges of the active stream channel to the top of the inner gorge, or to the outer edges of the 100 year flood plain, or to the outer edges of the riparian vegetation, or to a *distance equal to the height of two site-potential trees,* or 300 feet slope distance (600 feet, including both sides of the stream channel), *whichever is greatest.* This is the same in all Riparian Reserve scenarios. (FEMAT 1993, V-35; emphasis added)

In most cases, the "whichever is greater" clause means that the two-tree height standard is the binding constraint. The focal question in this vignette is why was the buffer width set at two-tree height when the data showed that most buffer strip benefits are accomplished at widths of one tree height? The establishment of two-tree height buffer strips was a dramatic expansion of the level of protection (FEMAT 1993, see table V-6, V-44), especially given that (1) fish-bearing streams represent the majority of the region's waterways, and (2) the standard did not vary across the analysis scenarios (ensuring that it would apply regardless of the scenario chosen). Given the way that streams bisect watersheds, these buffer strips had the potential to be hugely disruptive to the ability to access an entire watershed. Across the landscape, these buffer strips were projected to be a smaller area than the Late Successional Reserves established for old-growth-dependent species (see table V-4, V-33), but their distribution across the landscape was disproportionately problematic to managers trying to implement FEMAT.

FEMAT does not include explicit rationale for the two-tree height standard. It certainly did not contain a benefit-cost consideration of the marginal benefits and costs of the second tree's worth of buffer strip. It should be noted that these standards were regarded as interim standards to apply until site-specific watershed analyses could be conducted. The latitude created by the interim label is that they could be relaxed based on local conditions: "Interim widths are designed to provide a high level of fish habitat and riparian protection until watershed and project analysis can be completed" (V-35). But given that a subsequent site-specific watershed analysis would need to provide a compelling explanation why a narrower buffer strip could adequately protect aquatic resources, the two-tree height standard became the regional default.

A private late-night conversation between a senior member of the FEMAT aquatics team and one of the authors of this paper offers a potential, but very anecdotal, insight into the thinking behind the two-tree standard. When pressed to explain the rationale for the "second tree," the aquatics team member characterized it much like an opening offer in an offer-counteroffer negotiation—as a conservative place to start. It was as if the aquatics team expected there to be some pushback or political compromise over the buffer strip width, so, like all experienced bargainers, they started with a comparatively favorable initial offer. Interestingly, though, there was no subsequent process of negotiation over the buffer strips, and their first offer became the standard.

This vignette raises the possibility of scientists recognizing (correctly, it would seem) that they are players in a political process and strategically misrepresenting their recommendations in anticipation of those recommendations being watered down by political and bureaucratic actors. In so doing, scientists become politicized actors themselves, with a veneer of position over their underlying interest—just like every other political actor. This dynamic undermines the classic conception of scientific objectivity at its core.

CONCLUSION

These three vignettes, drawn from the showdown over spotted owls and forest management, demonstrate three very different ways in which scientists, and the information they produce, can be integrated into policy processes:

- They can provide a level of justification for a politically inspired fait accompli outcome (Jack Ward Thomas as leader of the science SWAT team and the domination of the team by scientists favoring a particular approach).
- Their scientific work can be excluded or significantly downplayed (social scientists and community assessments).
- They can become political negotiators and hedge their recommendations in anticipation of eventual political compromise (the buffer width standard related to tree height).

All three examples suggest that with wicked public problems that are loaded with uncertainty and beset by high stakes and contested values, science, as traditionally conceived, gets lost in the decision process. It is not a simple matter of scientists dutifully reporting only what the data tell them, nor is it a case in which policy actors dutifully "follow the science" and do what scientists say ought to be done.

Perhaps this occurred because, like many environmental and natural resource policy controversies, and despite the science requirements of the federal ESA, the spotted owl controversy was, at its core, *not* a scientific battle. It was fundamentally a values question, in which the fight over the future management of the remaining stands of old-growth Douglas-fir on public lands in the Pacific Northwest was political, driven by actors with very different visions about what should become of those stands and the habitat that they represented (Yaffee 1994). In the words of public policy scholar Daniel Sarewitz (2004) (taken from a different context), the battle had long been "scientized"—that is to say, politically framed using scientific terminology, which in effect can be seen as an attempt to cloak or recast the value question at its root. We would further observe that the impulse to portray the outcome of FEMAT as a scientific decision may have been particularly strong on the part of a new presidential administration that had garnered the support of *both* organized labor and the environmental community in its recent election. One can make a reasonable case that the environmental side got a lot more of what it wanted from the eventual outcome than did the unions, communities, or small timber industry players dependent on federal timber, but politically it was important that the final plan have the imprimatur of science.

These questions aside, even if decision-makers have a genuine desire to "allow science to decide," or at least strongly influence, policy outcomes, Sarewitz (2004) reminds us that it is not so simple:

> Central to the idea that science can help resolve environmental
> controversies is the expectation that science can help us understand
> current conditions under which our decisions are being made,
> and the potential future consequences of those decisions. This
> expectation must confront the proliferation of available facts that can
> be used to build competing pictures of current and future conditions,
> and the embeddedness of such facts in disciplinary perspectives
> that carry with them normative assumptions. These problems are
> in part a reflection of the diversity of human values and interests,
> but they also reflect the richness of nature, and the consequent
> incapability of science . . . to develop a coherent, unified picture of
> "the environment" that all can agree on. This lack of coherence goes
> by the name of "uncertainty." (392–393)

Given all of this, it would have been a naïve hope on our part that the community analysis that we could cobble together in sixty days would have had a major impact on the trajectory of the final outcome of a controversy that had been building for a decade or more. Nonetheless, we were concerned at the time, and remain so, over the constraints placed on the analysis we were authorized to conduct. We as a team had no role in constructing the management scenarios (including of course the timber-harvest reduction levels inherent in each scenario) that were the heart of the process. We were simply asked to prepare impact estimates for various levels of harvest reductions. When we did so and constructed "dot" maps to portray our estimate of the impact for the scenario ultimately chosen, the maps disappeared.

There are of course many other vignettes and dynamics that could be drawn from FEMAT or any other large science assessment conducted to inform policy. The ones presented here provide a thought-provoking narrative. One interesting way to approach these vignettes is to ask the reader to imagine having had these experiences—how would they affect your behavior when operating at the science-policy interface? It is fair to say the authors were flattered to have been asked to participate in the FEMAT community assessment. We were relatively early in our careers, and the invitation was both a personal and professional validation. We went into the process somewhat starry-eyed, and left somewhat less naïve. Sometimes the difference between realistic and cynical is hard to see.

At the same time, these vignettes remind us of how difficult it often is to apply either the traditional or the post-normal model of science to wicked problems at such a large scale and with such high stakes. For the post-normal model, the main challenge is to the basic idea of extended peer communities as a potential solution for wicked problems, whether it is socio-ecological in character or otherwise. In cases where the stakes are high enough to elicit considerable, sustained attention from the top of the US political system and from well-established powerful organized interests, how does one craft and operate decision processes such that an extended peer community does what the post-normal science model promises? In other words, under a heavily politicized condition, can institutions, rules, and decision processes be designed to engage the full peer community in an inclusive and meaningful process of scientific discovery and integration of results among the various relevant disciplines? Is it possible?

We are not sure. However, the second half of this book is more optimistic than the story told here; it draws on research and experience with various types of problem-solving institutions and methodologies that may well be able to overcome these challenges of politics for wicked problems.

One thing we are sure of is that scientists who are invited to participate in policy processes should not be flattered by the opportunity and engage the process with starry-eyed idealism. The rules of engagement are very different in politics than in science. The authentic inquiry that characterizes good science—inquiry that is truly open to new surprises, that is accurately reported, and that can change one's mind—is often absent in politicized processes. Science, and discovery, is about taking risks and requires openness to the risk of being proven wrong. Politics, on the other hand, is much more about managing and minimizing risk for one's interests and policy goals. It is about looking at least as many moves ahead on the chessboard as one's opponents, having backup strategies for your backup strategies, and spending the appropriate time developing and nurturing networks and coalitions with others, especially those in the system wielding decision-making power.

In short, scientists interested in being both part of and effective in having their science influence such processes need to find a way to gain adequate training in the politics and leadership of public policy-making processes. Failing that, they should spend the time and effort creating and enhancing their professional networks, recognizing that political and bureaucratic power matter.

References

Forest Ecosystem Management Assessment Team (FEMAT). 1993. *Forest Ecosystem Management: An Ecological, Economic, and Social Assessment.* Washington DC: Forest Ecosystem Management Assessment Team.

Sarewitz, D. 2004. "How Science Makes Environmental Controversies Worse." *Environmental Science and Policy* 7:385–403.

Sonner, S. 1993. "Scientists Will Help Map Logging Policy." *Eugene Register-Guard*, April 3, 7A.

Walker, G. B., and S. E. Daniels. 1996. "The Clinton Administration, the Northwest Forest Conference, and Conflict Management: When Talk and Structure Collide." *Society and Natural Resources* 9:77–91.

Yaffee, S. L. 1994. *The Wisdom of the Spotted Owl: Policy Lessons for a New Century.* Washington, DC: Island Press.

Chapter 5

Citizens and Scientists in Health-Care and Environmental Policy

Differing Levels of Citizen Engagement in Expert Decision-Making

ANN C. KELLER

For decades, policy makers have grappled with how to produce high-quality scientific information for society in ways that resist politicization. The need for, and influence of, credible scientific information may be socially constructed—created and reinforced through narratives about our increasingly complex and technically driven society that privilege the perspective of highly trained elites over average citizens (see chapter 1 this volume). Or it may simply reflect the way accountability is maintained in modern democratic societies, where policy makers are judged according to the effects of the policies they endorse.[1] It also might reflect the fact that, whether apparent or actual, those with scientific credibility tend to have more influence in policy-making, especially when it comes to highly complex, technical policy issues. Whatever the source, policy makers in the United States have increasingly been awash in analytic information (Bimber 1996; Jasanoff 1990; Jenkins-Smith 1990; Ricci 1993; Smith 1991).

At the same time, the effort to provide policy makers with expert advice has been challenged by demands that citizens who lack relevant scientific or technical training be allowed into these expert arenas (Fisher 2000, 2009; Kleinman 2000) and by arguments that practice-based and/or culturally grounded "knowledges" are essential to effective policy-making processes (Scott 1998). Yet, have all policy domains encountered the same pressure to include more citizens in traditional expert-based policy forums? Drawing from theories of interest-group participation and the role of professions in society, this chapter argues that health-care policy domains have experienced considerably less demand-side participation by ordinary citizens than environmental policy domains. Using case material from an overview of notable expert advisory boards in the domain of health-care reform policy-making, this research begins to articulate explanations about the differential experience of experts and, by extension, scientific information across environmental and health-care policy domains, thus laying the groundwork for more systematic research in this arena.

I begin with a review of relevant empirical and theoretical literatures. On the empirical side, the discussion examines innovations in citizen participation and argues that most of this literature treats cases in the environmental policy domain. Theoretical literatures are discussed that offer explanations for the increase in demand for citizen representation on otherwise expert deliberative bodies. I then turn to an empirical review of several expert advisory bodies in the area of health-care reform with varying degrees of citizen participation on influential expert panels. Finally, using the environmental policy domain as a point of comparison, several possible explanations are offered for why expert panels appear to be less "evolved," that is, less inclusive of citizens, in the arena of health-care policy than in environmental policy. The comparison between health-care reform and other policy issues suggests that attitudes about expertise and the potential for experts to play a fiduciary role in policy-making differ across domains of expertise. This might affect either the rate at which governmental bodies create opportunities for citizen participation or the level of demand among nonexperts for a larger role in policy-making.

Before beginning the literature review, one important point of terminology must be addressed. Environmental politics embodies both efforts to protect ecosystems and efforts to protect human health from environmental insults. Thus, it is not appropriate to consider this paper an examination of "health" policy-making, broadly speaking, as compared with "environmental" or "ecosystem" policy processes. Instead, the comparison is between "health-care" policy-making and environmental policy-making. The former refers to the system of paying for and delivering health care, while the latter can encompass questions of human or ecosystem health.

Health-care policy fits into the wicked-problem realm because it is often unstructured. Many diseases are rife with complexity and uncertainty, making causes and effects difficult to identify given the many different factors involved in disease formation. The uncertainty infuses treatment specifications too, with different scientists/doctors prescribing different methods, medicines, diets, and therapies for patients in the areas of autism, cancer, Alzheimer's, Parkinson's, muscular dystrophy, mental illness, post-traumatic stress disorder (PTSD), the idea of what constitutes a healthy diet, or even physical ailments such as back pain (e.g., Donvan and Zucker 2015; Teicholz 2014). And because health and disease affect almost everyone, with most health-care systems having been first established at local and regional versus national levels in the United States, the problem necessarily cuts across multiple levels of government and policy domains—pharmaceuticals, insurance, hospitals, medical professions, schools, medical device manufacturers, disability, welfare, employment, and so on—each with their distinctive preferences for solutions. Finally, despite all the best intentions and resources directed at the health-care problem, relentlessness is the watchword. Significant numbers will always remain uninsured, complex diseases will always have their share of conflict over causes and treatment options, and many of the toughest diseases will never be cured.

EXPLAINING CITIZEN PARTICIPATION IN EXPERT FORUMS

A substantial literature treats the role of citizens in expert policy deliberations. This literature is both empirical (e.g., Fisher 2000, Kleinman 2000; Wynne 1992, 1996) and normative (e.g., Fischer 2009; Kitcher 2003), in that scholars find both literatures increasing demands for citizen participation and argue for the worth of that enterprise in supporting policy-making. On the empirical side of the ledger, Kleinman lays out a continuum of types of citizen participation that runs from the least substantive forms of citizen inclusion to much more deliberative processes where the traditional expert-citizen relationship is transformed (2000). For example, advisory bodies that accept a traditional division of labor might include citizen-participants, but divide the work of the advisory body into technical work dominated by experts and nontechnical work involving citizen-participants. Close to that traditional division of labor are models of inclusion in which scientists and citizens share the responsibility of reviewing technical information, but, in practice, citizen participation is symbolic.[2] For example, Kleinman argues that citizen participation on National Institutes of Health (NIH) grant review panels falls short of meaningful participation, since grants are reviewed first for their technical merit by experts and only then are citizen-participants' views on what to fund brought into the decision process (2000, 141–142).

Moving along the continuum, Kleinman presents consensus conferences where citizen-participants are expected to master technical information in order to guide policy decisions. In these, citizens are convened to review technical policy matters and experts are brought in to the process to answer citizen questions rather than to set the agenda and the terms of discussion (Sclove 1996). Still, citizen-participants in consensus conferences are dependent on traditional experts for technical and scientific information (Kleinman 2000, 145). Popular epidemiology represents another innovation in citizen participation in that citizens formulate their own theories about cause and effect and gather data to support arguments that are consistent with their local experiences (Brown 1992). In such cases, citizen-participants often rely on experts to study and substantiate their causal claims. Yet experts are responding to citizen arguments and ideas rather than setting the research agenda themselves. A variation on this is community-based participatory research where nonexperts are involved in the design and execution of research at the outset, so that both experts and nonexperts are working together throughout the research process (Balazs and Morello-Frosch 2012). In both of these instances, what becomes part of the scientific record may be initiated and even substantially carried out by nonexperts. This approach rejects the traditional model of expertise, wherein the roles of scientist and citizen are clearly delineated.

In reviewing the types of science-citizen governance models currently in use, Kleinman applies the continuum as an analytic device to show variation in the conception of the respective roles of scientists and citizens and to demonstrate that there are multiple approaches for integrating citizens into arenas of scientific practice. While one might presume that there is an evolution away from the traditional model to the newer forms Kleinman presents, Kleinman himself does not make this argument and discusses several barriers to more integrated practices involving both citizens and scientists.

In contrast, Funtowicz and Ravetz (1993), in their presentation of the concept of "post-normal" science, do present the emergence of "extended peer communities" in scientific processes as a progression with post-normal science as the normative goal. In their account, insurmountable uncertainties limit the ability to use normal methods to judge the quality of science. In such situations, they suggest that the role of science in addressing a societal problem becomes less important than deliberations over the values at stake in policy debates. They use the case of trying to predict sea-level rise to guide preemptive policy action as an illustration and argue,

Public agreement and participation, deriving essentially from value commitments, will be decisive for the assessment of risks and the setting of policy. Thus the traditional scientific inputs have become "soft" in the context of the "hard" value commitments that will determine the success of policies for mitigating the effects of a possible sea-level rise. (1993, 751)

Their approach assumes that, as scientists are asked to address problems with insurmountable uncertainties—like predicting the future state of an incredibly complex global climate—policy action will turn less on tentative scientific claims than on the result of public debates regarding allocations of public resources.

For Funtowicz and Ravetz, the limits of scientific prediction open the door for larger communities of actors to assess the quality of scientific claims and adjudicate the social relevance of those claims—the extended peer communities that characterize post-normal science. They argue that the more traditional separation between science and nonscience will hold when scientists tackle applied problems whose solutions can be judged through direct experience on the part of end users—vaccines, for example. An intermediate step between this and post-normal science is that of "professional consultancy," in which the uniqueness of problems being addressed reduces the ability to judge the quality of the outcome. In this case, professional competence becomes a substitute for a review of the quality of either the scientific process (scientific peer review) or experience with end products (quality assessment in cases of applied science). Though Funtowicz and Ravetz argue that post-normal science occurs in the face of irreducible scientific uncertainties or when "decision stakes are high" (1993, 749), they point out that issues operating in the realm of applied science, where they would expect involvement of limited peer communities, can turn into issues of post-normal science if the stakes of some problems capture the attention of previously excluded groups (1993, 746–747). In this sense, they seem to acknowledge that levels of uncertainty alone do not distinguish applied science, professional consultancies, and post-normal science. Also, they seem to imply that decision stakes are not fixed, so that any issue of scientific inquiry may animate nonscience actors, who come to feel they have a stake in the products of scientific research.

Because Funtowicz and Ravetz's account of post-normal science does not provide much insight into why one scientific issue will animate large rather than narrow peer communities, it may be useful to consider political science and sociological explanations for citizen engagement in policy-making processes. Relevant theories tend to nominate either supply-side or demand-side changes in society and political life to account for the rise in citizen participation. On the supply side are arguments that point to changes in structural arrangements and institutions that make it easier for citizens to participate in political life. For example, the Administrative Procedures Act and the so-called sunshine laws passed in the 1970s create a platform for citizen participation by increasing transparency in public decision-making and encouraging citizen involvement in governmental deliberations. Moreover, specific pieces of environmental legislation, like the Clean Air Act Amendments of 1970, included provisions for citizens to sue the government if it was not fulfilling its responsibilities under the act. According to these theories, legislation or the creation of government programs precede political mobilization and, thus, should be viewed as stimulating grassroots movements rather than responding to them (Wilson 1989; Campbell 2005). Theodore Lowi's argument that "policies create politics" (1964, 1972) captures this inversion by suggesting that the type of intervention a policy creates in the marketplace or in society can be used to predict stakeholder mobilization around that policy. Wilson makes Lowi's prediction more systematic by adding the insight that the concentration versus distribution of costs and benefits associated with a given policy will predict the types and strength of interest groups that coalesce around that policy (1989).

Social movement theory articulates demand-side changes in social and political experience. Though social movement theory tends to view social movements as more likely in democratized settings, social movements are viewed as having the power to change policies and even political systems rather than as just forming around and entrenching existing political structures (Morris 2000). Taking this perspective, widespread declines in citizen trust in both government and in experts might precede grassroots demands for citizen participation in public decision-making. Similarly, organization theorists who view an organization's external environment as related to organizational structure might fit in with the demand-side theories, in that complexity theory predicts that organizational complexity results from environmental complexity rather than the reverse (Hannan and Freeman, 1977; Weick 1969, 1976). Applying this perspective to public agencies, one might expect that those with more complex stakeholder environments would develop more complex mechanisms for including stakeholders in agency decision processes.

If we consider citizen participation in environmental policy domains, we find evidence that both supply-side and demand-side factors may be at work (Beierle and Cayford 2002). While one can point to the slate of environmental statutes passed in the United States in the 1970s and show how these created opportunities for citizen participation in environmental policy processes, it is clear that the modern environmental movement, usually tied to the publication of *Silent Spring* in 1962, preceded these policies. It is also worth noting that the groups that take advantage of these formal policy-making mechanisms tend to be stable, professionalized public-interest groups like National Resources Defense Council (NRDC) and Environmental Defense. It is hard to imagine these groups existing without both the environmental movement they grew out of and the formal statutes that greatly enhance their potential role in environmental policy-making. It is interesting to note that Wilson's (1989) theory of concentrated versus diffuse costs and benefits would predict that environmental policy-making would face a stakeholder environment largely mobilized against protective regulation in that environmental policies produce concentrated costs and diffuse benefits. Thus, the stability and effectiveness of public interest organizations like the NRDC and Environmental Defense need to be accounted for.[3] Also on the demand side are examples of popular epidemiology and environmental justice where grassroots activism shapes policy-making without relying on formal policy statutes or even formal mechanisms for inclusion in policy-making. In fact, many of these cases involve relatively informal mechanisms for putting pressure on decision-makers, such as media coverage and demonstrations (Layzer 2002, 57–70; Ringquist 2006). Further, over the past twenty-five years, there has been an explosion of civic environmentalism (John 1994), also known as grassroots ecosystem management (Weber 2003) or cooperative conservation (Ash Institute 2006). With civic environmentalism, broad cross-sections of stakeholders self-organize and either create collaborative governance arrangements or push for increased citizen integration into environmental policy-decision processes.

Thus, while it is clear that the government created a number of structures that supported the effectiveness of environmental activists, it is also true that citizen demand for environmental health protections both precede governmental action and emerge in settings where government-created points of leverage are not present. This raises an interesting question regarding where the demand for inclusion in expert processes comes from. It may be that these same mobilized citizens are actively pushing for more access to scientific and technical decision-making rather than simply responding to these opportunities when government officials create them.

CITIZEN PARTICIPATION IN HEALTH-CARE POLICY

While there is no shortage of examples of demands for increased citizen participation on technical advisory panels in the environmental policy domain, it is clear that this is not the only arena where such transformations are taking place. Studies of citizen participation in scientific and technical debates treat other policy-issue areas, including defense policy, health research policy, energy policy, and emerging technology. Notably absent are scholarly works about citizen involvement in US health-care policies. It is not clear whether this reflects bias in scholarly interest or an actual difference in the level of citizen engagement in this policy area. Clearly, this absence merits systematic investigation. Here, however, as a point of departure, I begin with a brief discussion of the standard for expert advisory bodies in prominent agencies in the US Department of Health and Human Services (HHS). I also consider several prominent cases of influential expert bodies in health-care policy in which citizen participation is notably absent and examine the particular politics surrounding the creation of the Patient Centered Outcomes Research Institute, an exception in the arena of health-care policy, given its focus on including nonexperts in its work.

A number of HHS agencies rely on advisory bodies that are staffed with experts. Patient participation is common among committees allocating extramural funds in the National Institutes of Health. Civil servants at the NIH report that the National Cancer Institute (NCI) was the first to incorporate citizen participation and that this practice was picked up by other institutes over time (interviews with NIH staff, July 2007). This innovation in approach appears to have resulted from the lobbying efforts of Mary Lasker. Lasker gave voice to concerns that the basic research mission of the NIH was serving the research community more than it was serving the public. She successfully pressured Congress to make the National Cancer Institute more responsive to the public by making the NCI director a presidential appointee. Though many have argued that citizen participation on NIH committees has been largely symbolic (Kleinman 2000; Krimsky 1982; interviews with NIH staff, July 2007), not every NIH advisory board has been studied, and such participation may be evolving toward even more substantial citizen participation. On the other hand, staff at NIH in 2007 were unable to articulate how NIH decision-making might have been different without the mechanisms that drew patient representatives into its process (interviews with NIH staff, July 2007).

Though the FDA does not appear to go beyond the rules laid out in the Federal Advisory Committee Act (FACA), which require that advisory committee meetings be open to the public, it is clear that the FDA has engaged with and responded to citizen advocates on both individual decisions regarding drug approvals and in terms of shaping overall agency policy (Carpenter 2010). This is most clear in the case of AIDS activists, who were able to change the standards for clinical trials as well as push for new drug approval processes designed to take into account populations of patients with much higher thresholds for risk than traditional FDA procedures would allow. Though the FDA was responsive to the demands of AIDS activists, this experience does not appear to have led the FDA to reform its approach in convening advisory panels for its regulatory decision-making. For example, the FDA's advisory committee process came under a great deal of scrutiny during deliberations over the application to approve the contraceptive drug, Plan B, for over-the-counter sales. The controversy arose around the appointment of Dr. David Hager to the relevant FDA advisory committee and centered on whether he was sufficiently expert to be on the committee (Tumulty 2002). Notably absent in the debate was any discussion of nonexpert representation on the advisory board (Union of Concerned Scientists 2013).

Turning to the Centers for Medicare and Medicaid Services (CMS), which, among other things, sets policies regarding how much to pay physicians and hospitals for care they provide to program enrollees, citizen inclusion there appears to be largely left out of the policy-making process. Several prominent advisory bodies include no citizen participation, symbolic or otherwise. For example, to make its decisions about how much to pay health-care providers, CMS relies heavily on a committee housed within the American Medical Association (AMA) called the Relative Value Scale Update Committee, or RUC. This committee determines how much physicians should be paid for their work and makes recommendations to CMS of what to pay for every service a physician might provide a patient. The RUC has been criticized for valuing specialty services over that of primary care and keeping the influence of primary care physicians to a minimum on the committee (Laugesen et al. 2012). It has also been criticized for the fact that its members face a substantial conflict of interest in shaping the reimbursement rates of those within their specialty (Mathews and McGinty 2010). While it is common for regulators to depend on regulated parties to some degree, this level of participation and CMS compliance with RUC recommendations (estimated at 70–90 percent) is quite a bit cozier than one would expect in most areas of regulatory policy.[4]

Efforts to remedy the fox-in-the-henhouse image of the RUC tend toward creating alternate sources of expertise for CMS, but do not include discussions of greater citizen participation in this process.[5] For example, one alternate source of advice, designed to advise Congress directly rather than to support CMS decision-making, is the Medicare Payment Advisory Commission, or MedPAC. MedPAC was created in 1997 to advise Congress on payments to private health plans participating in Medicare; it also has a mandate to consider issues of access and quality for Medicare enrollees. The commission is made up of physicians, academics, industry executives, and one former member of Congress.[6] Though its meetings are public and it accepts comments from "interested parties," there are no formal roles for citizens in its advisory process.

Another example of an expert body designed to support congressional decision-making on health care is the US Preventive Services Task Force (USPSTF), an independent, volunteer panel of national experts convened to provide recommendations about clinical preventive services and report to Congress concerning gaps in knowledge about preventive services.[7] This taskforce may have been developed in an effort to increase the visibility and role of prevention in a health-care system heavily skewed toward high-cost treatments conducted by specialists. Thus, we can see an effort in recent years to diversify the professional voices contributing to US health-care policy, but the panels reviewed here do not appear to go beyond FACA rules in their efforts to include citizens in their deliberations. This does not mean that citizens have no influence; it is certainly possible that advocacy efforts using traditional routes of citizen access can be effective, but the advisory groups reviewed here appear to lag even in the symbolic inclusion of citizens on NIH committees. Thus, it appears that expert/nonexpert roles in many arenas of health-care policy deliberation make use of traditional notions of expertise in spite of the innovations in thinking and practice in other issue areas.

One notable exception is the recently created Patient-Centered Outcomes Research Institute (PCORI). PCORI is an independent agency tasked with funding research that will shed light on the most effective course of treatment for a given diagnosis. The logic of comparative effectiveness research rests on its promise of improving health-care outcomes by pointing both providers and patients toward the most effective treatments and away from treatments that, although popular, are less effective or even harmful (Gerber and Patashnik 2010). Though its logic seems unassailable, comparative effectiveness research, especially when conducted under the auspices of the federal government, tends to be viewed by physicians as an encroachment on their professional domain and by the medical products industry as a potential threat to their market share (Ashton and Wray 2011; Gray et al. 2003).

Comparative effectiveness research is used in many countries to shape health-care coverage policies (Chalkidou et al. 2009). This potential mobilizes both provider associations and the medical products industry against publicly funded comparative effectiveness research in the United States (Ashton and Wray 2011; Gerber and Patashnik 2010; Gray et al. 2003). For example, PCORI's predecessor, the Agency for Healthcare Quality and Research, ran into difficulty when it published a study showing evidence that surgery for low back pain was not effective. In 1995, spinal surgeons lobbied allies in Congress to terminate the agency. These efforts led to a 21 percent decrease in the agency's appropriations for 1996, effectively ending the agency's comparative effectiveness research (Gray et al. 2003).

Champions of comparative effectiveness research, in the wake of AHRQ's experience, continued to look for ways to produce more and better data on the most effective treatments, with PCORI being the most recent result of those efforts (Ashton and Wray 2011). While one might guess that the "patient-centered" approach written into the organization's name and mission reflected a growing trend in clinical research to include patients, it was the *opponents* of comparative effectiveness research—the medical products industry—rather than its supporters who insisted on this language in the organization's authorizing statute (Ashton and Wray 2011, 199). The goal was not to tip the balance in policy-making away from experts toward citizens. Instead, the industry hoped to ensure that any application of its comparative effectiveness research findings would be applied only in the private sector, specifically, in conversations between providers and patients.

In spite of the circumstances surrounding the origins of PCORI's "patient centeredness," it is possible that this legislative fluke will provide a supply-side mechanism to mobilize more active citizen involvement in the organization.

PCORI leadership argue that their approach can be distinguished from agencies housed within Health and Human Services in that patient involvement in PCORI decision-making is both deeper and more comprehensive. For example, not only are patients involved in setting research priorities and articulating PCORI methods, PCORI prioritizes those grant proposals that build patient-centeredness into the research itself. PCORI's standard for patient involvement expects that patients will be involved from the articulation of a research question and study design all the way to the dissemination of study results. Moreover, patient advocates make up 14 percent of PCORI's board and almost 40 percent of its advisory panels. Given that most NIH research is geared toward professional advancement and publication in academic research journals, the PCORI approach could alter the way researchers think about the goals of their research and who the audiences might be for their work. Moreover, the expectations of patient advocates who are participating in PCORI governance, either on its board or advisory panels, could stimulate more citizen demand for access to health-care policy decision-making within the federal government. However, because PCORI is a nongovernmental organization—an effort to prevent PCORI from influencing decisions about Medicare reimbursement—its influence in shaping the practices around advisory boards within the Department of Health and Human Services may be muted.

DIFFERENCES ACROSS POLICY DOMAINS

The preceding discussion shows that there exists within the health-care domain a set of influential advisory groups that has not been affected by broader societal trends in the United States to include citizens in technical policy-making processes. Moreover, PCORI's apparently unique emphasis on the patient perspective appears to stem from supply-side politics that intend to draw on the legitimacy of patient-centered processes to insulate comparative effectiveness research from potential attack from powerful provider groups. This raises an interesting question about why the movement toward citizen inclusion has not flourished in the health-care policy domain.

Funtowicz and Ravetz's framework suggests that we consider whether or not the policy issues in the health-care sector are ones that allow for applied science or professional consultancy models to dominate. They argue that post-normal science processes occur when uncertainty or policy stakes are high. The stakes could not have been higher for AIDS activists, and post-normal science processes did emerge around FDA and NIH regulations of clinical trials and drug approvals for HIV/AIDS. The mobilization of AIDS activists has had lasting effects on the conduct of clinical trials and on how quickly drugs can be approved for life-threatening illnesses lacking effective treatment. However, in keeping with Funtowicz and Ravetz's observation that post-normal scientific processes tend to occur in isolation, the work of the AIDS activists does not appear to have sparked a more systematic effort to increase citizen participation in scientific and technical domains in health-care policy formation.

It is worth noting that Funtowicz and Ravetz, after laying out what they see as a lack of sustained demand for post-normal science in environmental policy domains, argue that a "smooth" transition to post-normal science in the medical domain might be possible because there is a mass base of consumers who might demand more inclusion. This chapter suggests that the emergence of extended peer communities in health-care policy might lag considerably behind such demands in environmental policy domains.

If it were true that the stakes were low for social groups in the health-care domain or that uncertainties in science might explain the demand for extended peer communities, then Funtowicz and Ravetz's framework would go a long way to explaining the differences we see across these domains. However, there is a strong case to be made that the advisory committees that shape NIH grant making, FDA drug approvals, and Medicare reimbursement models influence decisions with very high stakes. Citizens tend to prefer more NIH dollars be spent on applied research, while researchers defend allocations for basic scientific research (Guston 1999). Though researchers might argue that basic science, in the long run, will lead to better disease prevention and treatment, patient advocates who are diagnosed with debilitating and deadly diseases are often desperate for faster improvements in treatments that might improve their quality of life in the near term. How society should balance these two goals is a question that lends itself to post-normal scientific debate. Predictions about which research endeavors will lead to the highest health-producing outcomes are inherently uncertain. Thus, debates over allocations of public funds for research are not likely to be resolved by conducting cost-benefit calculations of expected outcomes. Patient advocates have argued that patients should have more say in NIH funding decisions and, starting in the 1970s, have achieved representation on NIH panels reviewing grants. However, this space maintains traditional roles for scientists and citizens on these panels and looks less innovative than several modes of citizen involvement in science in environmental and environmental health domains. In four decades, there is not much evidence of an evolution in the role that nonscientists play at NIH.

While patient mobilization around NIH decision-making has not produced an evolved post-normal mode of participation, even the demand for inclusion of citizens on the RUC is lacking. This outcome cannot be explained by the stakes of the policies influenced by the RUC. The US health-care system costs more and yet performs poorly on multiple health indicators when compared with its counterparts in the Organization for Economic Cooperation and Development (Blendon et al. 2002; Reinhardt et al. 2002). Some scholars attribute this, in part, to an imbalance in the supply of primary care versus specialty physicians, an outcome that is heavily reinforced by the decision-making influence of specialists represented on the RUC.[88] Though citizens with excellent health-care coverage are unlikely to experience the costs and provider shortages that exist at the population level in the United States, there are millions of Americans who continue to be uninsured or who have difficulty accessing primary care providers, even after the passage and implementation of the Affordable Care Act.

There may be several barriers at work that prevent citizens from organizing and demanding greater representation in this type of decision-making. Americans who are ill-served by the current arrangement do not share an identity as unifying as that of AIDS activists. In addition, lack of resources, time, and education are all factors that inhibit mobilization of the citizens who are subject to the worst outcomes associated with current medical reimbursement policies (Campbell 2005). But it would be hard to argue that a lack of high stakes is what explains this outcome, since disparities in care can lead to a lifetime of disability and even death. Citizens who might mobilize around inequities in the US health-care system might not choose the RUC as one of their targets, but the lack of concern about the conflict of interest inherent in the RUC stands in stark contrast to citizen concerns about regulatory capture in environmental and energy policy.[99]

Peterson's (2001) critique of the AMA's role in shaping US health-care policy points to a more psychosocial explanation for the lack of demand for more citizen representation in health-care policy. Peterson argues that the fiduciary role—the obligation of medical doctors to look out for the welfare of their patients—that physicians play at the individual level has readily translated into deference regarding physician views about health-care policies. According to Peterson, policy makers and society mistakenly ceded an enormous amount of power to physicians in a domain where medical training should not be expected to confer relevant skills. Peterson draws from Paul Starr's (1984) argument regarding the social consequences of the successful professionalization of doctors in the twentieth century. Deference to physicians in the clinic and commensurate declines in the roles of other health providers are natural outgrowths of successful professionalization. But both agree that physician social standing extends well beyond the clinical domain. Thus, the particular status of the medical profession may create a situation that is very different than what we see in environmental politics, where industries, especially polluting ones, are viewed with suspicion. The relative esteem accorded to polluting industries and the agencies that regulate them is reversed in the case of physicians and the federal government in setting health-care policy.

In Wilson's (1989) typology of concentrated versus diffuse costs and benefits, regulatory politics should produce a situation where the regulated industry is the only well-mobilized stakeholder. According to the theory, it is hard to mobilize and maintain the participation of actors who might represent the diffuse benefits produced by regulation. In the domain of environmental politics, this theoretical prediction is overwhelmed by circumstances in which there *are* stable, well-organized, and often professionalized actors fighting on the side of diffuse benefits. This review of a comparative lack of citizen inclusion in health-care deliberations suggests that Wilson's prediction may hold true for some cases of regulatory politics. Recent changes in supply-side structures might be changing the standard in health-care policy. However, there is no associated grassroots mobilization that is simultaneously challenging accepted norms regarding the privileged domain of experts in health-care policy. PCORI may serve as a model for citizens who view the existing channels of access as too limited. This could bring more demand-side pressure to agencies that have relied on what appears to be an outdated model for generating expert advice.

CONCLUSION

This chapter makes use of several important examples of health-care policy-making where citizen inclusion is absent, or limited, and asks whether demands for increased citizen participation in health-care policy are less pronounced than they have been in environmental policy domains. The social status of the regulated entity may play an important role in shaping citizens' demands for inclusion. In short, although citizens are skeptical of the potential influence of regulated industries in many areas of public policy, medical associations are viewed as trustworthy. This difference translates into lower demands for citizen engagement in expert forums in the health-care policy domain than what we have seen in the once expert-dominated environmental policy forums. Nonetheless, given the case study design employed here, more research is needed to systematically measure the extent to which expertise in health-care policy has resisted democratization and further examine the root causes for the lack of citizen participation.

Notes

1   Edelman's work on symbolic politics (1964), of course, suggests that most voters have very little information about policy outcomes. At the same time, there are several indicators that voters are increasingly concerned about policy outcomes. For example, the Government Performance and Results Act (1993) requires agencies to set goals, measure, and report progress. David Guston's study of the National Institutes of Health analyzes the specific case of how the culture at NIH changed as the laissez-faire approach to science policy there was replaced by active oversight of NIH productivity (1990).

2   Selznick documents such cooptation in his study of decision processes of the Tennessee Valley Authority (1949).

3   One explanation comes from Nownes and Cigler (2007) who find that wealthy patrons help support environmental groups. Such support could be sufficient to overcome the free-rider problem that Mancur Olson argues can undermine public interest organizations (1965).

4   See Laugesen et al. (2012) for a study of the rates of CMS compliance with RUC recommendations. Laugesen (2013) argues that the AMA has captured the process of setting Medicare fees and finds that the method of determining physician reimbursement rates itself produces the conditions for capture.

5   One exception was a 2012 lawsuit brought by a group of primary care physicians who argued that the RUC, as the sole adviser to CMS in setting reimbursement policies, should come under FACA rules. The courts dismissed the case on procedural grounds without addressing the merits of the FACA claim. It is also notable that lay citizens were not behind this effort.

6   Information on the commission's membership can be found on its website, http://www.medpac.gov/commission.cfm.

7 Though the USPSTF is independent, since 1998 it is convened by, and receives administrative and resource support from, the Agency for Healthcare Quality and Research, which is part of the Department of Health and Human Services.

8 See, for example, Sandy et al. (2009).

9 For example, several environmental groups and journalists mobilized to uncover the role of oil executives on the Bush administration's energy task force convened in 2001.

References

Ash Institute. 2006. "Innovations in American Government: Site Report." *Montana Partners for Fish and Wildlife* (July). Cambridge, MA: Harvard University.

Ashton, Carol M., and Nelda P. Wray. 2011. *Comparative Effectiveness Research: Evidence, Medicine, and Policy.* Cambridge: Oxford University Press.

Balazs, Carolina, and Rachel Morello-Frosch. 2012. "The Three Rs: How Community-Based Participatory Research Strengthens Rigor, Relevance, and Reach of Science." *Environmental Justice* 6 (1): 9–16.

Beierle, Bruce, and Jerry Cayford. 2002. *Democracy in Practice: Public Participation in Environmental Decisions.* Washington, DC: Resources for the Future Press.

Bimber, Bruce. 1996. *The Politics of Expertise in Congress: The Rise and Fall of the Office of Technology Assessment.* New York: State University of New York Press.

Blendon, R. J., C. Schoen, C. M. DesRoches, R. Osborn, K. L. Scoles, and K. Zapert. 2002. "Inequities in Health Care: A Five-Country Survey." *Health Affairs* 21 (3): 182–191.

Brown, Phil. 1992. "Popular Epidemiology and Toxic Waste Contamination: Lay and Professional Ways of Knowing." *Journal of Health and Social Behavior* 33 (September): 267–281.

Campbell, Andrea L. 2005. *How Policies Make Citizens: Senior Political Activism and the American Welfare State.* Princeton, NJ: Princeton University Press.

Carpenter, Daniel. 2010. *Reputation and Power: Organizational Image and Pharmaceutical Regulation at the FDA.* Princeton, NJ: Princeton University Press.

Chalkidou, Kalipso, Sean Tunis, Ruth Lopert, Lise Rochaix, Peter Sawicki, Mona Nasser, and Bertrand Xerri. 2009. "Comparative Effectiveness Research and Evidence-Based Health Policy: Experience from Four Countries." *Milbank Quarterly* 87 (2): 339–367.

Donvan, John, and Caren Zucker. 2015. *In a Different Key: The Story of Autism.* New York: Crown Publishing.

Edelman, Murray. 1964. *The Symbolic Uses of Politics.* Champaign: University of Illinois Press.

Fischer, Frank. 2000. *Citizens, Experts, and the Environment: The Politics of Local Knowledge.* Durham, NC: Duke University Press.

———. 2009. *Democracy and Expertise: Reorienting Policy Inquiry.* Cambridge: Oxford University Press.

Funtowicz, S., and J. R. Ravetz. 1993. "Science for a Post-Normal Age." *Futures* 25:735–755.

Gerber, Alan S., and Eric M. Patashnik. 2010. "Problem Solving in a Polarized Age: Comparative Effectiveness Research and the Politicization of Evidenced-Based Medicine." *The Forum* 8, no. 1 (April). doi:10.2202/1540-8884.1353.

Gray, Bradford H., Michael K. Gusmano, and Sara Collins. 2003. "AHCPR and the Changing Politics of Health Services Research." *Health Affairs.* http://content.healthaffairs.org/content/early/2003/06/25/hlthaff.w3.283.citation.

Guston, David. 1990. *Between Politics and Science: Assuring the Integrity and Productivity of Research.* Cambridge: Cambridge University Press.

Hannan, Michael T., and John Freeman. 1977. "The Population Ecology of Organizations." *American Journal of Sociology* 82 (5): 929–964.

Jasanoff, Sheila. 1990. *The Fifth Branch: Science Advisors as Policy Makers.* Cambridge, MA: Harvard University Press.

Jenkins-Smith, Hank. 1990. *Democratic Politics and Policy Analysis.* Independence, KY: Brooks/Cole.

John, DeWitt. 1994. *Civic Environmentalism: Alternatives to Regulation in States and Communities.* Washington, DC: CQ Press.

Keller, Ann. 2010. "Credibility and Relevance in Environmental Policy: Measuring Strategies and Performance among Science Assessment Organizations." *Journal of Public Administration Research and Theory* 20: 357–386.

Keller, Ann C., and Laura Packel. 2014. "Going for the Cure: Patient Advocacy and Health Interest Groups in the United States." *Journal of Health Politics Policy and Law* 39 (2): 331–367.

Kitcher, Philip. 2003. *Science, Truth, and Democracy.* Cambridge: Oxford University Press.

Kleinman, Daniel L., ed. 2000. *Science, Technology, and Democracy.* Albany: SUNY Press.

Krimsky, Sheldon. 1982. *Genetic Alchemy: The Social History of the Recombinant DNA Controversy.* Cambridge, MA: MIT Press.

Laugesen, Miriam. 2013. "Policy Complexity and Capture in Federal Rulemaking." Unpublished conference paper prepared for the 2013 Annual Meeting of the American Political Science Association, Chicago.

Laugesen, Miriam J., Roy Wada, and Eric M. Chen. 2012. "In Setting Doctors' Medicare Fees, CMS Almost Always Accepts the Relative Value Update Panel's Advice on Work Values." *Health Affairs* 31:965–972.

Layzer, Judith A. 2002. *The Environmental Case: Translating Values into Public Policy*. Washington, DC: CQ Press.

Lowi, Theodore J. 1964. "American Business, Public Policy, Case Studies, and Political Theory." *World Politics* 16 (4): 677–715.

———. 1972. "Four Systems of Policy, Politics, and Choice." *Public Administration Review* 32 (4): 298–310.

Mathews, Anna Wilde, and Tom McGinty. 2010. "Physician Panel Prescribes the Fees Paid by Medicare." *Wall Street Journal*, October 26.

Morris, Aldon. 2000. "Reflections on Social Movement Theory: Criticisms and Proposals." *Contemporary Sociology* 29 (May): 445–454.

Nownes, Anthony J., and Allan J. Cigler. 2007. "Big-Money Donors to Environmental Groups: What They Give and What They Get." In *Interest Group Politics*, 7th ed., edited by A. J. Cigler and B. A. Loomis, 108–129. Washington, DC: CQ Press.

Olson, Mancur. 1965. *The Logic of Collective Action: Public Goods and the Theory of Groups*. Cambridge, MA: Harvard University Press.

Peterson, Mark. 2001. "From Trust to Political Power: Interest Groups, Public Choice, and Health Care." *Journal of Health Politics, Policy and Law* 26 (5): 1145–1163.

Price, Don K. 1965. *The Scientific Estate*. Cambridge, MA: Belknap.

Reinhardt, Uwe E., Peter S. Hussey, and Gerard F. Anderson. 2002. "Cross-National Comparisons of Health Systems Using OECD Data, 1999." *Health Affairs* 21 (3): 169–181.

Ricci, David M. 1993. *The Transformation of American Politics: The New Washington and the Rise of Think Tanks*. New Haven, CT: Yale University Press.

Ringquist, Evan J. 2006. "Environmental Justice: Normative Concerns, Empirical Evidence, and Government Action." In *Environmental Policy: New Directions for the Twenty-First Century*, 6th ed., edited by N. J. Vig and M. E. Kraft, 239–263. Washington, DC: CQ Press.

Sandy, Lewis G., Thomas Bodenheimer, L. Gregory Pawlson, and Barbara Starfield. 2009. "The Political Economy of US Primary Care." *Health Affairs* 28:1136–1145.

Sclove, Richard. 1996. "Town Meetings on Technology." *Technology Review* 99 (5): 24–31.

Scott, James. 1998. *Seeing Like a State: How Certain Schemes to Improve the Human Condition Have Failed*. New Haven, CT: Yale University Press.

Selznick, Philip. 1949. *TVA and the Grass Roots*. Berkeley: University of California Press.

Smith, James A. 1991. *The Idea Brokers*. New York: Free Press.

Starr, Paul. 1984. *The Social Transformation of Medicine: The Rise of a Sovereign Profession and the Making of a Vast Industry*. New York: Basic Books.

Teicholz, Nina. 2014. *The Big Fat Surprise: Why Butter, Meat and Cheese Belong in a Healthy Diet*. New York: Simon and Schuster.

Tumulty, K. 2002. "Jesus and the FDA." *Time*, October 5.

Union of Concerned Scientists. 2013. "Underqualified Nominee Installed on FDA Reproductive Health Advisory Committee." http://www.ucsusa.org/center-for-science-and-democracy/scientific_integrity/abuses_of_science/a-to-z/reproductive-health.html#.WGqMvmczXs0.

Weber, Edward P. 2003. *Bringing Society Back In: Grassroots Ecosystem Management, Accountability, and Sustainable Communities*. Cambridge, MA: MIT Press.

Weick, Karl E. 1969. *The Social Psychology of Organizing*. 2nd ed. Reading, PA: Addison-Wesley.

———. 1976. "Educational Organizations and Loosely Coupled Systems." *Administrative Science Quarterly* 21:1–19.

Wilson, James Q. 1989. *Bureaucracy: What Government Agencies Do and Why They Do It*. New York: Basic Books.

Wynne, Brian. 1992. "Misunderstood Misunderstanding: Social Identities and Public Uptake of Science." *Public Understanding of Science* 1:281–304.

———. 1996. "May the Sheep Safely Graze? A Reflexive View on the Expert-Lay Divide." In *Risk, Environment, and Modernity: Towards a New Ecology*, edited by S. Lash, B. Szerszynski, and B. Wynne, 44–83. London: Sage.

Part Two

Responding to the Challenges with New Problem-Solving Methodologies

Chapter 6

An Experiment in Post-Normal Science

Building a Knowledge-to-Action Network in Idaho

DENISE LACH

One of the critical components of a post-normal approach to science is the extension of peer communities (Funtowicz and Ravetz 1993). In the normal, or traditional, approach to science, peer communities are typically limited to those experts who can judge the quality of the science; for the most part, these are disciplinarily trained peers (e.g., biologists, physicists, geologists). When uncertainty and decision stakes increase, the post-normal approach suggests that the peer community can and should be extended to nondisciplinary experts, those with experiential, contextual, or local knowledge. This is because single scientific disciplines and strictly scientific knowledge are, by definition, incapable of capturing the full complexity of such problem settings.

A good example of an extended peer community approach to science is the Intergovernmental Panel on Climate Change (IPCC). It is best described as an interdisciplinary assessment of scientific research that attempts to integrate the best available knowledge for use by policy makers (Kennel and Daultrey 2010). These kinds of expert consultative initiatives do not create new data, but instead gather existing results together for interdisciplinary interpretation, and are one of the emergent methods for understanding wicked complex problems. The extended peer group in this case is not only an interdisciplinary group of scientists studying the problem, but also an interdisciplinary group of scientists *and policy experts* working together to interpret and understand the implications of the data.

Yet, while the global climate models used by the IPCC have been instrumental in understanding the worldwide impacts of climate change, many decision-makers are equally if not more concerned with the regional or even local impacts of climate change. Although climate modelers are well aware of policy demands for regional forecasts, the capacity to downscale global processes to regional landscapes is in its infancy (e.g., Ramesh and Goswani 2014). While regional climate is affected by a myriad of complex local variables, it is also conditioned by global phenomena and so beset with high levels of uncertainty and high decision stakes for affected stakeholders. These conditions make it difficult if not impossible to draw a boundary around a region and determine future climate impacts in that place (Pielke Sr. 2012). For example, a recent study (van der Ent et al. 2010) reported that 80 percent of China's water resources comes from evaporation from the Eurasian continent. Where is the boundary on that region for either European or Chinese decision-makers?

The concern is that we do not yet have the kinds of robust measurement and prediction methods required to assist regional policy makers tasked with making policy decisions that will affect, and are likely to be affected by, climate change. In such regionally based cases, even as the decision stakes rise, the level of uncertainty continues to increase as global models are downscaled and forecasts stretched into an unknowable future. This additional uncertainty suggests we have moved into a situation where a new problem-solving strategy grounded in post-normal science may be appropriate for developing the information needed to move forward on regionally based climate change decisions.

One possible approach involves the creation and use of a knowledge-to-action network (KTAN) (Cash et al. 2003). KTANs are designed to bring together an evolving group of participants to pose and answer questions collaboratively and iteratively, with the goal of creating usable information (or knowledge) for policy decisions. One of the exercises critical for KTAN success is a process for developing shared information and meaning. While participants come into the network with different knowledge, perspectives, and values, the KTAN creates a venue for participants to pose problems, develop a shared understanding of the issue and its uncertainties, collect relevant information, and agree on ways to interpret the data. This chapter describes the development and implementation of a KTAN with local stakeholders and experts to coproduce knowledge to address future water scarcity issues in a western US river basin. It is organized around the key stages of a research project—problem identification and research question development, data collection and analysis, and interpretation—as they may be practiced through a post-normal science approach.

FRAMING THE PROBLEM/KTAN DEVELOPMENT

The Climate Impacts Research Consortium (CIRC), a NOAA-funded initiative, was tasked with providing information to users in the US Pacific Northwest (PNW) to help with local decisions about adapting to climate change. While CIRC spent time producing downscaled regional climate models, it also worked with decision-makers in the PNW to identify critical issues and information gaps. After a set of regional meetings and surveys with state and local agencies (e.g., water resources, planning, power), staff of nongovernmental organizations (e.g., The Nature Conservancy, Surfrider, EcoTrust), local businesses (e.g., tourism, agriculture), and residents, an idea coalesced among Idaho decision-makers around planning for a future with less water. This was a critical issue, as water in this semiarid region has already been fully allocated through senior and junior water rights. Any changes in the amount or timing of precipitation had the potential to disrupt well-established practices for distributing and using water. And, because the problem was crosscutting, involving critical issues across the area's ecological, social, and economic landscapes, there was no obvious single scientific discipline, agency, or set of experts capable of helping with all the questions and trade-offs arising from any change in climate, especially precipitation. Idaho decision-makers approached CIRC about initiating a project to build capacity to adapt to climate change.

CIRC convened a meeting in south central Idaho, inviting potential participants from multiple groups, including state and federal agencies (e.g., water, agriculture, land use), nongovernmental organizations (NGOs) (e.g., The Nature Conservancy, Idaho Conservation League), local and county government (e.g., elected officials, planners), university extensions, canal companies, and residents (e.g., farmers, small business owners), interested in thinking about the future of the region. While the university researchers convened the meeting, they did so around issues raised earlier by residents and managers, and invited potential users to participate in the project. The KTAN approach was presented as an "experiment" in problem solving, with the idea that the group would coproduce the approach, data and data analysis, and interpretation. About fifteen people originally signed up as members of the KTAN, and that number fluctuated over a couple of years as the effort moved through the different stages of the project.

In many ways a post-normal approach follows a typical scientific method: we frame a problem and relevant questions, identify multiple methods for answering the questions, characterize and collect needed data, run the analysis, and interpret the output. But, along each step of the way, the post-normal approach calls for some practices distinct from the traditional approach to science. Originally this problem was framed, for example, through a region-wide discussion about the specific and local effects of climate change and what kinds of actions were necessary to adapt to identified and unanticipated changes. The Big Wood Basin was described by local informants as exemplifying challenges faced by many areas of Idaho that wanted to sustain traditional agricultural uses while accommodating new demands from growing urban and in-stream uses of water. Just as important, they pointed out that, unlike some PNW basins, water users in the Big Wood Basin had not yet reached a level of contention that would prevent them from sitting in the same room.

The Big Wood Basin in central Idaho covers about 5,500 square kilometers, with a landscape that varies from mountains in the north to large expanses of lava fields to shrubland in the south. A large percentage of the land is owned and managed by federal agencies, and agriculture is interspersed throughout the lower basin. Winter snowfall is the dominant source of water, recharging groundwater systems and feeding the rivers through spring runoff. The water supports many uses, including municipal and domestic requirements, habitat, industry, recreation, and commercial use. Nearly one hundred thousand acres of the basin are irrigated as well, making irrigation the single largest water use.

The 2010 population of the basin was approximately twenty-five thousand, with about 70 percent residing in urban centers and 30 percent in rural areas (US Census Bureau 2012). Although the population density in the basin is quite low, development is generally concentrated in the Wood River Valley, a small area of the northern basin, which experienced an average annual growth rate of 7 percent between 1970 and 2007. This area is anchored by the Sun Valley ski resort, which is home to many second homes and seasonal tourists. Rapid growth around the resort has led to concerns over the sustainability of water resources, highlighting the rise of competing water uses. These concerns are underscored by additional uncertainty about future climate, which could dramatically affect the winter snowpack.

At the beginning of the first KTAN meeting, we asked each member to complete a survey that asked about reasons for and expectations associated with participating. This information was designed to be shared with the participants, so they knew what others were interested in and/or expecting from the process. We continued to ask a similar set of questions at each meeting with the KTAN to track changes from initial positions. While many local informants told us not to mention climate change with this group, we surprisingly found that, for most participants in this first meeting (88 percent), their primary reason for getting involved was to learn more about the effects of a changing climate. After completing the survey, we began with a round of introductions and a backcasting exercise, asking each person to think about headlines in the local newspaper in the year 2050. What would be a best-case headline for the Big Wood Basin, and what would be a worst-case headline? We used backcasting as a method to start people thinking about the future and characterizing the conditions that might lead to desired futures, as well as understand how less-desirable futures can emerge from the choices made over the years (Holmberg and Robert 2000). The backcasting exercise resulted in laughter and high spirits, as well as the recognition that participants maybe had more in common than expected.

DEVELOPING RESEARCH QUESTIONS/CREATING SHARED KNOWLEDGE

The facilitators then organized the headlines into six categories: protection of aquatic habitat, responsible development, economically resilient communities, community collaboration, sufficient water (for agriculture, municipalities), and maintenance of an agriculture-based economy. The group agreed that these endpoints described the sorts of things people cared about ensuring into the future. One of the farmers, for example, expressed surprise and pleasure that people and groups he considered "less than friendly" were concerned about sustaining agriculture traditions in the basin.

The Big Wood Basin KTAN separated into small groups, each taking one of the desired endpoints and identifying the inputs, drivers, and outputs for that specific endpoint. Each group created a hand-drawn representation of the connections they saw between causes/drivers and desired effects (endpoints). As the groups completed their diagrams, we brought the hand-drawn figures together to begin making linkages among the ideas, conditions, and problems. This resulted in a spaghetti diagram that provided a good start for revealing the complexity of the Big Wood Basin socio-ecological system to those who participated. A lively discussion followed, with lots of redrawing of connectors and identifying new variables as KTAN members became familiar with the original six diagrams. This activity served as an ice breaker not only for the group to begin working together on a nonchallenging task, but also to deepen all participants' knowledge of relationships among natural and human systems, and others' perspectives and values around those systems.

The exercise allowed the group to move forward in identifying variables they wanted to consider, data they needed to support those variables, and what they probably could not include in the model given limitations in data or research methods techniques. For example, while community collaboration emerged as a high priority endpoint, the group discussed ways to characterize this through outputs of the research rather than through attempts to collect data to address it directly.

Based on the conceptual modeling and discussion, three research questions were developed by the KTAN as interesting, relevant, and feasible:

1. How are drivers of change, both biophysical and human, likely to affect the quantity and timing of water for agriculture, fish habitat, and municipal uses in the Big Wood Basin?
2. Where and when is water scarcity most likely to occur in the Big Wood Basin under projected climatic conditions?
3. What policies and strategies would be most effective for achieving the desired endpoints for the basin?

These research questions served as the basis for the next steps of the process, which included a transition from the conceptual, qualitative model to two quantitative modeling efforts. Participants agreed that the quantitative modeling approach was an appropriate way to think about change over time, given the complexity involved in the questions and multiple human and natural systems.

These conversations started the collaborative process of framing the problem and characterizing the system in a way that all could understand. In addition, participants began to talk about needed data sources, what to do if those data were not available, and possible placeholders for complex ideas such as community resilience. Creating the conceptual model, and the resulting discussion, helped open the black box that research can appear to be, helped participants understand what might not be possible, and helped researchers clarify what was important. Finally, it helped identify gaps in knowledge for all members of the KTAN.

UNDERSTANDING IMPACTS AND ADDRESSING MULTIPLE VIEWPOINTS: A SYSTEMS DYNAMICS MODEL

We began to model the basin using a systems dynamics model, as these are relatively easy to understand and use by non-technical folks (e.g., Stave 2003; Beall et al. 2011). Because these models can be constructed relatively quickly, there isn't much delay in getting a model for review and discussion. And, finally, a systems dynamics model can help explain how different components connect with and affect each other. The CIRC technical team generated an initial systems dynamics model that contained information about hydrology, land use transitions, and population growth. This model was then reviewed with KTAN subgroups with local expertise in hydrology, agriculture, and land use planning to make sure the connections made sense, identify any local data or knowledge to incorporate into the model, and characterize any missing variables important to decision-making.

KTAN subgroup members were able to quickly begin using the model to understand relationships among the variables, without an express need to discuss the underlying algorithms or equations. After a brief presentation of the model, we talked with subgroup members about the validity of the approach, missing variables, and available data. For example, the agriculture group helped identify the soil types across the basin and estimated evapo-transpiration (ET) for vegetation types. Their local knowledge about these site-specific variables was critical for representing water demand in the basin. Following a robust discussion, the group agreed that improved ET estimates could be incorporated but that fine-scale variability of soil types could not be addressed without reducing efforts in other parts of the project. These are the kinds of decisions that are routinely made by scientists as they frame their research and start their data collection. In this case, the KTAN members worked with the technical team to decide which trade-offs were appropriate and which were not. Similarly, the land use group noted that the model should be amended to reflect current policy prohibiting wetland conversions to other land uses. After the subgroup meetings were completed, a webinar was held to review all the model updates, assumptions, and decisions with the whole KTAN so everyone understood the assumptions made, variables of choice, operationalization of variables, and, importantly, why some variables were not selected (because of lack of data).

Early conversations among the KTAN were generally pleasant and accommodating, but when it came time to discuss what was in the model (and what wasn't), the different viewpoints and perspectives came to play an important role in the model-building. The small-group/large-group strategy allowed KTAN members to look under the hood of the model, contribute or approve data, and create or challenge assumptions about how the model could be used. This strategy also illuminated the range of perspectives and assumptions in the group. But, because the subgroups were relatively homogeneous, at least in relation to the topic they worked on, the process tended to cover up or technically patch over any major disagreements in assumptions about how the socio-ecological system worked as a whole and what the future held in regard to climate or population change. The systems dynamics modeling effort served the purpose of explicitly identifying stocks, flows, and feedbacks within the system, introducing KTAN members to the process of developing a model and collecting and vetting data to be used in the model. However, it became apparent when the subgroups came together that the model was too simplistic to address the questions they had identified earlier and could not address the differing assumptions KTAN members held about the future of the basin.

As in many normal research projects, there were low points in which decisions about the research were questioned. This meeting with the KTAN to look at the systems dynamics model was a low point, as was reflected in the end-of-meeting survey that suggested only about one-third of KTAN members believed the process would produce anything they could use to help make decisions. This was down from about 80 percent across the subgroups, who reported strong belief that something usable would come from the project after their small-group meetings. The clash of ideas and assumptions could not be accommodated with the systems dynamics model, so we proposed a different kind of modeling that would be more spatially and temporally explicit and would be dynamic across time and policy preferences.

BUILDING A NEW MODEL: INTEGRATING LOCAL KNOWLEDGE, EXPERIENCE, AND EXPECTATIONS

The new model was based on a software program called Envision, which had been developed by Oregon State University researchers (John Bolte and colleagues) and implemented at multiple sites. Envision is a framework that can bring together any number of models (e.g., hydrologic, climate) to help understand what happens on the landscape under different management or policy approaches. The model helps decision-makers explore the interconnected feedbacks that affect any connected human and natural systems over time (Bolte et al. 2007). Benefits of the Envision platform include integration of already existing models so new ones don't have to be built, ability to include local data in models, and capability of exploring multiple scenarios played out over time.

For the Big Wood Basin, models were created to represent surface water hydrology, reservoir operations, irrigation demands, crop mix, and development patterns, all information that can help the KTAN answer its research questions. Regional economic drivers and population growth were included as boundary conditions but not modeled; for example, a population growth rate of 2.8 percent per year was included in the model but was not dynamic in that it did not respond to other variables. Finally, in consultation with a regional climate scientist, the KTAN participated in a webinar that explored predictions of different climate models for the area. Three climate models were selected to represent predictions of high, medium, and low temperature and precipitation change in the region.

Envision is designed to run with different policy preferences as characterized by the users. In this case, KTAN members worked together to come up with a set of four plausible futures characterized by the economic driver (tourism or agriculture) and policy restrictions (more or less) to develop four scenarios: managed tourism boom, unmanaged tourism boom, managed agriculture boom, unmanaged agriculture boom.

Each scenario contains a set of "policies" that directs choices made by agents in the model. For example, under the managed tourism boom, it is assumed that recreation will demand more water over time, policies to promote water efficiency will be implemented, incentives for shifting existing water rights from agricultural to nonagricultural use will occur, agriculture will shift to crops that need less water, and conservation practices will be required for all water users. If water becomes scarce in the future, residential and recreational uses are given preference over agricultural uses in this scenario. These policy assumptions were developed by the KTAN team using existing knowledge about water laws, water availability, historical water flows, and zoning regulations. Similar policies and assumptions were made for each of the other three scenarios. We began by having the entire KTAN set the scenarios about possible futures and then worked with subgroups to create the assumptions and gather necessary data and information.

An important point to note here is that, unlike the systems dynamics model, Envision requires great technical expertise to set up and run. After KTAN development of the scenarios, we moved away from the transparent systems dynamics approach to something that looked more like a "black box" to nontechnical members of the KTAN. However, the KTAN agreed to the trade-off of using a less transparent model in exchange for an increase in what they expected would be usable information. The Envision application also built on the hydrology model identified in the systems dynamics effort, which had been vetted by the stakeholders. The major advantages of using Envision for this project was its ability to customize the application for this basin, including the integration of local knowledge and experience.

INTERPRETING THE RESULTS/EXTENDED PEER COMMUNITY

We used the four different scenarios to force the model for the period from 2010 to 2070 (dates selected to coincide with climate models). The four scenarios were run with the three different climate futures to provide twelve different paths to the future. The goal was to simulate many possible futures to help resource users and managers explore the range of imaginable change. The next problem was how to look at overwhelming output from multiple model runs, which looked at change in the basin over decades. This is a problem not only of visualization, but also of determining criteria for examining output: What is credible? What is less credible? The growing problem of scientists working with large data sets and/or model outputs becomes especially salient when working with nontechnical people who are not steeped in the everyday analysis of data.

In an attempt to "tame" the initial explosion of data, the technical team went back to the original research questions and determined a set of stories to tell with the data. For example, one of the major issues in the basin is a change in future timing and supply of water resources in a basin with fully allocated resources that are highly influenced by snowpack and temperature changes. What did the model simulations tell us about how changes in snowpack would affect the availability of water over the year, change the types of crops that could be grown, and determine how much artificial snow would need to be made to ensure successful ski seasons? A series of visualizations was developed for each story line and presented in poster form. The idea was to share initial run information through a familiar strategy for scientists—a poster session. Small groups could spend time going over the model outputs in some detail with a set of organizing questions: Is this information clear? Are we making correct assumptions? Do you have knowledge that supports or contradicts our assumptions? Is this information helpful in making decisions? What other questions should we be asking or stories should we be telling?

During this stage, KTAN members acted as an extended peer community for the Envision modelers by validating or correcting assumptions, providing additional information or knowledge to condition the model, and thinking about how to produce and display information that can be used to make decisions. This is very different from a typical presentation at a scientific conference or publication of a peer-reviewed paper in a specialist journal. While the modelers are likely to publish their work in relevant disciplinary journals, the KTAN process is more interested in the output than in the workings of the model. If the model output looks "strange" based on their experience or knowledge of the system, they can question but can't suggest fixes to the mechanics of the model. Instead, they can tell modelers that something is wrong—this kind of land cover would never grow on this lava, for example— so that the computer code can be reviewed for errors.

As with all models, Envision makes many assumptions about the future, and the system interactions are only as sophisticated as the individual models allow. What is different about this kind of exercise is the degree to which stakeholders, in this case the KTAN members, are involved in setting the policies, agreeing to the assumptions, and determining the parameters of different variables included in the model. Although the actual model is encased in a black box, and KTAN members don't see the computer code, they do contribute to framing the problem and questions, collecting and characterizing data, and "tweaking" or conditioning the model using their own local knowledge and experience.

Once the initial results were discussed with KTAN members, a "data atlas" was created for each story line that included not only the data, so that individuals could use it in their own decisions, but also a take-home message about the specific topic (e.g., surface temperatures have increased in the basin over the last thirty years and are expected to continue to rise through the twenty-first century). Information was also included about which data were used and which assumptions made, and how the modeling was done (quite technical). In addition, key findings were described (e.g., air temperature expected to increase in all future climate scenarios), along with interactive graphs and charts about the topic.

Not only can the different climate models be turned on and off by the user in this example, which allows the viewer to look at a single variable (in this case, climate), each data point on any graph, table, or chart is revealed by placing the cursor on that year. In this way, large amounts of data are compressed and hidden until needed by a user. KTAN user groups helped identify the important story lines, the take-home messages, and key points, while the computer experts added the information about the data and how it was used in the model.

KTANS AS POST-NORMAL SCIENCE

Trying to understand a complex issue like the effects of climate change on a local basin is at heart an interdisciplinary problem that cannot be addressed through normal disciplinary science. Considering the uncertainty of future climate, population growth, economic health, and other drivers over time is a feat not well managed by the traditional approach to science. Yet people and organizations are asked all the time to make decisions that have long-term consequences in an environment that is highly ambiguous and unknowable. What role can scientific thinking, methods, and information play in these increasingly common environments?

Post-normal science suggests that extending the peer community beyond even a wide range of disciplinary experts to include those who will be affected by the changes can help scientists formulate questions, collect multiple kinds of data, and interpret results in a context of decision-making that accepts and leverages uncertainty, different perspectives, and local knowledge. The Big Wood Basin KTAN was an attempt to create a venue for post-normal science in addressing water scarcity concerns in the face of climate change and population growth in south central Idaho. KTAN members contributed to framing the problem and determining the research questions. They even participated in a "dead-end" data analysis exercise that led to a more sophisticated understanding of the place they live. While KTAN members were not involved in writing the code for the model, they were intensively engaged in interpreting and critiquing output from the model using their own knowledge and expertise to suggest fixes to model structures.

As we tracked participation in the KTAN over time, we saw that members started out enthusiastic about the experiment and were willing to commit time to the process. They fully expected to produce something they could use to help make decisions about adapting to climate change, whether it was about what types of crops to plant, how to plan a ski season, where to rezone for population growth, or how much water would be available for any of those activities. Once the problem was framed and research questions determined, the hard work began. Many KTAN members reported being surprised at how complicated the questions turned out to be and how interconnected the natural and human systems are, which made it difficult to hold on to preconceived ideas about a good future for the basin. As the project went on, KTAN members continued to participate but their expectations for useful outcomes declined as they wrestled with acceptable methods for modeling a complicated world, availability of relevant data, and searches for data proxies, and waded through the reams of output. As an interdisciplinary researcher operating in more "normal" or consultative modes, I have experienced this same sort of trajectory over time: high expectations are refined over time to a smaller though achievable set of outcomes. Research is always more complicated than we imagine at the beginning of a project, and post-normal situations are even more complicated initially.

As a method for conducting post-normal science, KTANs have several strengths along with limitations. The KTAN allowed for interested parties to be involved from the earliest stages in framing the problem and crafting research questions that would provide information they believed could be used in their decisions. They also tested one model and found it less than useful for answering their questions and moved on to a more sophisticated approach, giving up some transparency in exchange for exploring complicated interactions over time and space. They identified acceptable and accessible sources of data. While they did not contribute to writing the computer code for the model, they were instrumental in interpreting model output in ways that challenged modelers' assumptions and helped condition model parameters, and in finding ways to integrate local knowledge. Ultimately, the KTAN was the peer group to assess whether the research results could be used in their decision-making.

The KTAN was also a long and arduous process for individuals who had full-time jobs elsewhere. Members of the KTAN dropped in and out as necessary, often sending a substitute to a meeting who had little knowledge of the KTAN experiment or work to date. Multiple meetings of both large and subgroups presented challenges to preconceived notions and values. Focus on technical issues such as data collection or model parameters can paper over disputes, which are likely to reemerge during interpretation of results.

In these cases, we often saw KTAN members close down rather than resolve conflicts—they are all neighbors, after all, and have to live with each other after this project is over. However, once participants close down to argument, the discovery process slows down. This KTAN did not include any specific training or conversations about ways to deal with different perspectives, although that may be one of the most critical components of any planning or decision-making process.

CONCLUSION

The Big Wood Basin KTAN in Idaho is just about wrapping up as this chapter is written at the end of 2014. The real proof of the efficacy of the process will occur in the future. Will members use the information, the network of KTAN members, or the links with different types of expertise developed through the process to help make decisions? We plan to follow up with KTAN members in one year and then three years to see which changes, if any, are lasting.

As scientists and policy makers continue to grapple with increasingly complex and wicked problems like climate change, an intentional post-normal approach—that integrates rather than tries to eliminate uncertainty, revels in different perspectives rather than limits approaches, and extends the community that judges the value of output to those who bear the ultimate risk of using the information—may be the most efficient and equitable use of the scientific method. The post-normal approach should not replace normal or consultative science when the conditions are favorable, but we should not be afraid to experiment with ways that leverage the strengths of science in situations that are not conducive to traditional approaches.

References

Beall, A., F. Fiedler, J. Boll, and B. Cosens. 2011. "Sustainable Water Resource Management and Participatory Systems Dynamics. Case Study: Developing the Palouse Basin Participatory Model." *Sustainability* 3:720–742. doi:10.3390/su305072.

Bolte J., D. Hulse, S. Gregory, and C. Smith. 2007. "Modeling Biocomplexity: Actors, Landscapes and Alternative Futures." *Environmental Modeling Software* 22:570–579. doi:10.1016/j.envsoft.2005.12.033.

Cash, D. W., W. C. Clark, F. Alcock, N. M. Dickson, N. Eckley, D. H. Guston, J. Jager, and R. B. Mitchell. 2003. "Knowledge Systems for Sustainable Development." *PNAS* 100: 8086–8091.

Funtowicz, S., and J. R. Ravetz. 1993. "Science for a Post-Normal Age." *Futures* 25: 735–755.

Holmberg J., and K. Robert. 2000. "Backcasting: A Framework for Strategic Planning." *International Journal of Sustainable Development and World Ecology* 7:291–308. doi:10.1080/13504500009470049.

Kennel, C., and S. Daultrey. 2010. "Knowledge Action Networks: Connecting Regional Climate Change Assessments to Local Action." University of California San Diego Sustainable Solutions Institute Series. http://escholarship.org/uc/item/8gd6j0k5.

Lach, D., and S. Sanford. 2010. "Public Understanding of Science and Technology Embedded in Complex Institutional Settings." *Public Understanding of Science* 19 (2): 130–146.

Pielke Sr., R. 2012. "Regional Climate Downscaling: What's the Point?" *Eos* 93 (5): 52–53.

Ramesh, K., and P. Goswani. 2014. "Assessing Reliability of Regional Climate Projections: The Case of the Indian Monsoon." *Scientific Reports* 4 (article no. 4071). http://www.nature.com/srep/2014/140212/srep04071/full/srep04071.html.

Stave, K. 2003. "A Systems Dynamics Model to Facilitate Public Understanding of Water Management Options in Las Vegas, Nevada." *Journal of Environmental Management* 67:303–313.

US Census Bureau. 2012. http://www.census.gov/.

van der Ent, R., J. Savemoke, B. Scheafli, and S. Steel-Dunne. 2010. "Origin and Fate of Atmospheric Moisture over Continents." *Water Resources Research* 46:W09525. doi:10.1029/2010WR00912.

Chapter 7
The Role of Place-Based Social Learning

DANIEL R. WILLIAMS

> [Even] after the best of scientific studies a judgment must be made about the relevance of a piece of scientific research to a manager's . . . practical question at hand. In this judgment science is not at all helpful. . . . How to integrate the kind of knowledge that science can give with the practical judgment about what the [managerial] situation requires [remains one of the] great unresolved questions.
> —Hummel, *Public Administration Review*, 1994

Hummel's observations on the limits of science to inform practice provides a useful starting point for a book chapter devoted to examining post-normal environmental policy where the "facts are uncertain, values in dispute, stakes high, and decisions urgent" (Funtowicz and Ravetz 1993, 739, 744). Central to the argument here is that the integration of science with practice requires greater attention to the science of practice, and not just the practice of science. In particular, a geographic or place-focused approach can help explain why the science-practice gap persists and why efforts to close the gap often fail (Williams 2013). A place-focused approach helps us appreciate the inevitably incomplete and uncertain character of knowledge when applied to land management practice and highlights the way emplaced, networked practitioners can build a shared understanding of the situation. That is, rather than trying to solve wicked land management problems with an integrated top-down, or "normal," science-based view of knowledge, effective action can be conceived as the outcome of a social learning process that operates within a networked set of actors and institutions governing complex systems. In short, social learning can produce a collaborative form of rationality that operates both horizontally (place-to-place) and vertically (upward and downward in scale) to achieve a more sustainable form of landscape governance.

The kinds of post-normal conditions noted by Funtowicz and Ravetz (1993) are emblematic of the modern challenges faced by many public land management agencies. In recent decades the practice of public natural resource management has shifted from the long-standing multiple-use, commodity production paradigm to a multiscaled ecosystem management perspective that emphasizes the sustainable provision of a much wider assortment of ecosystem services embedded in complex sets of social-ecological interactions at multiple spatial scales (Williams et al. 2013). This has made fact-finding all the more complex and uncertain and has further amplified the competing values at stake.

A typical response to the growing complexity of these problems has been to focus on synthesizing the burgeoning body of scientific knowledge as a way to better inform managers on the best available science. Driven by unrealistic ambitions to close the gap between science and practice, these efforts routinely fail to achieve their stated goals because they assume the solution to complexity and uncertainty resides in the availability, communication, or application of science rather than in how to organize or improve practice. In addition, these efforts largely ignore the political or institutional context—steeped in value conflict and controversy—within which this practice must be carried out. The more fundamental problem is that the character and conduct of "normal" (context-independent) science does not lend itself to coherent, ready application in a post-normal world marked by complexity, uncertainty, and controversy. This chapter therefore explores an alternative perspective on science and practice that emphasizes place-oriented (context-dependent) knowledge production and application for improving sustainable landscape governance. It begins with a case example that tries to close the gap through "normal" science synthesis, followed by an explication of a spatial/relational view of knowledge that emphasizes bottom-up social learning strategies for landscape governance. These strategies are then illustrated through two case examples to show how informed practice can be conceived as a collaborative form of rationality that emerges within place-based networks of actors and institutions.

FISH, FIRE AND THE CONUNDRUM OF "NORMAL" SCIENCE

An effort to synthesize the available science related to protecting the endangered bull trout provides an apt illustration of the problems posed by knowledge complexity in pursuit of a "normal" top-down landscape-scale solution. The bull trout is native to much of the Pacific Northwest and western Canada. Ecological studies point to various conditions necessary to maintain the population, including maintaining habitat refugia, promoting episodic debris flows while avoiding chronic sedimentation, and regulating water temperatures within tolerance limits (Isaak et al. 2009). Numerous factors have contributed to local declines, including invasions by nonnative trout species, degradation and fragmentation of stream habitats, depletion of food supplies, warmer stream temperatures, more variable stream flows, and increased wildfires and stream channel changes. Moreover, addressing these threats to bull trout in concert with other land use considerations, and in ways that are financially and socially acceptable, creates an extremely difficult management environment.

To address one of the main threats to bull trout, in late 2007 the Pacific Northwest Research Station of the US Forest Service convened two workshops to assess the state of knowledge and identify research needs to support land management practices aimed at maintaining fish populations in fire-prone landscapes. The meetings were motivated by a widespread belief that "despite a growing body of empirically-sound but still disparate scientific studies," current policies and practices regarding fish and fire were based on "intuition, opinions, and informed guesses" (USDA 2008, 1). The first meeting brought together experienced land managers and fire practitioners to identify their information needs. The second meeting brought together an interdisciplinary group of research scientists from several federal land management agencies to assess and synthesize existing science relative to those needs.

The stated goal of both workshops was "to advance useable and applicable knowledge on how fish might best be managed in fire prone areas and how fire might best be managed in areas with important fish populations" (USDA 2008, 1). The research needs assessment coming out of the first workshop identified eight priority elements of a potential research program to "help policy makers, managers, and practitioners make more informed choices." These elements included aquatic/riparian ecosystem functionality, integration, risk assessment, monitoring, rapid assessment capabilities, public engagement, riparian areas, and invasive species. Each element was described in terms of a problem statement, information needs, existing knowledge, and current knowledge gaps. The problem statements were typically framed as "looking for well informed, science grounded guidance," applying the "soundest available science" and "integrating current information from multiple scientific disciplines." For scientists the central task was to generate and communicate the relevant scientific information to managers. But aside from grudging admission that managers lack the time to read scientific articles and reports, little attention was devoted to the everyday challenges faced by managers, who are ultimately responsible for integrating specific information on fish and fire with all the other informational, institutional, and practical demands that the managerial situation presents.

The scientific workshop devoted two and one-half days to discussing the state of knowledge on the topic. Building on complexity theory in ecology, landscape ecologists highlighted the need to identify criteria for defining a resilient landscape. At the same time, ecologists pointed to the complexity of the phenomenon (patchy, multiscaled, dynamic landscapes) in which the best prescription for any one-stream network was elusive if not unknowable. According to these ecologists, no singular riparian condition could be described as necessarily better or healthier than another because the viability of endangered fish populations depended on dynamic spatial variation in which some patches (streams) were in the process of becoming improved habitat for a given species and some in becoming worse habitat. The role of discipline and problem framing in synthesizing knowledge was also evident, as current science could support contradictory recommendations depending on one's primary focus. For example, because stream culverts are impediments to the adaptive dynamics sought by systems ecologists (culverts disrupt the movement of fish populations through a watershed), removing them would increase the connectivity of streams and thus enhance the survival of the endangered fish species. On the other hand, if the biggest threat to the endangered bull trout is the spread of invasive aquatic species, removing culverts would make it easier for such species to spread, to the detriment of bull trout.

From a fire-management perspective, there is a good bit of irony in the basic conclusion that management prescriptions for what to do with wildfire on the landscape are elusive and highly dependent on the specific historical and spatial context. Early in the twentieth century, the advice to fire managers would have seemed universal and precise: put the fire out and do it, preferably, by ten o'clock in the morning. In other words, instead of clarifying best management practices, a contemporary synthesis of one hundred years of additional science appears to have increased the uncertainty about best practice for any one location. In managing habitat for endangered species, best practice nowadays is increasingly understood as contingent on current local conditions as well as conditions in adjacent landscapes. The post-normal challenge then is figuring out how to coordinate each local manager's actions in a way that, at a larger scale, produces the kind of patchy dynamic system that supports healthy habitat for bull trout. A synthesis of the science is ill-suited to a problem that requires a network of managers sharing information and experience to produce dynamic coordination across the larger landscape.

Rather than providing actionable clarity, the ever-expanding body of scientific knowledge magnifies the complexity of practice. This is the central conundrum of normal science when applied to wicked-problem situations. On the one hand, the presumed power of scientific expertise to reduce uncertainty and complexity remains widely accepted within the professional ranks and institutions of environmental management. On the other hand, the gap between science and practice seems to defy most attempts to close it. Despite our best efforts at synthesis, most efforts to integrate, synthesize, and communicate the growing body of science fail to simplify practice (Collins 2014; Flyvbjerg 2001; Sarewitz 2004; Scott 1998).

For example, Scott (1998) illustrates how most attempts to impose a top-down planning mentality fail because they typically exclude local knowledge from consideration. He attributes this to the hegemony of a "high modernist" ideology that promotes overconfidence in scientific and technical progress. Similarly, Fischer (2000) attributes planning failures to the "over-application of scientific rationality to public policy making" (x). Collins (2014) makes the case that scientific integration is not some missing "ingredient" that can be applied to the situation by researchers (e.g., by organizing a synthesis workshop), but is instead a potentially emergent characteristic of a specific social-ecological context. For him the problem is how to better design social learning processes to make integration more likely to emerge. Others have gone so far as to suggest that science can actually make environmental controversies worse by providing contesting parties with their own bodies of relevant and legitimate facts (Sarewitz 2004). Scientific uncertainty persists and grows because of a lack of coherence among these competing scientific understandings, with conflicts further amplified by the various political, cultural, and institutional contexts within which the science is carried out. In sum, the science-practice gap persists because science aspires to produce context-independent principles, whereas practice requires context-dependent synthesis (Williams 2013).

Thus, rather than conceiving knowledge as the integration of an ever-expanding collection of facts and findings into a grand unifying model—presumably one that any practitioner could easily and effectively apply—in wicked-problem conditions knowledge can be understood more contextually as the accumulated wisdom that comes from shared social learning and the emergence of communities of practice organized not by discipline or algorithms, but by place-based interdependences. What might we gain by comprehending the structure of knowledge as embedded in and distributed across places and the people who occupy and interact with those places? Next we examine the potential of a spatial/relational model in which knowledge is produced, applied, and refined within a network of embedded, partially informed practitioners.

PLACE AND POST-NORMAL SCIENCE

In contrast to widely accepted views of science that presuppose a fundamental unity underlying all knowledge—for example, as embodied in E. O. Wilson's (1998) concept of consilience—a number of scholars point to a spatial, or relational, view of knowledge marked by an inherent *positionality* of observer-actors embedded in both vertical and horizontal relations to the world (Finnegan 2008; Livingstone 2003; Powell 2007; Rose 1997; Whatmore 2009; see also chapter 1 this volume). Unlike the naturalistic (positivist) epistemology guiding most ecological science (e.g., Lowe et al. 2009) some forms of constructivist epistemology regard knowledge as *ecologically* relational (situational and relative) to where one is positioned within a social-ecological field (see Allen et al. 2001; Hayles 1995). Accordingly, every observer of the world occupies a somewhat unique (subjective) position or place within that world by virtue of varying culture, history, training, embodiment, and personal experience that limits and conditions that observer's knowledge of it (Livingstone 2003). Likewise, in the real world of action where citizens and practitioners are embedded, knowledge is similarly partial and incomplete and likely over time to grow more fragmented than integrated (Hummel 1994; Whatmore 2009).

Given the inevitably varied positioning of each observer of the world, there is no unified platform from which all knowledge can be integrated into a single understanding: hence there will always be multiple forms of knowledge and competing understandings of particular situations. Rather than viewing this plurality as a failure, in post-normal situations recognizing competing vantage points may actually enrich each perspective and expose assumptions that may have otherwise remained hidden, especially to those who have dominant roles in mapping knowledge (Hayles 1995).

The concept of place in geography provides a powerful lens for understanding this kind of epistemic pluralism (Williams 2014). Place functions not only as a location or container of material and social phenomena, but also as a way of seeing and thinking about the world (Cresswell 2004; Entrikin 1991; Sack 1992, 1997). As Sack (1992) argues, individual awareness and knowledge of the world is necessarily a spatial awareness, informed by the particular cultural, experiential, temporal, and spatial positions that we happen to occupy. Taking an epistemological perspective on place helps transcend what some geographers regard as a deep and long-running tension within Western intellectual traditions between universalist (context-independent) and particularist (context-dependent) views of knowledge (Entrikin 1991; see also Flyvbjerg 2001; Williams 2013). This tension has been particularly salient within natural resource management, where the progressive/scientific view of resource management inherited from Pinchot—built on the universalist impulse of science and knowledge—has always collided with land management practice, which by necessity operates in the arena of the particular (Williams et al. 2013).

When dealing with wicked-problem conditions, all attempts to close the gap and overcome plurality and uncertainty ultimately rely on being able to attain some universal, context-independent, god's-eye view of reality. Alternatively, adopting a spatial or place-based perspective helps us recognize that all knowledge—even exalted scientific knowledge—is to a significant degree local or context-dependent because all observers and actors, by virtue of their biography and geography, occupy a particular, delimited position from which to observe the world. Though pluralism is also unavoidable in the realm of practice, recognizing and profiting from different kinds of knowledge and skills can become an advantage. As the fish and fire example shows, natural resource practice requires the cultivation of a capacity for collective sense-making that moves beyond the mere application of science and technical information. In other words, it is through real-world practice, embedded in actual places, that knowledge pluralism and value differences are ultimately reconciled.

The principles of pluralism and positionality underscore the value of emplaced practitioners learning and operating in real places and developing context-dependent knowledge. This is not to argue against investing in science, only that it is unreasonable to expect those investments alone to deliver efficient and effective solutions to the post-normal conditions of high complexity, uncertainty, and value controversy. At the very least we need to recognize that those who are engaged in practice cannot be expected to readily absorb the ever-expanding, often conflicting science that might apply to their practice. Rather, what is being argued here is that we need to develop more adaptive strategies for using and accessing the accumulated wisdom of the practitioners themselves as they go about their work, and help them harmonize their local efforts across adjacent spaces and at multiple spatial scales. Addressing the science-practice gap requires a rethinking of how practical knowledge is produced and applied in dynamic, adaptive systems. This brings to the fore questions of how individual practitioners might learn and apply local experiential knowledge.

PLACE AND THE SCIENCE OF PRACTICE

One place-based strategy for addressing the chronic insufficiency of knowledge in the face of unrelenting complexity, uncertainty, and conflicting values has been to adopt some version of adaptive management (Stankey et al. 2005). In theory, adaptive management involves multiscalar, place-sensitive policy experimentation (and by implication more case/context-sensitive knowledge) as a way to mitigate scientific uncertainty. As actually practiced however, it hasn't lived up to its promise (Allen and Curtis 2005).

First, as a pragmatic approach to sorting through competing management prescriptions for a place or landscape, adaptive management still tends to privilege formal scientific knowledge over other forms of knowledge held by local practitioners and residents (Stankey et al. 2005). Second, it hasn't been adaptive enough with respect to questions of value (Norton 1999). Third, it pays insufficient attention to the types of institutional structures and processes necessary for it to work on a large-scale basis (McLain and Lee 1996). Thus, as a potential post-normal strategy for addressing the science-practice gap, it hasn't fully embraced different ways of knowing and acting that emphasize local experiential knowledge and values of embedded practitioners (Fischer 2000). A number of social scientists (Collins 2014; Fischer 2000; Flyvbjerg 2001; Scott 1998; Wenger 1998) make the case that more could be done to integrate and profit from the practical and informal knowledge that exists among both occupants/users of places and emplaced professional practitioners.

Flyvbjerg (2001) builds his argument on the value of context-specific knowledge and practice by reference to the Aristotelian distinction among three forms of knowledge: *episteme, techne,* and *phronesis.* Whereas *episteme* refers to knowledge that is abstract and universal and *techne* describes the know-how associated with practicing a craft, Flyvbjerg seeks to resurrect Aristotle's idea of *phronesis* (practical wisdom) as the unique domain of the social sciences. In contrast to the natural-science model, which is rooted in *episteme* and *techne,* Caterino and Schram (2006, 9) describe *phronesis* as the practical wisdom that comes from "an intimate familiarity with the contingences and uncertainties of various forms of social practice embedded in complex social settings." In addition, *phronesis* concerns the kinds of value judgments and decisions that are so interwoven with political and administrative practices that any attempt to comprehend them in terms of *episteme* or *techne* seems misguided (Flyvbjerg 2006). According to Flyvbjerg, Aristotle put *phronesis* above the other modes of knowledge because it balanced instrumental rationality with value rationality, a balance Aristotle saw as crucial to the sustained happiness of citizens but that, according to Flyvbjerg, is currently undermined by the dominance of the instrumental rationalities of *episteme* and *techne* relative to *phronesis.* To achieve more balance, Flyvbjerg recommends an approach to social science that focuses on context-specific, case-study knowledge instead of trying to imitate the generalizable and predictive power of natural science.

Also drawing on Aristotle, Scott characterizes local, practical knowledge as something akin to *mētis*—a form of local, experiential knowledge that resists simplification into deductive principles that can be readily transferred through book learning. Scott documents numerous examples of "natural and social failures of thin, formulaic simplifications" imposed on society through the hegemony of state power. One of his main examples deals with the failures of the utilitarian logic that encouraged mono-cropped, even-aged forestry in early modern Europe. He notes that large-scale processes and events are inevitably far more complex than any models experts can devise to map them. What these schemes "ignore—and often suppress—are precisely the practical skills that underwrite any complex activity . . . variously called know-how . . . common sense, experience, a knack or *mētis*" (2008, 311). Instead of promoting an interchange between local or practical knowledge and formal scientific knowledge, he argues that governments often seek to constrain the former as a form of social control.

The two concepts, *phronesis* and *metis,* have much in common. That said, *phronesis* appears to be more closely linked to the political or administrative skills involved in reasoning about values, the good life, and the exercise of power. *Mētis* comes closer to the idea of *local* knowledge or wisdom. It is not as refined and systematized as *techne* (which, by Scott's reckoning, is more universal, organized, and ultimately expressible in the form of rules, principles, and propositions), but rooted in a history of local problem solving. In any case, both emphasize *emplaced* knowing over the "thin simplifications" of instrumental rationalities that "can never generate a functioning community, city or economy" (Scott 1998, 310). Both kinds of knowledge exist among practitioners and can be cultivated within organizations and institutions.

For example, as understood in the field of knowledge management, practice communities constitute groups of people who share a concern or interest in some domain of activity and learn how to do it better through regular interaction (Wenger 1998). According to Wenger, three characteristics are crucial to distinguishing communities of practice from other kinds of communities. First, their identity as group is rooted in shared competencies that distinguish members from nonmembers. Members value their collective competence and learn from each other, even if few people outside the community value or even recognize their expertise. Second, they act as a community with respect to their knowledge domain by engaging in joint activities and discussions and forging relationships that enable members to learn from each other. Third, members of a community of practice develop a shared repertoire of resources, experiences, stories, tools, and ways of addressing recurring problems. For many professional fields, including business, law, medicine, and planning, this repertoire is transmitted through case-based learning. For example, in a profession such as medicine, clinical knowledge is built up through the accumulation of experience from the careful analysis and treatment of many actual cases. Over time the practitioner is expected to learn how to diagnose and treat conditions by drawing on case-based experience. In important ways, what distinguishes such professions from the academic disciplines is their relatively greater emphasis on learning from real-world practice. Professional knowledge builds much more on inductive, situational, bottom-up learning than from top-down, deductive extension of theory to practice.

In sum, in a truly adaptive approach to knowledge production and management, it is at least as important to help practitioners better organize themselves into communities of practice as it is to produce the new scientific synthesis of knowledge or deploy adaptive management experiments. Practice communities draw from members' knowledge and experience to advance situation-specific problem solving. They might do this by requesting information from community members, seeking out people with specific experiences suited to a particular problem at hand, making site visits, documenting cases and solutions, or mapping knowledge and gaps in knowledge. Collins and Ison (2009) equated communities of practice to a form of social learning that occurs through situated and collective engagement with others. They argue that post-normal conditions of complexity, uncertainty, and controversy require an epistemic reframing of adaptation to embrace new forms of (social) learning that explicitly recognize and make sense of the partial understandings and varying norms and values of the stakeholders embedded in the situation.

PLACE-BASED SOCIAL LEARNING AND ADAPTIVE LANDSCAPE GOVERNANCE

A post-normal conception of knowledge gives greater recognition to the wisdom and experience of emplaced practitioners (and citizens), learning and operating in real places, and developing context-dependent knowledge. However, advancing social learning and practical knowledge may be insufficient for addressing post-normal conditions. According to Scott (1998) there is also a need for *mētis*-friendly institutional designs that emphasize plurality, diversity, and decentralization. Much like resilience in natural systems, institutional diversity is "demonstrably more stable, more self-sufficient and less vulnerable" (Scott 1998, 353).

By emphasizing institutional diversity, wider public participation, and enlarged social capacity and flexibility to respond to unplanned change, adaptive governance involves a shift from traditionally top-down, expert-driven decision-making structures to a multilevel and polycentric approach to governance that emphasize inclusiveness, collaboration, local knowledge, and identities (Bartel 2014; Wyborn and Bixler 2013). In other words, post-normal conditions require intuitional designs and practices that encourage more bottom-up forms of adaptive governance, in which individuals, organizations, agencies, and institutions at multiple organizational levels come together to transform management organizations toward a learning community drawing on various forms of knowledge, expertise, and experience for developing common understanding and policies (Brunner and Lynch 2010; Folke et al. 2005; Ilcan and Phillips 2008).

These forms are particularly important in dealing with large-scale ecological disturbances such as wildfire and climate change, and situations in which the scale and complexity of the issues exceed the capacity of existing organizations to address the problem on their own (Flint 2013). Adaptive forms of governance are most likely to emerge at a local scale because the consequences of decisions begin to matter to local constituencies in ways that, at a larger scale, they are often too obscure and remote to engage all but the most committed interest groups (Williams and Matheny 1995). At a local level, shared propinquity (common habitation in a geographic space) helps establish a workable polity as people find "themselves in geographic proximity and economic interdependence such that the activities and pursuits of some affect the ability of others to conduct their own activities" (Young 1996, 126). In these contexts, adaptive, place-focused collaboration promotes finding commonality among diverse stakeholders by encouraging them to "make sense together" in spite of their different, often conflicting, values and ways of life (Healey 1997). Whatever social differences exist regarding local uses and values for a landscape, there is at least the possibility of a shared concern for particular places from which new governance structures may emerge (Kemmis 1990).

CASE 1: PINE BEETLE INFESTATION IN COLORADO

A good illustration of the role of shared propinquity in promoting an emergent and adaptive governance regime is the work by Flint and colleagues (Flint 2013; Flint et al. 2009), which examines the way regional-scale collaboration emerged in response to a massive mountain pine beetle infestation in Colorado that devastated over 1.4 million hectares of high-altitude coniferous forests in the central Rocky Mountains. They describe how, in the context of such large-scale ecological disturbance, new governance relationships were forged involving both large-scale regulatory institutions at the state and federal level and locally emplaced residents, interest groups, government agencies, and organizations drawing on existing and emerging networks to address place-specific issues in response to the regional beetle outbreak. Historically rural communities in the western United States, where federally managed lands are the dominant form of ownership, have often been dependent on the federal government to address natural resource issues. In this instance, however, the scale of the mountain pine beetle outbreak (also referred to as the bark beetle outbreak) exceeded the institutional capacities of federal agencies to prescribe and implement landscape-scale solutions in a top-down manner, as has been the history of their management in the past.

One specific example of the emergence of an adaptive governance network was the formation in 2005 of the Colorado Bark Beetle Cooperative. This multilevel intergovernmental cooperative brought together three federal land management agencies, as well as the Colorado State Forest Service and the Northwest Colorado Council of Governments (itself a nonprofit organization created to facilitate multijurisdictional projects among local governments and nonprofit organizations and community members, including representatives of utility and water providers, the wood products industry, and conservation and public interest groups). Flint (2013) shows how through regular, open meetings, the Colorado Bark Beetle Cooperative encouraged regular dialogue among public and private landowners, major utility companies, conservation districts, water districts, and industry leaders. In the process, local representatives were able to learn how different places in the region were coping with similar ecological processes and management challenges, despite differences in their perceptions and attitudes about what needed to be done. In addition, Flint found that community representatives were able to identify shared regional and place-based strategies for promoting and locating commercial forest management options in more extractive-resource tolerant communities, while protecting aesthetic and conservation strategies around tourist- and amenity-oriented communities.

Beyond the regional organization, new forms of place-based interaction have also flourished at a smaller, grassroots scale. Flint (2013) describes one Colorado county where local citizens formed a task force called the Forest Health Task Force as part of an initiative called Our Future Summit. This local group hosted regular meetings in which local citizens, homeowner associations, and nonprofit organizations from communities within and beyond the county could interact with and learn about forest health issues and initiate local and regional efforts to manage risks. In effect the Task Force provided a spatial context for local residents to do the social learning necessary to enhance the protection of their respective places from the effects of a large-scale landscape disturbance.

The bark beetle example shows how social systems can self-organize to adaptively respond to complexity and uncertainty and address the challenges of governing complex social-ecological systems tailored to specific contexts. Networks of actors and institutions were identified as key factors facilitating the emergence of self-organized governance structures. Examined in light of emerging theories in public administration (Pierre and Peters 2005), the bark beetle case shows that landscape governance can emerge outside formal government institutions and bureaucracies and involves increasingly complex linkages and collaborations among multiple public and private organizations.

CASE 2: ADAPTIVE GOVERNANCE, CONTEXT, AND CLIMATE CHANGE

Adaptive governance for climate change is another example of a post-normal problem amenable to a place-based social learning approach (Adger et al. 2011; Brugger and Crimmins 2013; Lyon 2014). Despite technical advances in climate science, enormous uncertainties remain regarding the impacts of climate change, especially when downscaled to particular landscapes where adaptation strategies are most likely to be enacted. In keeping with the "normal" science model, the existing literature on social vulnerability and adaptation in natural hazards and climate change has been criticized for emphasizing static profiles of human resources and quantitative indicators of community characteristics at various discrete scales to assess social vulnerability and adaptive capacity (O'Brien et al. 2007). Such studies tend to limit climate change to a generalized, distant environmental stressor. In contrast, some have called for contextual approaches that pay attention to the complex relationships and interactions among formal and informal networks, institutions, and organizations that produce vulnerability and enable and constrain adaptation (O'Brien et al. 2007; Murphy et al. 2015).

To illustrate how a contextual approach might be applied to climate change adaptation, Murphy and colleagues conducted two case studies (Big Hole Valley, Montana, and Grand County, Colorado) that used a collaborative scenario-building methodology as a tool to promote social learning (Murphy et al. 2015; Wyborn et al. 2014). The scenarios presented three alternative story lines written in accessible lay language (three hundred to four hundred words each) to depict the range of possible climate changes. The initial scenarios were local in scale and developed by experts using climate change projections to describe how local landscapes might change over the next twenty years in response to temperature and precipitation trends. By describing alternative plausible futures, these scenarios allowed locally situated stakeholders to consider potential climate change adaptation strategies in the context of uncertainty regarding exactly how local landscapes will change in response to climate trends. The scenario-building process started with individual interviews in which the scenarios were presented to stakeholders from different sectors (e.g., business owners, private landowners, elected officials, and public land managers) to generate diverse views on possible adaptation strategies. These interviews were followed by a round of sector-specific focus group sessions wherein participants reacted to and revised the scenarios in a group process, and a follow-up session composed of stakeholders from different sectors brought together to learn from each other as they explored the implications of the various scenarios.

These cases illustrated how adaptation actors and their potential adaptation strategies were situated within interacting social, political, and economic forces operating at multiple scales. In particular, stakeholders drew from their own experience of past landscape change (including the previously described bark beetle challenges) to suggest they could work together to find common solutions. In addition, the detailed and tangible descriptions of local landscape changes provided in the scenarios created a platform for even self-identified skeptics to discuss vulnerabilities and potential adaptations. Inviting participants to respond to recognizable and tangibly relevant narratives of local change legitimized their knowledge and experiences, and enabled them to move beyond dominant discourses about climate change. Some participants also expressed appreciation that the method explicitly acknowledged uncertainty and the limits of current scientific knowledge; this acknowledgment actually made the science behind the scenarios seem more credible for these participants. Engaging stakeholders in collaborative scenario-building exercises helped them move beyond the perception that uncertain science was a barrier to adaptation action and allowed them to focus instead on collaborative social learning with potential impacts to community, landscape, and sense of place serving as points of shared concern (Wyborn et al. 2014).

In the context of high complexity, uncertainty, and controversy, scenario approaches to planning and policy offer promising ways to advance social learning (Murphy et al. in review; Wyborn et al. 2014). The scenario method in particular combines the strengths of case-study methods and contextual approaches by focusing on a "landscape of change" rather than a specific problem such fish and fire; building deeper appreciation for the social and community dynamics involved, including the role of meaning and identity in place-making; attending to broadscale governance and institutional issues; engaging a diverse array of participants in a social learning process; and showing how these forces affect the perception of risk, uncertainty, vulnerability, and possible adaptive pathways available at a local scale (Murphy et al. in review). The end goal of the process was not the scenarios themselves, but using them as a tool to support social learning about possible future vulnerabilities and adaptation. The scenarios enabled participants to articulate these issues in their own language without being guided by a preconceived framing of an issue. Collaborative scenario-building enabled participants to learn about other stakeholders' adaptive responses; identify potential feedbacks, synergies, and conflicts between these responses; and generate the type of reflexive and relational dialogue deemed foundational to social learning (Collins 2014; Collins and Ison 2009).

CONCLUSION

One of the legacies of the "normal" science approach to problem solving in natural resource management is the inability to close the science-practice gap. When applied to specific local contexts, normal science often struggles to clarify best practice because it expands rather than reduces knowledge complexity, increases scientific uncertainty, provides contesting parties with competing sets of facts, and amplifies policy conflict. In its stead, place-oriented inquiry and practice offers a post-normal context-dependent problem-solving strategy by emphasizing bottom-up social learning for the adaptive, sustainable governance of complex dynamic landscapes. Epistemic theories of place provide conceptual tools to help scientists, practitioners, and embedded stakeholders recognize plural forms of knowledge that include local, context-dependent knowledge. In addition, by thinking about practice as a form of emplaced knowing, the practitioner or local stakeholder becomes part of a potential learning system in which knowledge and learning are spatially distributed processes.

Post-normal problem-solving requires professional practices and governance strategies that capitalize on the emergent wisdom of spatially networked actors and institutions engaging in a collaborative form of rationality. This emplaced form of adaptive social learning emerged on its own in the mountain pine beetle example and was expressly designed into the collaborative scenario-building exercises for climate change adaptation. One model of this type of practice can be found in fields such as law, medicine, and business, where members learn through sharing case-based knowledge. Another model involves less formally organized actors engaging in social learning to exploit the different forms of knowledge and values that make up important parts of the system. Both models showed how stakeholders can move beyond complexities, uncertainties, and even conflicting values and begin to govern the system through collaborative social learning with potential impacts to community, landscape, and sense of place serving as points of common interest.

A place-based approach suggests that the problem of sustainable governance is not one of insufficient science to inform policy and practice, but a failure to develop an adequate science of practice to address the inexorable knowledge complexity and uncertainty that arises when applied to specific places or contexts. In such contexts, the resilience of the social-ecological system depends on the knowledge and combined actions of many practitioners and stakeholders, each familiar with and responsible for various parts of the overall system. Specifically, place helps to address the growing complexity and uncertainty of knowledge, bridge the epistemological divide between local/contextual knowledge and global/generalizable knowledge, and validate and organize social learning and knowledge formation originating in a bottom-up synthesis of networks of actors.

References

Adger, W. N., J. Barnett, F. S. Chapin III, and H. Ellemor. 2011. "This Must Be the Place: Underrepresentation of Identity and Meaning in Climate Change Decision-Making." *Global Environmental Politics* 11 (2): 1–25.

Allen, C., and A. Curtis. 2005. "Nipped in the Bud: Why Regional Scale Adaptive Management Is Not Blooming." *Environmental Management* 36:414–425.

Allen, T. F. H., J. A. Tainter, C. Pires, and T. W. Hoekstra. 2001. "Dragnet Ecology—'Just the Facts Ma'am': The Privilege of Science in a Postmodern World." *BioScience* 51:475–485.

Bartel, R. 2014. "Vernacular Knowledge and Environmental Law: Case and Cure for Regulatory Failure." *Local Environment* 19:891–914.

Brugger, J., and M. Crimmins. 2013. "The Art of Adaptation: Living with Climate Change in the Rural American Southwest." *Global Environmental Change* 23:1830–1840.

Brunner, R. D., and A. H. Lynch. 2010. *Adaptive Governance and Climate Change.* Boston: American Meteorological Society.

Caterino, B., and S. F. Schram. 2006. "Introduction: Reframing the Debate." In *Making Political Science Matter: Debating Knowledge, Research and Method,* edited by S. F. Schram and B. Caterino, 1–13. New York: New York University Press.

Collins, K. 2014. "Designing Social Learning Systems for Integrating Social Sciences into Policy Processes: Some Experiences with Water Managing." In *Understanding Society and Natural Resources: Forging New Strands of Integration across the Social Sciences*, edited by Michael Manfredo, Jerry J. Vaske, Andreas Rechkemmer, and Esther A. Duke, 229–251. Dordrecht: Springer.

Collins, K., and R. Ison. 2009. "Jumping Off Arnstein's Ladder: Social Learning as a New Policy Paradigm for Climate Change Adaptation." *Environmental Policy and Governance* 19:358–373.

Cresswell, T. 2004. *Place: A Short Introduction*. Oxford: Blackwell.

Entrikin, J. N. 1991. *The Betweenness of Place: Towards a Geography of Modernity*. Baltimore, MD: Johns Hopkins University Press.

Finnegan, D. A. 2008. "The Spatial Turn: Geographical Approaches in the History of Science." *Journal of the History of Biology* 41:369–388.

Fischer, F. 2000. *Citizens, Experts and the Environment: The Politics of Local Knowledge*. Durham, NC: Duke University Press.

Flint, C. G. 2013. "Conservation That Connects Multiple Scales of Place." In *Place-Based Conservation: Perspectives from the Social Sciences*, edited by W. Stewart, D. Williams, and L. Kruger, 35–44. Dordrecht: Springer.

Flint, C. G., B. McFarlane, and M. Muller. 2009. "Human Dimensions of Forest Disturbance by Insects: An International Synthesis." *Environmental Management* 43:1174–1186.

Flyvbjerg, B. 2001. *Making Social Science Matter: Why Social Inquiry Fails and How It Can Succeed Again*. New York: Cambridge University Press.

———. 2006. "A Perestroikan Straw Man Answers Back: David Laitin and Phronetic Political Science." In *Making Political Science Matter: Debating Knowledge, Research and Method*, edited by S. Schram and B. Caterino, 56–85. New York: New York University Press.

Folke, C., T. Han, P. Olsson, and J. Norberg. 2005. "Adaptive Governance of Social-Ecological Systems." *Annual Review of Environmental Resources* 30:441–473.

Funtowicz, S., and J. R. Ravetz. 1993. "Science for a Post-Normal Age." *Futures* 25:735–755.

Hayles, N. K. 1995. "Searching for Common Ground." In *Reinventing Nature? Response to Postmodern Deconstruction*, edited by M. Soule and G. Lease, 47–63. Washington, DC: Island Press.

Healey, P. 1997. *Collaborative Planning: Shaping Places in Fragmented Societies*. Vancouver: University of British Columbia Press.

Hummel, R. P. 1994. "Commentary." *Public Administration Review* 54:314.

Ilcan, S., and L. Phillips. 2008. "Governing through Global Networks: Knowledge Mobilities and Participatory Development." *Current Sociology* 56:711–734.

Isaak, D., B. Reiman, and D. Horan. 2009. "Watershed-Scale Monitoring Protocol for Bull Trout." General Technical Report RMRS-GTR-224. Fort Collins, CO: USDA Forest Service, Rocky Mountain Research Station.

Kemmis, D. 1990. *Community and the Politics of Place*. Norman: University of Oklahoma Press.

Livingstone, D. N. 2003. *Putting Science in Its Place*. Chicago: University of Chicago Press.

Lowe, P., G. Whitman, and J. Phillipson. 2009. "Ecology and the Social Sciences." *Journal of Applied Ecology* 46:297–305.

Lyon, C. 2014. "Place Systems and Social Resilience: A Framework for Understanding Place in Social Adaptation, Resilience, and Transformation." *Society and Natural Resources* 27:1009–1023.

McLain, R. J., and R. G. Lee. 1996. "Adaptive Management: Promises and Pitfalls." *Environmental Management* 20:437–488.

Murphy, D., C. Wyborn, L. Yung, and D. R. Williams. 2015. "Key Concepts in Social Vulnerability and Adaptive Capacity." General Technical Report RMRS-GTR-xxx. Fort Collins, CO: USDA Forest Service, Rocky Mountain Research Station.

Murphy, D., C. Wyborn, L. Yung, D. R. Williams, C. C. Cleveland, L. A. Eby, S. Dobrowski, and E. Towler (in review). "Using Multi-Scale, Iterative Scenario Building (MISB) to Access Socio-Ecological Vulnerability and Adaptive Capacity in the Western U.S." *Human Organization*.

Norton, B. G. 1999. "Pragmatism, Adaptive Management, and Sustainability." *Environmental Values* 8:451–466.

O'Brien, K., S. Eriksen, L. P. Nygaard, and A. Schjolden. 2007. "Why Different Interpretations of Vulnerability Matter in Climate Change Discourses." *Climate Policy* 7:73–88.

Pierre, J., and B. G. Peters. 2005. *Governing Complex Societies*. New York: Palgrave Macmillan.

Powell, R. C. 2007. "Geographies of Science: Histories, Localities, Practices, Futures." *Progress in Human Geography* 31:309–239.

Rose, G. 1997. "Situating Knowledges: Positionality, Reflexivities and Other Tactics." *Progress in Human Geography* 21:305–320.

Sack, R. D. 1992. *Place, Modernity and the Consumer's World*. Baltimore, MD: Johns Hopkins University Press.

———. 1997. *Homo geographicus*. Baltimore, MD: Johns Hopkins University Press.

Sarewitz, D. 2004. "How Science Makes Environmental Controversies Worse." *Environmental Science and Policy* 7:385–403.

Scott, J. C. 1998. *Seeing Like a State: How Certain Schemes to Improve the Human Condition Have Failed*. New Haven, CT: Yale University Press.

Stankey, G. H., R. N. Clark, and B. T. Bormann. 2005. "Adaptive Management of Natural Resources: Theory, Concepts and Management Institutions." General

Technical Report PNW-GTR-654. Portland, OR: USDA Forest Service, Pacific Northwestern Research Station.

USDA. 2008. "Fish and Fire: A Research Needs Assessment." Portland, OR: USDA Forest Service, Pacific Northwest Research Station.

Wenger, E. 1998. *Communities of Practice: Learning, Meaning, and Identity.* Cambridge: Cambridge University Press.

Whatmore, S. J. 2009. "Mapping Knowledge Controversies: Science, Democracy and the Redistribution of Expertise." *Progress in Human Geography* 33:587–598.

Williams, B. A., and A. R. Matheny. 1995. *Democracy, Dialogue, and Environmental Disputes: The Contested Languages of Social Regulation.* New Haven, CT: Yale University Press.

Williams, D. R. 2013. "Science, Practice, and Place." In *Place-Based Conservation: Perspectives from the Social Sciences,* edited by W. P. Stewart, D. R. Williams, and L. E. Kruger, 21–34. Dordrecht: Springer.

———. 2014. "Making Sense of 'Place': Reflections on Pluralism and Positionality in Place Research." *Landscape and Urban Planning* 131:74–82.

Williams, D. R., W. P. Stewart, and L. E. Kruger. 2013. "The Emergence of Place-Based Conservation." In *Place-Based Conservation: Perspectives from the Social Sciences,* edited by W. P. Stewart, D. R. Williams, and L. E. Kruger, 1–17. Dordrecht: Springer.

Wilson, E. O. 1998. *Consilience: The Unity of Science.* New York: Knopf.

Wyborn, C., and R. P. Bixler. 2013. "Collaboration and Nested Environmental Governance: Scale Dependency, Scale Framing, and Cross-Scale Interactions in Collaborative Conservation." *Journal of Environmental Management* 123:58–67.

Wyborn, C., L. Yung, D. Murphy, and D. R. Williams. 2014. "Situating Adaptation: How Governance Challenges and Perceptions of Uncertainty Influence Adaptation in the Rocky Mountains." *Regional Environmental Change.* August 14. doi:10.1007/s10113-014-0663-3.

Young, I. M. 1996. "Communication and the Other: Beyond Deliberative Democracy." In *Democracy and Difference: Contesting the Boundaries of the Political,* edited by S. Benhabib, 121–135. Princeton, NJ: Princeton University Press.

Chapter 8

Changing Expectations for Science and Scientists in Marine and Terrestrial Management and Policy
Possibilities and Best Practices[1]

BRENT S. STEEL AND DENISE LACH

Over the last several decades there has been an increasing emphasis among decision-makers, interest groups, and citizens about the importance of science-based environmental policy at local, regional, national, and international levels of governance (Johnson et al. 1999; Sarewitz and Pielke 2000). And, as the scientific community has advanced our understanding of environmental issues and problems over the past three decades, it has become an ever more important participant in the policy process. When asked, many observers, including scientists themselves, agree with Harmon's observation:

> We in modern society give tremendous prestige and power to our official, publicly validated knowledge system, namely science. It is unique in this position; none of the coexisting knowledge systems— not any system of philosophy or theology, not philosophy or theology as a whole—is in a comparable position. (Harmon 1998, 116)

The importance of science and scientists is reflected by the National Academy of Sciences, which was established by a congressional charter in 1863 to "advise the federal government on scientific and technical matters" (National Academy of Sciences Charter). The academy has been called on in recent years to research and advise the government on environmental issues such as global warming, nuclear waste management and disposal, wildlife and fisheries management issues, and others.

Yet, as science and, by extension, scientists, have become ever more important participants in the policy process, the debate has grown over just what the role of scientists should be, and whether science should have such a privileged position when deciding policy. As outlined in the introduction to this volume, there are at least three competing views on the proper role of science and scientists in the policy process. The traditional, or "normal," science view is grounded in positivism and believes that science can accurately and objectively predict various phenomena, that science is "a matter of truth" (Pyeson and Sheets-Pyeson 1999, 5), and that science will bring about prosperity through the use of quantitative methods to understand both physical and social affairs.

Another perspective, influenced by postmodernism, suggests that scientists and scientific data are only one source of information and authority among the many sources involved in the policy process (Collingridge and Reeve 1986; Ezrahi 1980; Ravetz 1990). From this perspective, the value of scientific information can be considered to be entirely contingent on context, and nonscientific, political, personal, and ideological information can readily override scientific data in policy-making at many points. The emergence of this second understanding of the role of science in the policy process has been described by Shabecoff: "In recent decades, science has begun to slip from its lofty pedestal as it has become apparent that it is not adequate either to meet all the needs of humanity or to protect us from the dangers that science and technology themselves create" (2000, 139).

A third perspective believes that science can improve the quality of complex environmental policy decisions, but only if done in the right way (e.g., Ehrlich and Ehrlich 1996). The assumption is that scientists can and should facilitate the resolution of public resource decisions by providing objective scientific information to policy makers and the public, and by becoming more directly involved in policy arenas than they have been traditionally (Mazur 1981). This shift from traditional positivistic roles to a more "post-normal," "integrative," or "civic science" model of engagement and involvement (Funtowicz and Ravetz 1992; Lee 1993) is expected to produce higher-quality and more relevant research for at least four reasons (Welp et al. 2006, 171–172):

- Managers and other stakeholders can "boost the creative process" by helping scientists identify relevant and challenging research questions.

- Stakeholders can provide scientists a "reality check" by evaluating research methodologies and research results.
- Much basic science research is often devoid of important ethical or cultural considerations and fraught with scientific jargon and terms that leads to confusion and ambiguity. An integrative approach can lead to better understanding among all involved parties and lead to research results that are culturally and ethically sensitive.
- Collaborative efforts give scientists access to important "data and knowledge that otherwise would remain unknown or at least very difficult to access."

This chapter explores the attitudes of scientists involved in natural resource and marine policy arenas toward their role in the management and policy process. Building on a previous 2003 National Science Foundation (NSF) pilot study that examined the role of science and scientists at the H. J. Andrews (HJA) experimental forest, a Long Term Ecological Research (LTER) site in Oregon, we use data and interviews from national samples of land-based, or terrestrial, ecological scientists and marine/ocean scientists to find out scientists' preferred role in natural resource and marine management and policy: Do they see themselves as traditionalists, interpreters, integrators, advocates, or technocrats in the policy process? We also examine the degree to which scientists support and participate in terrestrial and marine management and policy processes.

In the initial study, we found that while there are limits to the roles that ecological scientists can play in environmental policy, there is still broad support for more active involvement by scientists in policy-making processes (Steel et al. 2004). We also found significant differences among scientists, natural resource managers, and the public in the Pacific Northwest region of the United States about what constitutes science and what the most suitable role for ecological science and scientists in the policy process should be (Lach et al. 2003). In the study presented here, we find that both terrestrial and marine scientists strongly prefer an integrative role to any of the other four possible roles.

BACKGROUND AND LITERATURE REVIEW

In our original 2003 pilot study (Lach et al. 2003), we investigated orientations toward the proper role of scientists in the policy process in the US Pacific

Northwest. Based on interviews and an exploratory survey of scientists, we developed a list of five potential roles for scientists in the policy process. These ideal types reflect a complex relationship among expectations of science, attitudes about resource management, and decision-making styles (see table 8.1). While the categories reflect levels of preference for scientist involvement ranging from minimal to dominant roles, they also distinguish between science as an activity separate from other, nonscientific activities and science as an activity integrated with management and other nonscientific activities.

The first role, the traditionalist, reflects the traditional science model, which limits research scientists to reporting results and letting others make resource decisions. As part of an "emerging role," we described two possibilities: an interpreter, for those research scientists who interpret scientific results so that others can use them; and an integrator, for those working closely with managers and others to integrate scientific results directly into resource policies and decisions. The advocate describes researchers who actively support specific resource policies or management decisions that they prefer or believe flow from their scientific findings. A final role, the technocrat, reflecting the increasingly technical and complicated decisions facing natural resource managers, describes scientists who make resource decisions themselves (see table 8.1).

In our original 2003 Pacific Northwest survey of scientists, managers, interest groups, and members of the attentive public, we asked respondents to tell us how much they agreed with scientists taking each of these potential roles. The two most popular roles for scientists in the natural resource policy process for all study groups were the integrator and interpreter roles—assisting managers to interpret and then integrate scientific research into management practices. Managers, NGO staff, and members of the attentive public most often preferred the integrator role, while scientists themselves preferred the slightly less involved role of interpreter. In general, most respondents were least supportive of scientists as technocrats (i.e., making decisions themselves); however, NGOs and the public also were not enamored with the traditionalist role, just reporting scientific results, and were more likely than scientists and managers to support the advocate role for scientists. Scientists and managers were not supportive of the advocate role for scientists (Lach et al. 2003). In summary, respondents were all likely to agree that integrative roles are more preferable than any of the other roles, including the traditional role of just reporting results.

Finally, we also discovered that a "culture of science" affects research scientists in a manner that does not so clearly apply to other groups in the policy process (managers, citizens and interest groups) (Steel et al. 2004). This culture emphasizes the traditional science goals of academic publication and citations, rather than activities such as working with the public or managers. Research scientists operate in a communal scientific environment that imposes demands on their time and energy, and their reputations and identities as scientists depend on a different system of institutional relationships and rewards than those of managers and other groups. Involvement in resource management and public environmental policy processes requires somewhat different communication and interpersonal skills than those that are effective in the scientific community. Other scientists sometimes have reservations about researchers who do become involved in policy matters, and may question their standing and credibility as a result. These and other factors can mean that scientists will be wary of researchers taking a more active, integrative role in policy-making. As former EPA scientist Robert Lackey has argued,

> I am concerned that we scientists in conservation biology, ecology, natural resources, environmental science, and similar disciplines are collectively slipping into a morass that risks marginalizing the contribution of science to public policy. . . . Scientists are uniquely qualified to participate in public policy deliberations and they should, but advocating for their policy preferences is not appropriate. (2007, 12)

Resource managers, on the other hand, work in an environment that is quite different from that of research scientists; this leads them to view the role of scientists differently than do scientists themselves, accepting their authority as scientists but not as advocates for particular policy positions. For example, because of organizational imperatives, managers do not always have the time to wait until "all the evidence is in" or the uncertainties are finally removed from the latest scientific findings. Nor do they have to satisfy their curiosity in research or gain the consequent rewards that scientists receive from interactions with other scientists. Even when trained as scientists, in their current roles managers are less likely than scientists to be involved in the scientific community and thus may not share as deeply the values and norms that define the culture of science.

In summary, many academics, managers, and members of the public have normative expectations that including scientists and scientific information in the policy process will improve complex natural resource decisions. However, increasing experiential evidence suggests that tensions between the distinct institutional needs and cultural values of decision-makers and scientists may preclude the effective use of science in many environmental decisions (e.g., Brown and Harris 1998; Collingridge and Reeve 1986; Meidinger and Antypus 1996). As Hess commented, "Scientists have come to recognize the political nature of the institutions of science, and their research problems have become increasingly tied to public and private agendas outside their disciplines" (1997, 2). The two national studies of terrestrial and marine policy contexts presented in this chapter may well help us expand our understanding of the expectations of relevant groups for the use of ecological information in environmental policy-making, how science is perceived in terms of objectivity, and the range and acceptability of appropriate roles that scientists can take in policy-making and natural resource management.

METHODS

Scientists working through the National Science Foundation's Long Term Ecological Research (LTER) program were surveyed in 2007 as a group of relatively homogeneous scientists involved in potentially policy-relevant terrestrial research. These scientists work at universities, state and federal agencies, and private organizations. The LTER program has twenty-six sites located in the continental United States, Alaska, the Antarctic, the Caribbean, and the Pacific, with approximately two thousand scientists involved. Only LTER scientists that work at sites in the continental United States and Alaska were included in this study. The randomly selected sample contained 424 scientists, with 355 responding to the mail/internet-based survey, for an 84 percent response rate. The sample of scientists was provided by the LTER national office in Albuquerque, New Mexico.

In 2011, the LTER scientist study was replicated in the marine and ocean science, policy, and management context. The scientists we sampled work at universities, state and federal agencies, and private organizations that deal with ocean and marine policy issues (including only ocean coastal states). The systematic random sample was developed using relevant websites (e.g., Sea Grant Programs, NOAA, US Fish and Wildlife, relevant state agencies, and so on) in each coastal state including Hawai'i and Alaska (but excluding

Great Lakes states), and from directories available in print and on the Internet. Approximately 1,200 potential scientists were identified and three hundred were sent mail surveys and instructions for completing the Internet-based version if they preferred. Two hundred and eleven scientists completed the survey, for a 70 percent response rate.

FINDINGS: WHAT SCIENTISTS THINK ABOUT THEIR ROLE IN THE POLICY PROCESS

A major focus of this study was not only to investigate attitudes toward science and the scientific process but also to investigate orientations toward the proper role of scientists in the policy process, and then determine what relationship may exist between the two. Based on the interviews and exploratory survey of scientists discussed above in the methods section, we developed a list of five potential roles for scientists in the policy process. These ideal types reflect a complex relationship among expectations of science, attitudes about resource management, and decision-making styles (see table 8.1). We asked respondents to tell us how much they agreed with each of these potential roles. The roles are not mutually exclusive, although it is unlikely that anyone who favors a minimal role for scientists will also prefer the technocratic role of putting them in charge of resource decisions.

When asked to designate "the best single description of your preferred role" for scientists in natural resource and marine policy (see table 8.1), both terrestrial and marine scientists strongly preferred the integrator role. The majority of both scientist groups agreed that "scientists should work closely with managers and others to integrate scientific results in management decisions" (63 percent of terrestrial scientists and 60 percent of marine scientists). The second highest preference for both groups was for the interpreter role: "scientists should report and interpret the results for others involved in natural resource issues" (21 percent for terrestrial scientists and 22 percent for marine scientists). These roles—integrator and interpreter—appear to reflect an emerging expectation of scientists that they will interact with the extended peer community as required to address many wicked natural resource problems. The roles least preferred by both groups of scientists include the traditionalist role, just reporting scientific results, and the technocratic role, researchers making decisions themselves.

Given the high level of support among both groups of scientists in this study for roles in natural resource and marine management and policy that

Table 8.1. Preferred Role for Scientists in Natural Resource/Marine Management and Policy

Question: Which of the following is the best single description of your preferred role for scientists in natural resource/marine and ocean policy and management?		
Roles	Terrestrial Scientists	Marine/Ocean Scientists
A. Traditionalist	3.4%	3.9%
Scientists should only report scientific results and leave others to make natural resource management decisions.	n=12	n=8
B. Interpreter	20.6%	22.2%
Scientists should report scientific results and then interpret the results for others involved in natural resource management decisions.	n=72	n=46
C. Integrator	63.4%	59.9%
Scientists should work closely with managers and others to integrate scientific results in management decisions.	n=222	n=124
D. Advocate	9.4%	10.6%
Scientists should actively advocate for specific natural resource management policies they prefer.	n=33	n=22
E. Technocrat	3.1%	3.4%
Scientists should be responsible for making decisions about natural resource management.	n=11	n=7
	N=350	N=207

can be described as necessary for post-normal science, to what degree do scientists actually support and participate in specific integrative activities? In both surveys of scientists we provided a list of traditional and integrative science activities and asked scientists the (a) importance and (b) frequency of personal participation in each activity. The data presented in table 8.2 provides mean scores of the level of importance and frequency of participation for each activity. We have rank-ordered the results based on the frequency of participation, which was very similar for both groups of scientists.

Not surprisingly, scientists were most likely to frequently engage in the normal science activities of "presenting research results at professional meetings" and "publishing research results in academic journals." These two activities were also considered the most important activities by scientists. The remaining activities included efforts more consistent with post-normal and integrative science to produce and disseminate usable scientific information to the public, elected

Table 8.2. Normal and Post-Normal Activities of Terrestrial and Marine Scientists

How frequently have you engaged in the following activities on an annual basis? 1 = Never to 5 = Very Frequently			How important do you consider these activities? 1 = Not Important At All to 5 = Very Important	
Scientists	Mean	Activities	Mean	Tau b
Terrestrial	4.65	a. Publish research results in academic journals.	4.36	.43**
Marine	4.71		4.42	.50**
Terrestrial	3.98	b. Present research results at professional meetings.	4.20	.60**
Marine	4.04		4.24	.63**
Terrestrial	3.77	c. Provide expert scientific testimony on pending legislation in judicial proceedings.	3.97	.49**
Marine	3.82		3.99	.68**
Terrestrial	3.64	d. Translate research results into a format that natural resource managers can readily understand and use.	3.78	.58**
Marine	3.73		3.83	.61**
Terrestrial	3.60	e. Communicate research results directly to nonscientists through the Internet.	3.57	.37**
Marine	3.63		3.62	.36**
Terrestrial	3.33	f. Communicate research results directly to non-scientists through field trips or on-site demonstrations.	3.61	.55**
Marine	3.35		3.60	.47**
Terrestrial	2.33	g. Translate research results into a format that elected officials or staff can readily understand and use.	2.60	.30**
Marine	2.38		2.64	.31**
Terrestrial	2.02	h. Present information at public planning hearings for natural resource agencies.	2.55	.53**
Marine	2.03		2.61	.50**
Terrestrial	1.92	i. Communicate research results directly to non-scientists through organization/agency publications.	2.28	.38**
Marine	1.98		2.87	.36**
Terrestrial	1.24	j. Translate research results into a format that mass media (newspaper, television, etc.) can readily use.	2.20	.28**
Marine	1.23		2.23	.29**

Significance: ** p < .01

officials, agencies, and managers. Three activities had mean scores between "sometimes" to "frequently" for engagement: "translating research results" for managers, providing "expert scientific testimony" on pending legislation, and "communicating research results directly to nonscientists through the Internet." The remaining listed activities had fairly low levels of participation by scientists: translating "research results into a format that elected officials or staff can readily understand" (mean scores of 2.33 and 2.38), presenting "information at public planning hearings for natural resource agencies" (mean scores 2.02 and 2.03), and communicating "research results directly to nonscientists through organization/agency publications" (mean scores of 1.92 and 1.98). The activity in which scientists were least likely to participate, which has huge implications for democratic policy processes, is translating "research results into a format that the mass media can readily use" (mean scores of 1.24 and 1.23). The mean scores for this activity indicate that most terrestrial and marine scientists in these studies "never" engage in dissemination of information to mass media outlets such as newspapers and television.

Is it the case that scientists feel some activities are important yet do not engage in them for some particular reason(s), such as time constraints, lack of training, promotion and tenure considerations, and so on? The scores listed on the right side of table 8.2 indicate how important scientists consider each of the activities, and correlation coefficients (tau b in table) indicate consistency between reported levels of engagement and importance. Similar to self-reported engagement, the two activities considered most important by scientists were the traditional science activities of presenting research at professional meetings and publishing in academic journals. The mean scores for these two activities are situated between "important" and "very important." However, two additional activities also received a high level of importance—"providing expert scientific testimony on pending legislation in judicial proceedings" (mean scores of 3.97 and 3.99) and "translating research results for resource managers" (mean scores of 3.78 and 3.83). Activities that were considered "somewhat important" to "not important at all" included translating research results for elected officials (mean scores of 2.60 and 2.64), presenting information at public planning hearings (mean scores of 2.55 and 2.61), and communicating results to nonscientists through agencies (mean scores of 2.28 and 2.87). The activity seen as least important was "translating research results into a format that mass media can readily use" (mean scores of 2.20 and 2.23). Not only are most scientists in this study not engaging with the mass media, they also believe it is of little importance. This reflects a recent National Academy of Sciences study, which concluded, "Although there is more influence on public communication from the science organizations . . .

the available data do not indicate abrupt changes in communication practices or in the relevant beliefs and attitudes of scientists in the past 30 years" (Peters 2013, 14102). This study also concludes that "norms of scientific communities toward the public have been characterized as ambivalent—partly rewarding, partly condemning media interactions" (Peters 2013, 14105).

When we examine the correlation coefficients (tau b) between frequency of activity and importance of activity, we find positive and statistically significant relationships between engagement in and rated importance of each activity. However, the strength of the relationships varies widely, ranging from a very strong relationship (.68) for marine scientists concerning providing expert testimony in judicial proceedings to a moderately strong relationship (.28) for terrestrial scientists concerning translating research for mass media. One pattern evident in all of these results is that believing that an activity is important doesn't mean scientists will take on that activity.

Given that both groups of scientists reported extremely low levels of participation and importance for translating research results for use by mass media—which one could argue may be the best way to communicate scientific research to the public—what role do scientists themselves believe the public should play in natural resource and marine policy and management? To get at this question, we asked both samples of scientists this question: In your opinion, what is a realistic role for the public in natural resource/marine and ocean policy management issues? Similar to the scientist roles displayed in table 8.1, we provided a list of five possible public roles, ranging from a minimalist role ("none, let natural resource/marine and ocean professionals decide") to a dominant role ("the public should decide management issues and natural resource/marine and ocean professionals should carry them out"). Table 8.3 displays the results for this question for both groups of scientists.

The consensus role for the public according to both groups of scientists is "serve on advisory boards that review and comment on natural resource/marine and ocean managers' decisions" (71 percent for terrestrial scientists and 72 percent for marine scientists). There was little to no support for the minimalist role for the public ("none") or the maximum direct democracy response of "the public should decide management issues and natural resource/marine and ocean professionals should carry them out." There was also little overall support for the more collaborative public role of acting "as a full and equal partner in making natural resource/marine and ocean management decisions" (17 percent of terrestrial scientists and 15 percent of marine scientists). Many

Table 8.3. Scientist Perceptions of a Realistic Role for the Public in Natural Resource/Marine and Ocean Management

Question: In your opinion, a realistic role for the public in natural resource/marine and ocean policy management issues should be (please select only one).	Terrestrial Scientists	Marine Scientists
a. None, let natural resource/marine and ocean professionals decide.	0.8% n=3	1.0% n=2
b. Provide suggestions and let the natural resource/marine and ocean professionals decide.	10.8% n=38	12.1% n=25
c. Serve on advisory boards that review and comment on natural resource/marine and ocean manager's decisions.	71.1% n=251	72.0% n=149
d. Act as a full and equal partner in making natural resource/marine and ocean management decisions.	17.0% n=60	15.0% n=31
e. The public should decide management issues and natural resource/marine and ocean professionals should carry them out.	0.3% n=1	0.0% n=0

post-normal, civic, and collaborative science advocates would be somewhat dismayed by these results, because they suggest a continuing reliance on "experts," with the public serving only as reviewers on advisory boards.

BEST PRACTICES: INTEGRATING AND COMMUNICATING SCIENCE

While the findings presented so far in this chapter indicate support for integrative approaches to science among our samples of both terrestrial and marine scientists, the level of participation by scientists in such activities does not match their reported level of support. There also appears to be some concern by scientists about how involved the public should be in natural resource management and what the role of scientists should be in communicating research to broader audiences. Our results also suggest that many scientists do not see much possibility or value in extending a peer community to include nonscientists.

However, there are a growing number of successful examples of integrative community-based science that can be used to demonstrate how such an integrative approach can work in practice. Toward this end, and as part of this research project, we conducted case-study visits at several LTER sites that have a history of engagement with managers, citizens, and the public in order to identify some examples of successful efforts of communicating and integrating science.

At several LTER sites, including our original case study of the H. J. Andrews LTER site in Oregon, we found strong support for the integrative science approach. Stankey and Shindler's work with management plans for rare and little-known species (RLKS) such as slugs and fungi found that limited public awareness and knowledge led to community resistance to management programs and therefore species decline. They found that while there had been much research on the biological and economic aspects of RLKS management, there had been no research whatsoever to "foster cultural adoptability, or as commonly termed, social acceptability" of management plans among the public (2006, 29). In order to enhance public understanding and participation in RLKS management, Stankey and Shindler took a proactive and post-normal approach by having scientists, managers, and community members engage in joint fact-finding and collaborative discovery. They argue that the key for social acceptability and participation for successful management requires collaborative approaches that (1) clarify the rationale and potential impacts of policies on species and communities; (2) outline specific actions that will be taken with the management plan; (3) specify and adapt to the contextual setting of the issue; and (4), identify where and when management plans will be implemented (2006, 28).

Other activities at several LTER case-study sites such as Coweeta LTER (Southern Appalachian Mountains), Central Arizona-Phoenix LTER (Arizona), Northern Temperate Lakes (Wisconsin), and Sevilleta LTER (New Mexico), include K–12 and university student outreach and field trips to LTER research sites, on-site demonstrations for the public and managers, and sometimes even collaborative research. An interesting project conducted by Northern Temperate Lakes (NTL) LTER researchers associated with the University of Wisconsin–Madison found that healthy fish populations and biodiversity among Wisconsin's many small lakes were most likely to be evident in lakes where dead trees and branches were found along the shoreline (Bates 2008). Dead trees and natural debris are extremely important to aquatic food chains. The problem is that many of Wisconsin's smaller lakes are on private lands with summer cottages and cabins along the shoreline. Private landowners along lakes were found to be removing woody debris to make room for docks and for general aesthetic reasons, thus damaging aquatic ecosystems and fish populations. Through implementing demonstration projects on several experimental lakes on state land and encouraging participation of landowners in research by asking them to leave fallen trees and other debris on the shoreline and in the water, NTL researchers are now in the process of changing shoreline owner behaviors for ecologically healthier lakes.

A third and final example of an interesting and successful integrative science research project has been developed at the Central Arizona-Phoenix (CAP) LTER site. This project looks at vegetation patterns, water use, biodiversity, and how humans affect urban landscapes (Martin et al. 2008). More specifically, this research examines landscaping alternatives in the Phoenix, Arizona, metropolitan area and how landscaping choices affect human behavior and urban ecosystems. Included in the study are two hundred sites in neighborhood plots and K–12 schools where differing landscaping practices are being used (e.g., native Sonoran Desert vegetation versus "Wisconsin"-style vegetation with lawns, nonindigenous plants, and so on). Students, citizens, and scientists are conducting longitudinal surveys and measurements of plants, trees, lichens, insects, pollutants, animals, water use, resident attitudes and behaviors, and so on to determine the effect of humans on vegetation and the effect of differing landscapes on water use and biodiversity. This integrative and collaborative longitudinal research has engaged a large number of both nonscientists and scientists in valuable research that has the potential to affect policy in years to come.

CONCLUSION

The results reported in this study suggest that there is some support for integrative or post-normal science with scientists directly involving themselves in natural resource and marine policy and management process—especially with natural resource and marine managers. However, we also found that these same scientists do not fully embrace the post-normal approach when it calls for increasing involvement by the public in this process, including their ability to provide expertise or help integrate new information into existing decision routines and practices.

These approaches do bring scientists out of the laboratory and into the political realm, which may be uncomfortable for scientists who aren't familiar with or skilled at working in these arenas. It also raises issues of scientific credibility, which is still tied to the positivistic ideals of objectivity and neutrality. Scientists with the willingness and skill to walk the tightrope that is policy-making will help familiarize nonscientists with both the strength and limitations of science. As Larson (2007, 953) has argued, if scientists want to contribute to sound policy, "they cannot simply present the facts, but need to interact with non-scientists both in the design of their research as well as in its application to particular problems." This interaction will also help scientists understand more clearly the possible roles for science in the "sausage-making" of public policy. The successful integrative approaches at the LTER sites that engaged scientists, managers, and the public can generate excitement about issues and demonstrate how such an integrative approach can work in practice.

Notes

Partial funding for this research was provided by the National Science Foundation, "Changing Expectations for Science and Scientists in Natural Resource Decision Making: A Case Study of the Long Term Ecological Research (LTER) Program" (2004–2008); and by the North Pacific Research Board "Analysis of the North Pacific Research Board Research Program" (2010).

References

Bates, J. 2008. "Lake Study Says to Leave the Dead." Looking at Lake Series. Madison: University of Wisconsin. http://lter.limnology.wisc.edu/.

Brown, G., and C. Harris. 1998. "Professional Foresters and the Land Ethic, Revisited." *Journal of Forestry* 96:4–12.

Collingridge, D., and C. Reeve. 1986. *Science Speaks to Power: The Role of Experts in Policymaking*. New York: St. Martin's Press.

Ehrlich, P., and A. Ehrlich. 1996. *Betrayal of Science and Reason: How Anti-environmental Rhetoric Threatens Our Future*. Washington, DC: Island Press.

Ezrahi, Y. 1980. "Utopian and Pragmatic Rationalism: The Political Context of Scientific Advice." *Minerva* 18:111–131.

Funtowicz, S., and J. Ravetz. 1992. "Three Types of Risk Assessment and the Emergence of Post-Normal Science." In *Social Theories of Risk*, edited by S. Krimisky and D. Golding. Westport, CT: Praeger.

Funtowicz, S., and J. Ravetz. 1999. "Post-Normal Science: Environmental Policy under Conditions of Complexity." http://www.jvds.nl/pns/pns.htm.

Harmon, W. 1998. *Global Mind Change: The Promise of the Twenty-First Century*. San Francisco: Berrett-Koehler.

Hess, D. 1997. *Science Studies: An Advanced Introduction*. New York: NYU Press.

Johnson, N., F. Swanson, M. Herring, S. Greene, eds. 1999. *Bioregional Assessments: Science at the Crossroads of Management and Policy*. Washington, DC: Island Press.

Lach, D. P., B. List, S. Steel, and B. Shindler. 2003. "Advocacy and Credibility of Ecological Scientists in Resource Decision-Making: A Regional Study." *Bioscience* 53:171–179.

Lackey, Robert. 2007. "Science, Scientists, and Policy Advocacy." *Conservation Biology* 21:12–17.

Larson, Brendon M. H. 2007. "An Alien Approach to Invasive Species: Objectivity and Society in Invasion Biology." *Biological Invasions* 9 (December): 947–956.

Lee, K. 1993. *Compass and Gyroscope*. Washington, DC: Island Press.

Martin, C., C. Saltz, M. Elser, C. Martin, and S. Scheiner. 2008. "Ecology Explorers, Vegetation Sampling Protocol." Central Arizona-Phoenix Long-Term Ecological Research. Phoenix: Arizona State University. http://caplter. asu.edu/home/protocols/.

Mazur, A. 1981. *The Dynamics of Technical Controversy*. Washington, DC: Communications Press.

Meidinger, E., and A. Antypus. 1996. "Science Intensive Policy Disputes: An Analytical Overview of the Literature." Report prepared for the People and Natural Resources Program. Seattle: USDA Forest Service, PNW Station.

National Academy of Sciences Charter. http://www.nasonline.org/site/ PageServer? pagename=ABOUT_main_page.

Peters, H. P. 2013. "Gap between Science and Media Revisited: Scientists as Public Communicators." *PNAS* 110:14102–14109.

Pyeson, L., and S. Sheets-Pyeson. 1999. *Servants of Nature: A History of Scientific Institutions, Enterprises, and Sensibilities*. New York: Norton.

Ravetz, J. 1987. "Uncertainty, Ignorance, and Policy." In *Science for Public Policy*, edited by H. Brooks and C. Cooper, 48–63. New York: Pergamon Press.

———. 1990. *The Merger of Knowledge with Power: Essays in Critical Science*. London: Mansell Publishing.

Sarewitz, D., and R. Pielke. 2000. "Prediction in Science and Policy." In *Prediction: Science, Decision Making and the Future of Nature*, edited by D. Sarewitz, R. Pielke, and R. Byerly. Washington, DC: Island Press.

Shabecoff, P. 2000. *Earth Rising: American Environmentalism in the 21st Century*. Washington, DC: Island Press.

Stankey, G., and B. Shindler. 2006. "Formation of Social Acceptability Judgements and Their Implications for Management of Rare and Little-Known Species." *Conservation Biology* 20:28–37.

Steel, B. S., P. List, D. Lach, and B. Shindler. 2004. "The Role of Scientists in the Environmental Policy Process: A Case Study from the American West." *Environmental Science and Policy* 7:1–13.

Welp, M., A. de la Vega-Leinert, S. Stoll-Kleemann, and C. C. Jaeger. 2006. "Science-Based Stakeholder Dialogues: Theories and Tools." *Global Environmental Change* 16:170–181.

Chapter 9
Collaborative Governance, Science, and Policy Outcomes

EDWARD P. WEBER AND ANNA P. STEVENSON

The dynamic complexity of many public problems defies the confines of established "stove-piped," or fragmented, systems of problem definition, administration, and resolution (Rittel and Webber 1973). This conundrum has created incentives to search for more effective alternative governance institutions, in particular, collaborative governance arrangements, which promise to give more people a voice in decisions (empowerment and democratization), reduce conflict and litigation, and, ultimately, break the gridlock among erstwhile adversaries and produce more durable policy outcomes by creating trust and providing solutions that leave all participants better off than before.

Thus, it is not surprising that community-based collaboration has emerged in thousands of places around the globe wrestling with difficult environmental, economic, and other kinds of public problems (e.g., Ostrom 1990; Sabatier et al. 2005; Weber 2000). The early trend involved largely self-organized groups of stakeholders, while more recently governments have actively encouraged their formation. In the United States, for example, key US natural resource and public lands agencies such as the US Forest Service, National Park Service, Bureau of Land Management, and US Fish and Wildlife Service have now created programs to train officials in collaborative governance (CG) and to facilitate small scale CG formation and operation (Cheng 2007).

And while there are many forms of CG arrangements, at their core they share a few key characteristics, including shared authority for decisions, the ability to recognize and respect diverse interests and needs, an openness to different forms of knowledge (e.g., science, indigenous, practice-based), reliance on a consensus or near consensus decision rule, and a focus on the production of mutual gain (win-win-win) outcomes (versus win-lose in adversarial settings) (Ansell and Gash 2008; Daniels and Walker 2001; Weber 2003).

We acknowledge the importance of the large literature on the kinds of factors contributing to collaborative governance success, particularly with regard to institutional design, existing conditions, and leadership. But the primary question of interest here is more narrowly confined to the production and use of science and other knowledges in collaborative problem-solving processes. This is because the complex, crosscutting, uncertain character of wicked problems increases the reliance on multiple knowledges—science, indigenous, and practice-based expertise—that pose their own unique political, social, and leadership challenges that must be resolved in order to find success (Weber and Khademian 2008).

These types of problems thus necessarily require decision-makers, practitioners, and the public to rethink the role of traditional science and scientists in the policy process. A common response has been to demand a more collaborative approach to decision-making in the hope of producing solutions capable of addressing multiple competing demands—ecological, social, and economic—and integrating multiple knowledges into final decisions (Schusler et al. 2003; Stayaert and Jiggins 2007). In this sense, collaborative governance is a problem-solving methodology that takes full advantage of post-normal science's extended peer community concept. What are some ways that collaborative governance approaches can produce knowledge well-suited to wicked-problem settings and facilitate agreed interpretations of science, risk, and uncertainty, while also increasing the probability that science will influence policy in wicked-problem cases?

The rest of this chapter discusses two possible paths for how collaborative governance can help address the challenges of science/knowledge and problem solving in wicked-problem settings.

- The use of civic science rules and management to govern the production and use of science in a case of watershed-based planning for salmon recovery. The plans were adopted by the National Oceanic and Atmospheric Administration (NOAA) in 2006.
- The importance of a collaborative leader's mind-set in overcoming the challenges of knowledge sharing among diverse participants in a wicked-problem setting.

CASE 1: SALMON AND CIVIC SCIENCE IN PUGET SOUND, WASHINGTON

In 1999, NOAA Fisheries designated Puget Sound Chinook stocks as threatened under the federal Endangered Species Act (ESA). This development followed only a few years after the northern spotted owl battles of the late 1980s and early 1990s, and many in the Pacific Northwest were wary of the federal government's ability to command change and perhaps fundamentally change their way of life, especially given that the Puget Sound Chinook runs in jeopardy affected fourteen major watersheds in a heavily industrialized region containing more than three million people. The prospects of federal intervention and the massive, difficult nature of any recovery effort galvanized prominent leaders in the region into action, including former US Environmental Protection Agency administrator William Ruckelshaus, sitting and former Washington governors Gary Locke and Daniel Evans (respectively), Walter Reid of the Packard Foundation, and Native American leader Billy Frank Jr. to action. In search of a process and solution that, from their perspective, would have the best chance of helping recover salmon to harvestable levels while also respecting local and regional needs, they convened a series of regional meetings between 1999 and 2001 involving over two hundred individuals, leaders, and scientists from local, state, federal, and tribal governments, businesses, environmental groups, the agricultural and fishing industries, and universities.

The traditional approach to ESA recovery planning places all decision-making responsibility and authority with the federal agency having jurisdiction over the listed species. Yet, Puget Sound, Washington, stakeholders, in concert with NOAA Fisheries, deliberately departed from this traditional approach by agreeing to an inclusive, collaborative recovery planning process. The multilevel (government), multination (Native Americans), multistakeholder initiative was housed within a new nonprofit entity called Shared Strategy for Salmon Recovery in Puget Sound. The goal of the collaborative process was to increase the receptiveness of watershed stakeholders to the difficult, costly, and lengthy task of salmon recovery by more fully and effectively integrating science into the planning effort, while also increasing the likelihood of salmon recovery success (Weber et al. 2010).

Central to the collaborative effort, and credited as one of several keys to the successful conclusion in 2007 of the endangered species collaborative planning effort, was civic science (Brock et al. 2009). Civic science involves "efforts on the part of scientists to articulate and illuminate science content in the context of social issues" (Clark and Illman 2001, 18) and "is the process of linking experts and stakeholders in planning social, economic, and environmental improvements" (Schmandt 1998, 63; see also Feldman et al. 2006). Webler and Tuler (1999, 534), for their part, rely on the "analytic-deliberative" model developed by the National Research Council in 1996 to explore the value added by integrating scientific and technical analysis with inclusive, deliberative processes at each step of the watershed management decision process. As such, civic science necessarily emphasizes a multidirectional and iterative flow of information between scientists, policy makers, citizens, and other societal stakeholders for the purpose of reconciling and better managing the supply, demand, and use of scientific information in the policy process (Dietz and Stern 2009).

The adoption of the civic science model by NOAA Fisheries is of particular importance to policy makers and those interested in seeing that the requirements of the ESA, which grants science a dominant role in determining the validity of recovery plan choices, are properly discharged by the responsible agency (i.e., NOAA Fisheries). Traditional models of science in the policy process are relatively passive; they isolate science-decision processes from policy decisions in order to distinguish the function of scientists from that of policy makers and to preserve scientists' ability to give independent and objective, hence credible, scientific advice (Lane 1999; Pielke 2007). In fact, this has always been the typical mode of operation for NOAA Fisheries and their Technical Recovery Teams (TRTs), including the other seven TRTs NOAA Fisheries created to advise West Coast salmon recovery activities during this same time period in Washington, Idaho, Oregon, and California (Weber, Leschine, and Brock 2010).

In this traditional model, the NOAA Northwest Fisheries Science Center is responsible for conducting independent research and then forwarding its scientific conclusions to the Northwest Regional Office, where final permit and policy decisions are made. As well, the NOAA Fisheries *Integrated Recovery Planning for Listed Salmon* (NOAA 2002) described the TRT's task as developing biological delisting or recovery criteria and, more generally, providing scientific support and technical evaluation to recovery planners and policy makers. The science, and the limitations on policy decisions implied by the scientific parameters, would then be passed on to planners and policy makers in other federal, state, tribal, local, and private entities who take responsibility for developing recovery program options with due consideration given to economic and social factors (NOAA 2002). Thus, the initial expectation was that the scientific analyses would be completed separately from policy-making, yet, given the acknowledged presence and central role of the collaborative Shared Strategy effort in the Puget Sound listings, the NOAA guidance left unresolved how the working relationship between the TRT and Shared Strategy leaders should function in practice.

Without an established road map to guide them on integrating science into the Endangered Species Act (ESA) planning process, the Puget Sound TRT, in concert with Shared Strategy, structured the science-decision process so that the TRT was more fully and directly integrated into ESA planning and program selection. The rationale behind the new approach, strongly supported by Bob Lohn, the NOAA Fisheries regional administrator under the Bush administration, and other regional leaders, was that it increased the likelihood of clarifying and effectively communicating the lessons from science, which necessarily would increase the technical sophistication of the local watershed plans, providing greater certainty that proposed recovery measures would work to meet the needs of threatened salmon populations (Weber, Leschine, and Brock 2010).

The Puget Sound civic science model is defined by three key components:

- bridging the traditionally separate science and policy spheres in order to increase the certainty of science impact
- designing specific steps to establish and maintain the TRT's role as an authoritative, credible source of science
- adopting a results-oriented, adaptive learning approach to TRT process management, science application, and program implementation

BRIDGING THE SCIENCE AND POLICY DIVIDE

The Technical Recovery Teams (TRT) bridged the traditionally separate spheres between science and policy, while still ensuring that science remained independent and the critical driver of final decisions as required by the ESA, by implementing the following actions: (1) creating a specific structure for the science integration process; (2) adopting a new mode of interaction between the producers (the TRT) and users of science; (3) focusing on programmatic feasibility in achieving salmon viability goals; and (4) enhancing freedom of choice for watershed stakeholders within the overarching constraints provided by the TRT's science.

The structure of the science integration process

Directly integrating and successfully applying the technical team's scientific findings to policy choices required the capacity to effectively communicate and translate the science to an audience of largely nonscientific stakeholder decision-makers. In 2002, the TRT produced a primary guidance document, *Integrated Recovery Planning for Listed Salmon: Technical Guidance for Watershed Groups in Puget Sound* (NOAA 2002), that described the necessary biological components related to successfully establishing an ESA recovery plan and achieving harvestable salmon populations. The initial science guidance document was poorly received by Shared Strategy's policy work group, and virtually all of the watershed stakeholders, as being overly complex and therefore doing a poor job of communicating the necessary technical information (interviews August 27, November 19 and 30, 2007). The TRT responded to criticisms by revising the document and making it more accessible to all participants—providing clear goals, no jargon, and clarifying which tools, protocols, and applications could be used to estimate information such as the capacity and productivity of a resident salmon population. The new, more readily understandable document was delivered, to a much warmer reception from stakeholders, in February 2003.

The TRT scientists also served in the critical roles of evaluator and certifier of the programmatic elements of the watershed-level recovery plans in the new civic science process. After the fourteen watershed planning groups turned the technical guidance into programmatic options and testable hypotheses for further research, the TRT conducted two internal reviews. The reviews served as a way for the TRT to assess the technical nature of the programmatic options, identify the major uncertainties in each plan, and recommend possible options for addressing information gaps in order to improve the likelihood of producing viable salmon populations. The review and certification process resulted in NOAA Fisheries approving the final Shared Strategy Plan as the official ESA recovery plan.

A new mode of interaction

In November 2003, Shared Strategy held a meeting with all the watershed groups to create technical planning benchmarks so that each watershed group could measure their progress in meeting the scientific requirements for their recovery plans. The exercise convinced Shared Strategy staff and TRT scientists that something more than the revised guidance document was needed to improve the scientific rigor and quality of the various plans to an acceptable level. This realization led to the creation of an additional nonmandatory role for TRT scientists: science liaisons to the individual watershed groups.

The liaison role was designed to give watershed planning groups a direct, personal point of contact in the TRT to provide answers and continuous technical feedback as they worked through the salmon recovery planning process. Participants believe the liaison role was critical to translating the science to the watershed groups so that the science could influence the policy decisions made at the watershed level (interview September 13, 2007). The direct line of communication, iterative and informal discussions, fostered additional trust by stakeholders in both the science information and the scientists themselves (interviews September 13, October 3, November 8 and 19, 2007) and helped improve the overall credibility of the watershed planning process (interviews August 2, 14, and 27, 2007).

Focusing on uncertainty

All wicked problems possess a high degree of uncertainty that needs to be addressed when creating viable solutions. From the start, the TRT conceived of its role as threefold—to develop the science, to report and translate the science, and to connect the science to final policy decisions by highlighting the estimates of effectiveness associated with various proposed strategies. The focus on improving the estimates of effectiveness, and thus allowing all stakeholders to see the degree of uncertainty for each strategy, was incorporated through the watershed program certification process discussed above. Yet, while stakeholders agreed that this approach helped science to matter in the ESA planning process, from their perspective it was a dual-edged sword. Stakeholders acknowledged that the estimates of effectiveness component humanized the TRT scientists and, to some extent, helped engender a "we're all in this together" dynamic. Breaking down this barrier between scientists and communities made it easier for stakeholders to "listen" and ultimately "hear" and then "apply" what the scientists were saying. However, because the science-based estimates necessarily restricted the menu of possible policy options by advantaging those deemed most effective, many stakeholders also resented the intrusion of the scientists and science into what they viewed as the realm of policy-making (interviews August 21 and November 8 and 19, 2007).

Freedom of choice for stakeholders within a science-defined framework

The civic science model in Puget Sound granted those bearing the brunt of the ecological, economic, social, and political consequences of saving salmon critical input into the final watershed program choices. Within the limits provided by science, stakeholders were given the leeway to fit their choices to local circumstances in terms of ecology, culture, community values, the structure of the economy, and so on. Empowering stakeholders in this way improves the likelihood of science impact and policy effectiveness. Creating ownership of, and responsibility for, the final decisions leads stakeholders to more willingly and actively support program implementation, rather than fight it, as is more typical of ESA recovery programs. The science automatically influences the policy because it is inextricably intertwined and fundamental to the final policy programs being selected and implemented by such stakeholders, given the structure of the review, certification, and program selection process.

A COMMITMENT TO CREDIBLE, QUALITY SCIENCE

The credibility and quality of science in the policy process is almost always at issue for high complexity, high uncertainty, and contested problems. It is especially the case for salmon in the Pacific Northwest, given that iconic status typically translates into fierce debates over how best to "save the salmon," and can and does lead to firmly established normative predispositions toward what is "right" and therefore what "should" be done (see chapter 3 of this volume). The challenge is even more acute with a civic science model that, by definition, embraces closer, more prolonged interaction between the producers and users of science, thereby increasing opportunities for the science to be influenced, or captured, by the nonscientist stakeholders (e.g., Selznick 1957). The TRT employed a series of structural checks and specific choices to signal commitment to credible science, while also guarding against capture by any one set of political interests.

First, the TRT was tasked with providing credible and measurable science to assess factors that lead to population declines, establishing viability goals for salmon populations, and identifying for early action those implementation options with the greatest probability of benefiting salmon (NOAA

2002). Second, a National Academy of Sciences panel screened and ranked applicant-scientists to the TRT according to whether they had a strong record of achievement in their discipline (e.g., success in publishing high quality peer-reviewed science), a reputation for scientific integrity and independence, and the ability to work effectively in an interdisciplinary team setting. Third, the TRT was notable for its purposive diversity of representation across scientific disciplines and levels of government, agencies, and nations (Native Americans). The team's eight scientists possessed expertise in salmon biology, population dynamics, conservation biology, ecology, and other disciplines applicable for setting salmon recovery standards and measuring recovery progress. Fourth, the TRT added a layer of external technical review by having teams of four to five non-TRT scientists working with a TRT "lead" scientist on each proposed watershed recovery plan. Fifth, a Recovery Science Review Panel (RSRP) made up of National Academy–level senior scientists not steeped in salmon science served as an additional external check on the integrity and legitimacy of TRT science decisions.

Two important choices were also made by the TRT in support of the goal of a high quality and credible science and policy outcomes. In the first case, the TRT recognized and responded to the poor scientific quality of most watershed plans in November 2003 by adding a scientist liaison role to further engage watershed-level recovery plan decision-makers to enhance the probability that future decisions would meet the scientific demands of fish "recovery" needs. In the second case, the TRT provided another external check on their own expertise by subjecting a number of their in-house scientific studies to the traditional rigors of peer review. They succeeded in getting these studies published, adding further legitimacy because their work was formally vetted and deemed scientifically sound by their scientist peers.

A RESULTS-ORIENTED, ADAPTIVE APPROACH

The TRT adopted a results-oriented, adaptive approach to process management, science application, and program implementation. An adaptive learning style infused the approach to science during policy implementation because science was linked directly to programmatic performance. This was accomplished by setting fish recovery (viable population) targets for each watershed, requiring a mandatory science review every five years, and using the review data to adjust recovery plans accordingly if plans were not working, or if they were working better than expected.

The importance of the adaptable learning dynamic within the larger context of firm recovery targets, or "goalposts," is demonstrated by the way the goalposts inject results-orientation and greater certainty into the policy implementation process. The approach signals to stakeholders, first, that they will not be stuck sinking endless amounts of money and time into ineffective programs. Second, promising not to move the goalposts ensures to stakeholders that they can and will be rewarded for the hard work of implementation if their program choices are successful. The first reward will be a recovered salmon population per the recovery target, while the second comes when successful programs relieve stakeholders of their obligations to continue spending considerable time and money on ESA recovery programs. These components offer certainty and incentives to stakeholders to choose effective science-based programs.

Moreover, by using science to pare program choices to a subset of those most likely to be scientifically effective in recovering salmon populations, the decision process enhances the probability of overall policy effectiveness. Further, leaving final policy choices in the hands of the watershed stakeholders responsible for implementation increases the chance that the kinds of locally important political, economic, and social factors with direct impacts on policy effectiveness will influence program choices. The presence of the incentives to choose effective programs only adds to the likelihood that the locally important information essential to program effectiveness will find its way into the final decision-making mix.

CASE 2: FACILITATING KNOWLEDGE TRANSFER AND USE WITH COLLABORATIVE CAPACITY BUILDERS

Weber and Khademian (2008) focus attention on the challenges associated with knowledge-sharing among diverse participants to achieve collaborative governance, or network, effectiveness in a wicked-problem setting. They define effectiveness as "collaborative capacity, or long- and short-term problem solving capacity, improved policy performance, and the maintenance of accountability for public action" (336). Successfully achieving collaborative capacity is often the result of the transfer of information across a network through the channels or relationships that connect participants, how this transfer takes place, and the advantages of the transfer for individual participants (organizations) and the collaborative as a whole.

In some instances, the focus is on providing the technical capacity to share information among participants (Schau et al. 2005). Others focus on the speed or flow of information diffusion, with emphasis on the structural dimensions of collaboratives such as density, degree of centralization, the number of "bridges," and the geographic propinquity of members (Buskens and Yamaguchi 1999). Still others argue that managers must be skilled at facilitating and prompting communication across organizational boundaries (Tushman and Scanlan 1981) and the development of rules or norms to guide information-sharing (Gargiulo and Benassi 2000). Still others focus on the common interests, training, or background that members of a collaborative may have that facilitate the transfer of information (Buchel and Raub 2002). Yet these approaches to knowledge transfers assume that (1) information is the same thing as knowledge; (2) the problem is a technical issue amenable to technical solutions; and (3) collaborative "structure" is the place for answers to the collaborative capacity puzzle. These approaches also fail to take into account the knowledge challenge in wicked-problem settings.

Understanding the full knowledge "transfer, receipt, and integration" challenge of a wicked problem–based collaborative governance setting necessarily involves recognizing the presence of highly diverse participants, which means that the information flowing through the collaborative is likely to have different meanings, different uses, and different values for the individuals and groups receiving and using it. Consider, for example, stakeholders with a shared interest in renewing an urban area, loosely linked by occasional meetings and forums around the general problem of renewal. A cluster of landscape architects working on the renewal problem may have information on existing and potential green spaces in the urban area, horticultural variation, pedestrian and motor vehicle traffic, and property values that is valuable for the architects in trying to plan and utilize the spaces of the city. The immediate relevance of this information for a resident, on the other hand, may be significantly less. The information the resident most values could be the stories collected and told among other residents about the difficulties in finding work, the scarcity of stores selling fresh produce, traffic patterns near a school, graffiti on the buildings, and the recent wave of crime in a neighborhood. The relevance of any and all information will depend not only on the experience and expertise participants bring to the network, but also on the various interpretations of the problem of renewal and the understandings among participants of what renewal might accomplish. Environmentalists, elected officials, developers, and government agencies with a stake in the renewal of the city will all bring different experience with and expertise in the problem of renewal, different expectations for what renewal might accomplish, and hence different understandings of what information will be valuable for addressing the problem. The analogy could extend to any type of network setting.

The variance in value assigned by different participants to particular information in a collaborative governance setting has implications for the way we think about information and for the capacity of a collaborative to use information to solve wicked problems. First, there is a fundamental difference between information and knowledge. Knowledge, we argue, is socially mediated information (Schneider and Ingram 1997). Societies, communities, groups, professions, and neighborhoods develop forms of discourse that frame and give meaning to the information that is brought in, scientists included. Knowledge, in this view, cannot be separated from practice—the application, use and development of information (Nicolini et al. 2003). Each set of participants— residents of a community, elected officials, interest groups, experts, entrepreneurs—does not bring "information" to the collaborative about the problem; rather, these participants know the problem and perceive possible solutions through their engagement with the problem. Each has experienced, perhaps analyzed, discussed, and interpreted the dimensions of the wicked problem through specific lenses, or communities of discourse, and these diverse experiential lenses create formidable barriers to communication (Carlile 2002). The challenge is to find ways that this variegated knowledge can be distributed across participants, received (or accepted) among participants, and integrated to form a base of knowledge that can be used by the collaborative to address the wicked problem (Feldman and Khademian 2005).

Second, we argue that practice-based knowledge poses critical challenges for managers' attempts to convince participants to send or share their distinctive knowledge, receive the knowledge of others in the network, and integrate a collaborative's knowledge into the kind of unified, useful, and often new knowledge base necessary for effectively managing wicked problems. In short, failure to recognize and make allowances for these socially constructed sources of knowledge will necessarily hamper the problem-solving effectiveness of networks (see also chapter 1 in this volume).

More specifically, and drawing on prior research into public managers working in wicked-problem settings across a range of policy settings (Weber and Khademian 1997; Khademian 2002; Weber 1998, 2003; Weber et al.

2005), we argue for the critical importance of a collaborative capacity builder (CCB). A CCB is someone who either by legal authority, expertise valued within the collaborative governance arrangement, reputation as an honest broker, or some combination of the three, has been accorded a lead role in problem-solving exercises. In addition, CCBs tend to have a long-term stake in and commitment to building collaborative capacity for continuously addressing wicked problems.

The argument is that collaborative capacity is most likely to be achieved in a wicked-problem setting when a CCB adopts a mind-set, or set of commitments, that frames the tasks of sending, receiving, and integrating knowledge. The concept of a mind-set that influences top managers or leaders has a basis in both the public bureaucracy and business literatures, where mind-set is examined for its important role in the pursuit of innovation, decentralization, alternative ways of conceptualizing problems, global competitiveness, and, more generally, the creation of organizational culture (Aspinwall and Cain 1997; Selznick 1957; La Porte 1996).

In short, the mind-set frames the approach to collaborative problem solving and the relationships between government and other participants in the wicked-problem setting, and thereby facilitates the integration of science and other knowledges deemed important to a particular wicked problem into management plans and actions. Of chief importance are six commitments.

Commitment 1: Governance with government

The CCB mind-set accepts both that the interdependencies between government, private, and nonprofit sectors are inevitable and that government has a responsibility to play a prominent role in collaborative approaches to public problems (Klijn and Kopperjan 2000). Consider the comments by Julie Gerberding, the director of the Centers for Disease Control, on their evolving management approach in the years following the terrorist attacks of 9/11, the discovery of anthrax in postal facilities, and global challenges to public health such as severe acute respiratory syndrome (SARS) and Ebola: "We will . . . change the CDC's management platform into a less hierarchical one, [but] we never will be a completely distributed network. Nor should we be; that would not be in the interest of our accountability or the important work that we need to do" (Gerberding 2004, 10).

This is a commitment to governance with government; it is not a belief that government alone can solve problems with its connotations of finality and absolute success. Instead government is viewed as a key actor among many, but with responsibility to the broad public interest that other nongovernmental actors do not have. Indeed, this premise of the CCB mind-set recognizes that in a wicked-problem setting, vertical *government* responsibilities must necessarily be coupled with an obligation to build capacity in horizontal systems, as well as strengthen the linkages between vertical and horizontal systems (Weber and Khademian 2008). From this perspective, government can be a catalyst for producing broad, enduring collaborative capacity for addressing, managing, and coping with wicked problems (Sirianni 2010). And the authority of a government agency can play a critical role in soliciting, sharing, and integrating knowledge among participants in a network. But precisely because the definition of a problem, the design of a capacity to address it, and the responsibilities for funding and implementation will not be concentrated in a single government entity, the need to share, understand, and integrate diverse understandings of the wicked problem is paramount. It also means that managers who accept this commitment are less concerned about who or what agency or actor gets the credit for success but whether the problem gets addressed and, given its relentless character, continues to receive attention.

Commitment 2: Govern within the rules, yet think creatively

Collaborative capacity builders accept existing rules (established by an agency, a legislative or executive mandate, or existing policy) as a necessary, but not sufficient, part of the overall process to build long-term capacities to address wicked problems (Weber and Khademian 2008). Wicked problems, by their nature, defy categorization within a strict rules-based system that seeks to divide complex systems and problems into more manageable parts and assumes that the causal relationships within the wicked-problem set are clear and identifiable. The complexity and uncertainty of knowledge transfer and the creation of new knowledge associated with wicked problems means that anticipatory rules-based actions are bound to be inadequate. This commitment reflects a balance between the public manager as conservator (Terry 1993) and as entrepreneur (Moore 1995). It is recognition of democratically defined rules that place necessary boundaries on permissible actions, combined with openness to new ideas expressed within the network that could help build new competencies for the long-term management of wicked problems. It is also recognition that by-the-book problem solving, or a heavy rules-oriented approach, is unlikely to create the kinds of relationships among stakeholders required for the sending, receiving, and integration of knowledge needed for long-term problem-solving capacity (Bardach and Kagan 1982). Put differently, the premise for cooperation in wicked-problem settings is likely to be a common knowledge base, not a command-and-control processes.

Commitment 3: Collaborative governance as a mutual-aid partnership with society

Collaborative capacity builders (CCBs) view citizens and other stakeholding organizations as partners and potential helpers who nevertheless face legitimate constraints on collective action, including narrow or limited knowledge about the scope and severity of the problem, limited individual resources, and the fear that government authorities will not listen to, or incorporate and allow, innovative solutions produced by those outside the agency that has formal jurisdiction over the problem. This is why a CCB views authority and expertise as tools that allow managers to "serve" citizens (Weber and Khademian 2008). The flip side is that the blunt, coercive use of formal authority in collaborative scenarios is of limited value, particularly when encouraging participants to send, receive, and integrate knowledge for long-term capacity to address a wicked problem—such an approach risks breeding resistance and alienating the very people necessary for successfully managing a particular problem. This commitment does not view experts and managers as having all the answers; expertise is one source of knowledge, and public management is just that—managing problems and decision mechanisms within a democracy. More specifically, the management role is understood to be facilitative (Denhardt and Denhardt 2000). A helper, or servant manager, not only treats members of the network with appropriate respect and actively solicits their input, but also takes responsibility for helping build the capacities all participants need for addressing wicked problems (Roberts 2002).

Commitment 4: Public managers can be those without official government portfolios

Commitment 4 recognizes that not all collaborative capacity builders are employed by traditional government bureaucracies and that a public manager is someone critical for coordinating and catalyzing resources on behalf of public problem-solving efforts. This is because authority in collaboratives is often organic and informal, meaning that leadership is not granted automatically by formal titles or location within an organizational hierarchy (Weber and Khademian 2008). Rather it is earned or awarded by other stakeholders to those with access to critical resources and/or the ability to catalyze and apply them successfully for problem-solving purposes (Khademian 2002). This form of leadership is essential to bringing people and organizations together to initially share information, to encourage participants to listen and learn, and to integrate disparate forms of knowledge into a workable knowledge base particular to any given wicked problem.

Consider, for example, a wicked problem involving a community with a high degree of social capital. There are likely to be key leaders, whether political, social/cultural, or economic, within the community who can activate a collaborative by drawing on community social capital to support or oppose a public problem-solving effort. This point recognizes that communities have, over time, developed institutions, both informal and formal, and that long-term problem-solving success involves getting them to work with you rather than against you. Put differently, using only government-based public managers and coercion to solicit information and bring about compliance may lead to short-term, incomplete, high-cost successes at the expense of long-term problem-solving effectiveness (Bardach and Kagan 1982). The trade-off is more problematic to the extent that problems are of the relentless, wicked type, which necessarily demand long-term problem-solving capacity. Government-based CCBs are therefore committed to identifying and cultivating key nongovernmental public managers in cases where such citizen leaders exist. Of course, it also raises the possibility that collaborative action may not be possible in all settings because of hostility to the policy in question or serious value differences over the aims of government.

Commitment 5: Inseparability of performance, capacity, and accountability

In the whirl of management change and reform philosophies emphasizing results, the question of performance typically focuses on whether the problem has been solved, whether the targets met, whether progress is being made toward a solution, or whether benefits exceed costs. While the emphasis on results is welcomed by practicing managers and scholars, important cautions have been issued to attend to accountability—how we arrive at results can be as crucial as the results that are achieved, particularly when the desired goal or result is not clear or under dispute (Behn 1998). This is particularly the case when working to address wicked problems. By definition, wicked problems are hard to define, and solutions elusive. An important component of the CCB mind-set links performance and accountability by emphasizing the capacity of the collaborative governance arrangement to demonstrate accountability to a wide range of stakeholders whose participation is essential for long-term wicked-problem management (Weber and Khademian 2008).

Sending, receiving, and integrating knowledge is fundamental to the effort to build capacity for performance and accountability. Successful efforts to integrate across knowledge bases will provide an ongoing and evolving premise from which collaborative governance participants can take actions. But the process of integrating knowledge and identifying new sources of knowledge that are valuable across the CG arrangement is also an exercise in accountability. Sharing knowledge and creating a collective premise from which to address ongoing wicked problems requires stakeholder participation and understanding of the knowledge that is being shared and the knowledge that is being created.

The public in public problems requires consideration of to whom, and to what values, a program or policy is responsive. Wicked problems typically involve large sets of stakeholders up and down the formal political authority structure (cutting across state, local, and federal jurisdictions) and across multiple policy areas and agencies and individual citizens within the affected communities. The attendant complexity and interdependency is such that coercive solutions, or solutions responsive to only a few interests, cannot provide the needed simultaneous, broad-based accountability or accountability system—one that that maintains or improves accountability to local interests, private and public—to keep stakeholders collaboratively and constructively engaged over the long term without a corresponding diminution of accountability to broader state, regional, and national public interests (Weber 2003, 13). And if all stakeholders do not stay constructively engaged, it is unlikely that the capacity for solving wicked problems can be maintained for the long term. From this perspective, CCBs recognize that capacity is about finding ways to create and sustain mechanisms for participation for all stakeholders and finding solutions or processes that meet the needs of stakeholders across the board, including government at all appropriate levels, whether for mutual gain for all within a particular decision, mutual gain stemming from reciprocity across decisions over time, or a reasonable, mutually agreed sharing of burdens (e.g., implementation costs, programmatic responsibilities, time and personnel commitments, and so on).

Commitment 6: Passion for, and commitment to, the collaborative process

The CG literature focused on management addresses the authority of managers, the skills for collaboration, and possible resources to build and sustain collaboratives. Yet, successful CCBs working on wicked problems require an undeniable passion and commitment to the collaborative process (Weber and Khademian 2008). In an ongoing collaborative effort, the multiple organizations, people, and groups working together are really working out a new knowledge for the purposes of their collaborative. Conflicts inevitably arise between the objectives and values developed within the CG arrangement and those of individual organizations and other participants. Given this, managers need the energy to overcome resistance within their own organizations as well as within other participating organizations, in order to get a collaborative's members to share hard-won knowledge, to receive knowledge from others, and to create a new knowledge that will facilitate the successful management of wicked problems. In short, CCBs accept that they have primary responsibility for convincing the full range of affected interests to credibly commit to collaborative arrangements and the expected mutual-gain results, while also demonstrating a willingness to use their authority and the resources at their disposal to promote, enforce, and protect agreements arrived at collaboratively (Weber 1998).

CONCLUSION

The fundamental challenges posed by complex wicked problems place critical emphasis on the tasks of knowledge transmission and integration, whether of science or other knowledges such as indigenous- or practice-based expertise. Knowledge transmission tasks are communication issues grounded in social and political relationships involving heterogeneous actors with diverse interests and goals. The knowledge integration task is likewise grounded in these same relationships and involves taking what is known among CG actors, engaging the CG dynamic so that new information is developed, and putting it all together into a practical, useful database for problem-solving purposes. In short, CG effectiveness, or collaborative capacity—long- and short-term problem-solving capacity, improved policy performance, and accountability maintenance—requires successful completion of these "knowledge" tasks. This chapter has explored and explicated two possible avenues for successfully overcoming the fundamental challenges of knowledge transmission and integration in order to create collaborative capacity.

The first case, of Puget Sound, Washington, salmon recovery demon-
strates how civic science can be used as a tool to integrate the traditional
approach to science into a post-normal planning and policy process, find
agreed-upon and lasting solutions for both the species and the community,
and better address the complexity and uncertainty of many wicked problems.
In important respects, NOAA Fisheries, working with Shared Strategy to
develop a region-wide plan for salmon recovery in Puget Sound, departed
significantly from their own playbook for the role of science and scientists
in the ESA recovery process. Instead of a strict separation between the scientists and the science users, or stakeholders, the Technical Recovery Team
(TRT) model directly integrated scientists and science into the ESA recovery planning process using liaisons, a focus on programmatic feasibility, and
empowerment at the watershed level. The civic science model also took a
series of explicit steps to ensure the credibility of the science behind recovery
planning decisions and practiced a management style focused on, and conducive to, policy effectiveness. Of greater importance to those stakeholders in
Puget Sound wrestling with salmon recovery, however, was the belief that the
civic science model was a key factor in the ability of the collaborative multilevel regional planning effort to come to a successful conclusion (interviews
August 2, November 14, 2007).

The combination of these elements had dual benefits for stakeholders
and scientists alike. The responsiveness of the Technical Recovery Team to
the people with ultimate responsibility for crafting and implementing recovery programs, and the TRT's willingness to "get their hands dirty" by directly
engaging the problem of having science inform policy, created a reservoir of
goodwill with Shared Strategy staff and watershed stakeholders, thus increasing
the salience of the information (interviews November 19, December 16, 2007).
Both appreciated the extra effort by the scientists and the more useful end products. The TRT, for its part, gained valuable practice translating complex science
concepts for a nonscientific audience and increased their awareness of the civic
dimensions of public problem solving, or what Lane (1999) calls the complex
patterns of overlapping consequences, including those of social and cultural
import, that ultimately require more than technical solutions.

In the second case, we have argued that successfully completing the critical tasks of transferring, integrating, creating, and, ultimately, applying new,
useful knowledge in wicked-problem settings requires a CCB who does not
make choices in a vacuum. The lesson for public managers is that the better

they understand the mind-set in CG settings, the better position they will be in to make appropriate choices in terms of tools, strategies, skill application, and so on. And those who are not the main CCB need to nurture or discover one to facilitate the successful creation of collaborative capacity. In this sense, the dynamic is not that of public managers dropping back and ceding legal power to nonpublic CCBs, but instead of recognizing the value of such CCBs and shepherding their efforts on behalf of publicly mandated missions and goals.

References

Ansell, C., and A. Gash. 2008. "Collaborative Governance in Theory and Practice." *Journal of Public Administration Research and Theory* 18 (4): 543–571.

Aspinwall, R., and J. Cain. 1997. "The Changing Mindset in the Management of Waste." *Philosophical Transactions: Mathematical, Physical and Engineering Sciences* 355:1425–1437.

Bardach, Eugene, and Robert Kagan. 1982. *Going by the Book: The Problem of Regulatory Unreasonableness.* Philadelphia, PA: Temple University.

Behn, Robert D. 1998. "Management by Groping Along." *Journal of Policy Analysis and Management* 7 (Fall): 643–663.

Brock, Jon, Tom Leschine, Edward P. Weber, Lesley Jantarasmi, and Emily Templin. 2009. "Seeking Sustainable and Practical ESA Recovery Plans: Lessons from Puget Sound Salmon Recovery." For NOAA Fisheries, Northwest Region (October).

Buchel, B., and S. Raub. 2002. "Building Knowledge Creation Value Networks." *European Management Journal* 20 (6): 587–596.

Buskens, Vincent, and Kazuo Yamaguchi. 1999. "A New Model for Information Diffusion in Heterogeneous Social Networks." In *Sociological Methodology,* edited by Mark Becker and Michael Sobel, 281–325. Oxford: Blackwell.

Carlile, Paul R. 2002. "A Pragmatic View of Knowledge and Boundaries: Boundary Objects in New Product Development." *Organization Science* 13 (4): 442–455.

Cheng, Antony S. 2007. "Build It and They Will Come? Mandating Collaboration in Public Lands Policy and Management." *Natural Resources Journal* 46:841–858.

Clark, Fiona, and Deborah H. Illman 2001. "Dimensions of Civic Science: Introductory Essay." *Science Communication* 23 (1): 5–27.

Daniels, Steve, and Gregg Walker. 2001. *Working through Environmental Conflict: The Collaborative Learning Approach.* Westport, CT: Praeger.

Denhardt, Robert, and Janet Denhardt. 2000. "The New Public Service: Serving Rather than Steering." *Public Administration Review* 60 (6): 549.

Dietz, Thomas, and Paul Stern. 2009. *Public Participation in Environmental Assessment and Decision Making.* Washington, DC: National Academies Press.

Feldman, Martha S., and Anne M. Khademian. 2005. "The Role of Public Managers in Inclusive Management." Presented at the Public Management Research Conference, USC, Los Angeles, September 29–October 1, 2005.

Feldman, Martha S., Anne M. Khademian, Helen Ingram, and Anne S. Schneider. 2006. "Ways of Knowing and Inclusive Management Practices." *Public Administration Review* 66 (1): 89–99.

Gargiulo, Martin, and Mario Benassi. 2000. "Trapped in Your Own Net? Network Cohesion, Structural Holes, and the Adaptation of Social Capital." *Organizational Science* 11 (2): 183–196.

Gerberding, Julie. 2004. "Protecting the Public's Health with Small World Connections." The James E. Webb Lecture, November 18, 2004, National Academy of Public Administration.

Khademian, Anne. 2002. *Working with Culture: How the Job Gets Done in Public Programs.* Washington, DC: CQ Press.

Klijn, Erik-Hans, and Joop F. M. Koopenjan. 2000. "Public Management and Policy Networks: Foundations to a Network Approach to Governance." *Public Management* 2 (2): 135–158.

Lane, Neal. 1999. "The Civic Scientist and Science Policy." In *AAAS Science and Technology Policy Yearbook.* http://www.aaas.org/spp/yearbook/chap22.htm.

La Porte, Todd R. 1996. "Shifting Vantage and Conceptual Puzzles in Understanding Public Organization Networks." *Journal of Public Administration Research and Theory* 6 (1): 49–74.

Moore, Mark H. 1995. *Creating Public Value: Strategic Management in Government.* Cambridge, MA: Harvard University Press.

National Oceanic and Atmospheric Administration (NOAA). 2002. *Integrated Recovery Planning for Listed Salmon: Technical Guidance for Watershed Groups in Puget Sound.* Seattle: NOAA.

Nicolini, Davide, Silvia Gherardi, and Dvora Yanow, eds. 2003. *Knowing in Organizations: A Practice Based Approach.* Armonk, NY: M.E. Sharpe.

Ostrom, Elinor. 1990. *Governing the Commons: The Evolution of Institutions for Collective Action.* Cambridge: Cambridge University Press.

Pielke, Roger A. 2007. *The Honest Broker: Making Sense of Science in Policy and Politics.* Cambridge: Cambridge University Press.

Rittel, Horst W. J., and Melvin M. Webber. 1973. "Dilemmas in a General Theory of Planning." *Policy Science* 2 (4): 155–169.

Roberts, Nancy C. 2002. *The Transformative Power of Dialogue.* New York: JAI Press.

Sabatier, Paul, Will Focht, Mark Lubell, Zev Trachtenberg, Arnold Vedlitz, and Marty Matlock. 2005. *Swimming Upstream: Collaborative Approaches to Watershed Management.* Cambridge, MA: MIT Press.

Schau H. J., M. F. Smith, P. I. Schau. 2005. "The Healthcare Network Economy: The Role of Internet Information Transfer and Implications for Pricing." *Industrial Marketing Management* 34 (2): 147–156.

Schmandt, Juergen. 1998. "Civic Science." *Science Communication* 20 (1): 62–69.

Schneider, Anne, and Helen Ingram. 1997. *Policy Design for Democracy*. Lawrence: University Press of Kansas.

Schusler, T. M., D. J. Decker, and M. J. Pfeffer. 2003. "Social Learning for Collaborative Natural Resource Management." *Society and Natural Resources* 15:309–326.

Selznick, Philip. 1957. *Leadership in Administration: A Sociological Interpretation*. New York: Harper and Row.

Shared Strategy for Puget Sound. 2005. Progress Report on Individual Watershed Profiles. June. Seattle: Shared Strategy.

Sirianni, Carmen. 2010. *Investing in Democracy: Engaging Citizens in Collaborative Governance*. Washington, DC: Brookings Institution Press.

Stayaert, Patrick, and Janice Jiggins. 2007. "Governance of Complex Environmental Situations through Social Learning: A Synthesis of SLIM's Lessons for Research, Policy and Practice." *Environmental Science and Policy* 10 (6): 575–586.

Terry, Larry. 1993. *Leadership of Public Bureaucracies: The Administrator as Conservator*. New York: Routledge.

Tushman, Michael L., and Thomas J. Scanlan. 1981. "Characteristics and External Orientations of Boundary Spanning Individuals." *Academy of Management Journal* 24 (1): 83–98.

Weber, Edward P. 1998. *Pluralism by the Rules: Conflict and Cooperation in Environmental Regulation*. Washington, DC: Georgetown University Press.

———. 2000. "A New Vanguard for the Environment: Grass-Roots Ecosystem Management as a New Environmental Movement." *Society and Natural Resources* 13:237–259.

———. 2003. *Bringing Society Back In: Grassroots Ecosystem Management, Accountability, and Sustainable Communities*. Cambridge, MA: MIT Press.

Weber, Edward P., and Anne Khademian. 2008. "Wicked Problems, Knowledge Challenges, and Collaborative Capacity Builders in Network Settings." *Public Administration Review* 68, no. 2 (March-April): 334–349.

Weber, Edward P., Nicholas P. Lovrich, and Michael Gaffney. 2005. "Collaboration, Enforcement, and Endangered Species: A Framework for Assessing Collaborative Problem Solving Capacity." *Society and Natural Resources* 18, no. 8 (September): 677–698.

Weber, Edward P., Tom Leschine, and Jon Brock. 2010. "Civic Science and Salmon Recovery Planning in Puget Sound." *Policy Studies Journal* 38, no. 2 (May): 235–256.

Webler, Thomas, and Seth Tuler. 1999. "Integrating Technical Analysis with Deliberation in Regional Watershed Management Planning: Applying the National Research Council Approach." *Policy Studies Journal* 27 (3): 530–543.

Chapter 10

Wicked-Problem Settings

A New and Expanded Social Contract for Scientists and Policy Implementation?

EDWARD P. WEBER, DENISE LACH, AND BRENT S. STEEL

There is no shortage of important, wicked public problems, from fracking to salmon recovery to forestry management, health care, climate change, watershed restoration, and beyond. The contemporary cases presented here illustrate how the uncertainty and complexity of wicked problems translate into decision-making contexts and dynamics ill-suited to a normal science approach and therefore unable to provide the full range of knowledge required for effective and accountable decisions. These case studies also explore and describe the many challenges to the effective application of science in wicked-problem settings.

Given these problem dynamics and challenges, is marine ecologist and former administrator of the National Oceanic and Atmospheric Administration (NOAA) Jane Lubchenco (1998) right? Do we need a new social contract for scientists that is more capable of meeting the "new and unmet needs of society" and that, according to her, will lead to more sustainable watersheds, forests, landscapes, coastal zones, oceans, and communities? Such a social contract entails "integrative science," or more "fundamental research, faster and more effective transmission of new and existing knowledge to policy- and decision-makers, and better communication of this knowledge to the public" (492).

The research presented here on wicked problems and different emergent strategies for coping with their unstructured (nonlinear), crosscutting, and relentless character point in the direction of a new social contract for scientists. Yet it is one that explicitly and simultaneously narrows and expands

Lubchenco's concept, while also redirecting our attention to "how" the goals of the new social contract are to be achieved. The argument here narrows, or limits, the application of a new social contract to wicked-problem settings—not all public policy problems. But the argument also expands on the idea of a new social contract by (1) explicitly incorporating/integrating multiple knowledge types as a critical component of effective problem solving, in addition to science; and (2) finding that problem-solving efforts are more likely to be effective when communication is a more deliberative, two-way street.

Moreover, the problem-solving strategies, or institutions, norms, and decision tools, are essential to making the new social contract with scientists work in practice. This is because they are specifically designed to facilitate collective problem-solving capacity in the face of the uncertainty, disputed values, and high stakes of wicked-problem settings, which are a poor match with, or whose solutions are insufficient for, traditional science applications. Hence the emergent problem-solving strategies presented here increase the probability that both science and other important knowledges will impact programs and policies. In short, wicked problems present a need for open-ended, transparent, self-reflective, and more overtly political decision processes that integrate not just technical and scientific information, but experiential and values-based information as well (Funtowicz and Ravetz 1993; Sarewitz 2000).

COMMON GROUND AMONG THE EMERGENT PROBLEM-SOLVING STRATEGIES

At the same time, we recognize that none of the emergent problem-solving methodologies, whether collaborative governance, knowledge-to-action networks, or place-based social learning, are new in and of themselves and that each of these approaches to the challenges posed by wicked problems is unique in its own right. Nonetheless, the different institutions, norms, and decision tools share *important commonalities that are essential to their successful operation.* Each approach

- accepts the limitations of science in problem solving; solutions are about more than the "technical." Each involves a problem-solving dynamic that reflects the importance of multiple knowledges: that is, science is necessary but not sufficient for effective problem solving.

- explicitly acknowledges the importance of politics and values, along with the inevitability of conflict.
- involves significant public engagement and the idea of an extended peer community; experts work together with a broad array of stakeholders representing a variety of societal, governmental, economic, and cultural institutions.
- relies heavily on building trust and constructive working relationships among all participants.
- employs collaborative decision processes as a key part of the overall interactive dialogue.
- requires the inculcation and practice of new cultural/professional norms for scientists and technical experts
- focuses on smaller-scale governance arrangements in accord with Rayner's advice that, for wicked problems, "we should really move away from thinking that . . . [such] problem[s] [are] to be dealt with by governments and nation states alone, and should move the focus down to lower levels of decision-making, provinces and cities" (2006, 10).

FACILITATING EMERGENT PROBLEM-SOLVING STRATEGIES

Yet, while it is important to identify and explain how different strategies work and how they can help in the face of wicked problems, and while they share many of the same characteristics, what about the facilitation of such "strategies"? What should policy makers, agency officials, community members, and other stakeholders know, and what might they do, if they are faced with a wicked-problem setting and if wish to advance one of these strategies? We offer six lessons, or recommendations, to help decision-makers faced with wicked problems better facilitate the kinds of emergent problem-solving strategies outlined in this volume.

First, all these problem-solving strategies take many years to develop for two key reasons. The complexity and characteristics associated with wicked problems means that most meaningful outcomes, or results, will not occur overnight, much less in one or two years. Developing strategic plans to successfully tackle watershed restoration, or ecologically sensitive forestry, for example, often take a year or two all by themselves—which says nothing about the actual on-the-ground implementation of agreed-upon plans and the willingness, or need, to adapt programs and plans as new information/science becomes available. And even after program implementation, results in such complex settings do not appear overnight. Another consideration in getting these emergent problem-solving strategies right is the fact that each requires significant time to build the kinds of constructive working relationships necessary for coming to agreement. This need for patience and years of time does not, of course, fit well into current political election cycles of two to four years, wherein politicians have a desire (some say need) to show voters how their policy choices are making peoples' lives better, or are improving ecological conditions, and so on. In short, it is virtually impossible to build relationships, develop broad, crosscutting, holistic strategies, implement programs, and achieve concrete results over only a few years.

Second, the need for longer periods of time to implement programs and plans has direct implications for the funding required for success over the long term. The holistic, wicked-problem setting means that problem solving does not match up well with existing political and institutional funding cycles, which are often annual or semiannual in length. Ultimate success requires a new funding model designed to match the needs of these emergent problem-solving strategies and institutions. More specifically, funding models should recognize that there are several key stages in such collaborative processes: (1) intermediate institution-building steps in the near term (e.g., trust-building, information gathering, etc.) (one to three years); (2) priority-setting in the medium term (two to five years); and (3) strategically targeted results in the long term (three to ten years, with smaller, simpler, yet still strategically designed programs and results occurring in the earlier years). Each stage should be funded accordingly *within a larger funding plan focused on a minimum of a ten-year investment program*. Some organizations are already moving their funding models for watershed and forest restoration in just this direction, most notably the Oregon Watershed Enhancement Board (OWEB) and the National Forest Foundation (NFF).

Third, greater effort needs to be made to identify, cultivate, and retain leadership capable of fostering the necessary trust, constructive working relationships, and public engagement across a broad range of stakeholders and collaborative problem-solving processes. This will require champions who possess a keen understanding of collaboration (the philosophy and practice/process); a reputation as fair, honest, and capable of leading a big-picture approach emphasizing "all of us in it together for the common good"; and are willing to commit considerable political capital in support of collaboration (Bardach 1998; La Porte 1996; Salmon 2007; Weber 1998).

The skills and traits required of a successful collaborative leader, or facilitator/mediator, are essentially the same. They include the possession of good communication and listening skills, respect for and ability to work with all sides of an issue, and strong people skills, meaning that the leader/facilitator is comfortable with, and skilled at, interaction and outreach involving a diversity of different organizations and individuals. This also means that the collaborative leader is not afraid to share power because s/he realizes this is necessary to get to mutual gain or win-win-win outcomes. Further, collaborative capacity builders are also able to convince others to commit to and follow through on promises, cajole participants to stay the course when times get rough, and champion the collective, positive-sum benefits of successful collaboration (Weber 1998; Weber and Khademian 2008).

Importantly, "leaders" can and do come from anywhere within participant ranks. This means that collaborative leadership is not solely the domain of government officials with specific policy responsibility and legal authority, although to the extent these leadership traits are attached to key public officials within the effort, the likelihood of success improves. Instead, private citizens, or some combination of public and private participants or multiple private citizens, can take on the collaborative leadership role. The key to success appears to be more the *presence* of the collaborative leadership characteristics than the *organizational location* of the leadership (Daniels and Walker 2001, 173, 183; Weber and Khademian 2008).

Fourth, successful management of these emergent problem-solving methodologies for wicked problems requires a set of tools capable of assessing community problem-solving capacity for collaborative governance, place-based management, and/or adaptive governance. These tools can help identify places with high versus low capacity, thus helping target scarce resources most effectively. They can, and should, be used in tandem with assessments of wicked-problem severity and placed-based vulnerability.

Fifth, and as a corollary to item four, the complexity and uncertainty of wicked problems means that constant vigilance is required for understanding whether headway is being made against the larger problem set, or key subsets of the overall problem. In turn, this demands that close attention be paid and adequate resources devoted to selecting appropriate indicators, and then measuring and monitoring progress against those indicators. Too often, it is the measuring and monitoring element of the implementation process that is neglected in favor of convenient proxies and/or other policy priorities. Yet, with wicked problems and these emergent problem-solving strategies, the need for this element is even more critical to overall success than with less than wicked problems.

Sixth, there are implications for government agency personnel decisions. Instead of the traditional model of regular movement from place to place, or office to office, personnel with key roles in these long-term, emergent problem-solving strategies and institutions need to stay in place for longer periods in order to facilitate the kinds of relationships and place-based knowledge required for success. The logic here also extends to agency considerations for hiring (certain personalities are likely better suited to these collaboratives), promotion, and overall career advancement. Moreover, agency leaders need to be educated about the value added by integrating research scientists, in particular, into communities, management and policy processes, and direct engagement with communities/citizens. Successfully integrating physical and natural scientists in this way, along with other key personnel, will necessarily require additional and/or adequate training in, among other things, negotiating and building relationships with stakeholders outside primary organizations, conflict resolution skills, trust-building and good faith bargaining techniques/approaches, the importance of reciprocity as a practice, how politics and values influence policy-making and problem solving, and how to achieve goals while sharing power. The Canterbury Water Management Strategy, an innovative collaborative governance arrangement in New Zealand, does exactly this—training collaborative "watershed zone committee" members and government personnel in the art of successful collaborative problem solving prior to the initiation of collaborative governance (Knobloch 2016). At the same time, and as per Kaufman (1959) and others, there must still be sensitivity to the possibility of community, or stakeholder, capture of such agency employees.

Taken together, these six recommendations also suggest a number of research questions that need answers in order to fully implement these ideas. Currently, we have limited knowledge in the area of assessment tools focused on community capacity for collaborative governance and adaptiveness, or which communities are best suited to place-based management as described by Daniel Williams in chapter 7 of this volume. Nor is it clear that we have a set of best practices for identifying, hiring, promoting, and retaining the types of leadership and personnel required to facilitate problem-solving strategies for wicked problems, whether it is government agencies or nonprofit stakeholder organizations. What might these different "personnel" practices look like? As regards the suggestion that successful research scientists in these settings need more training and integration into such policy implementation processes, might this same "gap" be filled as effectively with cross-disciplinary teams, or not? Further, using the "important commonalities" shared by the strategies, or institutions, norms, and decision tools, outlined here, are there other emergent problem-solving methodologies/strategies that might work for wicked problems? Finally, we need to learn more about how to facilitate and successfully apply the "expanded model of practice" within communities that is developed by Williams in chapter 7 on place-based social learning.

CONCLUSION

The goal of this book is to more firmly establish the connection between unstructured (nonlinear), crosscutting, relentless wicked problems and plausible, empirically derived problem-solving methodologies capable of effectively managing, or coping with, such problems. Doing so takes two well-established and influential lines of research—wicked problems dating back to Rittel and Webber (1973) and extended peer communities originating with Funtowicz and Ravetz (1993)—and marries them to real-world policy implementation institutions, processes, norms, and decision tools. As with any science-based scholarship, the hope is to further our knowledge in these areas that are of importance to a growing list of wicked public problems. Yet we also hope to energize the scholarly and practitioner-based conversations and real-world practices around these topics in ways that help leaders and stakeholders imagine new possibilities, conduct new experiments in implementation, and, ultimately, make even more progress in the ongoing, difficult battle against wicked problems and their less-than-desirable effects for society as a whole.

References

Bardach, Eugene. 1998. *Getting Agencies to Work Together*. Washington, DC: Brookings Institution Press.

Daniels, Steve, and Gregg Walker. 2001. *Working through Environmental Conflict: The Collaborative Learning Approach*. Westport, CT: Praeger.

Funtowicz, Silvio O., and Jerome R. Ravetz. 1993. "Science for the Post-Normal Age." *Futures* (September): 739–755.

Kaufman, Herbert. 1959. *The Forest Ranger: A Study in Administrative Behavior.* Washington, DC: Resources for the Future Press.

Knobloch, Jenna. 2016. *We Can Work It Out: Implementation and Collaborative Governance.* Unpublished MPP Essay, Oregon State University. June.

La Porte, Todd R. 1996. "Shifting Vantage and Conceptual Puzzles in Understanding Public Organization Networks." *Journal of Public Administration Research and Theory* 6 (1): 49–74.

Lubchenco, Jane. 1998. "Entering the Century of the Environment: A New Social Contract for Science." *Science* 279:491–497.

Rayner, Steve. 2006. "Wicked Problems: Clumsy Solutions—Diagnoses and Prescriptions for Environmental Ills." Jack Beale Memorial Lecture on the Global Environment, James Martin Institute for Science and Civilization. July. Sydney, Australia. http://eureka.bodleian.ox.ac.uk/93/1/Steve%20 Rayner%2C%20Jack%20Beale%20Lecture%20Wicked%20Problems.pdf.

Rittel, Horst W. J., and Melvin M. Webber. 1973. "Dilemmas in a General Theory of Planning." *Policy Science* 2 (4): 155–169.

Salmon, Guy. 2007. "Collaborative Approaches to Sustainable Development: Lessons from the Nordic Countries." Address to the Ninth Southeast Asian Survey Congress on Developing Sustainable Societies, October 31.

Sarewitz, Daniel. 2000. "Human Well-Being and Federal Science: What's the Connection?" In *Science, Technology and Democracy*, edited by Daniel Kleinman. Albany: State University of New York Press.

Weber, Edward P. 1998. *Pluralism by the Rules: Conflict and Cooperation in Environmental Regulation.* Washington, DC: Georgetown University Press.

Weber, Edward P., and Anne Khademian. 2008. "Wicked Problems, Knowledge Challenges, and Collaborative Capacity Builders in Network Settings." *Public Administration Review* 68, no. 2 (March-April): 334–349.

About the Editors and Authors

EDWARD P. WEBER is the Ulysses G. Dubach Professor of Political Science in the School of Public Policy at Oregon State University. He has published widely on natural resource/environmental policymaking, policy implementation, democratic accountability, and the design and operation of alternative decision-making and governance institutions, particularly collaborative governance arrangements. He is also the chair of the Committee for Family Forestlands for the Oregon Department of Forestry and the former leader of the Thomas Foley Public Policy Institute.

DENISE LACH is professor of sociology and director of the School of Public Policy at Oregon State University. Her research focuses on the role of science and scientists in natural resources policymaking, including finding ways to visualize data to effectively communicate results. Her interdisciplinary research and teaching engages scholars, students, and decision-makers from fields as diverse as nuclear engineering and salmon biology.

BRENT S. STEEL is professor in and director of the graduate program in the School of Public Policy at Oregon State University. He has published numerous journal articles, book chapters, and books concerning public policy in areas such as forestry, rangelands, endangered species, coastal and marine issues, environmental issues, sustainable development, and the politicization of science.

MARCELA BRUGNACH is an assistant professor in the Water Engineering and Management group at the University of Twente (Belgium). She holds a PhD in bioresource engineering and forest ecology from Oregon State University. Her research focuses on collective decision-making processes in natural resources management, with expertise in computer modeling and simulations and decision-making under uncertainty. She is a former postdoc at the

University of California, Davis, and was a research associate with the Institute for Environmental Systems Research at Germany's University of Osnabrück.

MATT CARROLL is a natural resource sociologist and professor in the School of the Environment at Washington State University, with experience in forest management. His research centers on natural resource–based human communities, wildland fire, and natural resource labor, as well as social assessment in a natural resources context and collaborative processes. He has served as chair of the Society of American Forester's National Task Force on Community Stability and on President Clinton's Ecosystem Assessment Team.

STEVEN E. DANIELS is a community development specialist in university extension and professor in the Department of Sociology, Social Work, and Anthropology in the School of Environment and Society at Utah State University. Previously, he was the director of the Western Rural Development Center (1999–2004). His expertise focuses on community linkages to natural resources and collaborative processes in natural resources management.

TANYA HEIKKILA is a professor of political science and codirector of the Workshop on Policy Process Research in the School of Public Affairs at the University of Colorado–Denver. Her research expertise is in comparative institutional analysis and the management of collaboration and conflict around common pool resources, with an emphasis on water resources, ecosystem restoration programs, and the political landscape of hydraulic fracturing in the United States.

HELEN INGRAM is a research fellow at the Southwest Center at the University of Arizona. She is a professor emeritus at the University of California at Irvine, Department of Planning Policy and Design in the School of Social Ecology and the Department of Political Science in the School of Social Sciences. Water resources have been her long-term research project, although she has also published a number of articles and book chapters on the role of science in public policy.

ANN C. KELLER is an associate professor of health policy and management at the UC Berkeley School of Public Health. Keller studies expertise in public decision-making, focusing on environmental and health policy issues. She is particularly interested in the difficulties associated with producing expertise in politically contested domains and in patterns of mobilization of lay actors in traditionally expert-dominated areas of policy formation.

ROBERT T. LACKEY is a professor of fisheries science at Oregon State University and the former deputy director of the US Environmental Protection Agency's national research laboratory. Over the years he has worked on an assortment of natural resource issues from various positions in government and academia, with a primary emphasis on the interface between science and policy.

ANNA P. STEVENSON is a PhD student focusing on environmental policy in the School of Public Policy at Oregon State University. Anna has previously worked in ecology and natural resource management with local, state, and federal agencies. Over the last ten years, these projects have ranged from evaluating the effects of land use on coastal ecosystems to leading community decision processes for the designation of protected areas and drafting state legislation as a staffer in the Oregon State legislature.

CHRISTOPHER M. WEIBLE is an associate professor of political science and public policy and codirector of the Workshop on Policy Process Research at the School of Public Affairs at the University of Colorado–Denver. His research focuses on advancing policy theories, including as coeditor of the last two editions of Theories of the Policy Process. He has published widely on science, politics, and policy, as well as on energy, food, environmental, and natural resource policy.

DANIEL R. WILLIAMS is a research social scientist with the US Forest Service, Rocky Mountain Research Station, in Fort Collins, Colorado, and former coeditor-in-chief of the journal Society and Natural Resources. His research draws from theory and methods of environmental psychology and human geography to study the meanings, values, and uses of natural environments for application to public lands management, planning, and policy. His current work examines place-based inquiry and practice to inform the adaptive governance of complex social-ecological systems.

Index